THRE
IMPORTANT

THREE HUNDRED

IMPORTANT COMBINATIONS

BANGALORE VENKATA RAMAN

MOTILAL BANARSIDASS PUBLISHERS
PRIVATE LIMITED • DELHI

5th Reprint: Delhi, 2010
Tenth Edition: Delhi, 1991
Ninth Edition: Bangalore, 1983

ISBN: 978-81-208-0843-9 (Cloth)
ISBN: 978-81-208-0850-8 (Paper)

MOTILAL BANARSIDASS
41 U.A., Bungalow Road, Jawahar Nagar, Delhi 110 007
8 Mahalaxmi Chamber, 22 Bhulabhai Desai Road, Mumbai 400 026
203 Royapettah High Road, Mylapore, Chennai 600 004
236, 9th Main III Block, Jayanagar, Bengaluru 560 011
Sanas Plaza, 1302 Baji Rao Road, Pune 411 002
8 Camac Street, Kolkata 700 017
Ashok Rajpath, Patna 800 004
Chowk, Varanasi 221 001

Printed in India

By Jainendra Prakash Jain at Shri Jainendra Press,
A-45 Naraina, Phase-I, New Delhi 110 028
and Published by Narendra Prakash Jain for
Motilal Banarsidass Publishers Private Limited,
Bungalow Road, Delhi 110 007

PREFACE TO THE NINTH EDITION

I have the pleasure to present herewith the ninth edition of THREE HUNDRED IMPORTANT COMBINATIONS. This new edition has been revised and at some places re-written.

The "Appendix" on the much feared Kala Sarpa Yoga will no doubt enhance the value of the book. An alphabetical index of the Yogas, to facilitate easy reference, will also be found to be highly useful.

Thanks to the immense interest envinced by the educated public in my humble writings on Astrology, the seventh edition, published in September 1978, was sold within a few months of its issue. I am confident that this edition will also be given the usual encouraging reception.

I am thankful to my daughter, Gayatri Devi Raman for her assistance in thoroughly revising this edition, to my sons, B. Niranjan Babu and B. Satchidananda Babu for careful proof corrections and to Messrs. P. N. Kamat and G. K. Anantram of IBH Prakashana for bringing out this new edition attractively.

Bangalore
25-7-1983

B. V. RAMAN

PREFACE

The importance of Astrology in the social life of man is manifold. Human needs and aspirations furnish a continuous motive power for astrological inquiry. Astrology has a definite relation to the several grades of urgency into which the needs of human being in society can be divided. Success in life depends to a large material prosperity or adversity. Yogas in astrological parlance tend to show the degree of wealth, fame, rank, position, adversity, ill-health and misfortunes a man is likely to enjoy in his present life as a sequel to his own actions in previous states of existence. In other words, the different *specific* planetary combinations show a summation of *inherited* physical and psychological tendencies which condition our present environment ; the extent to which we can offset the inherited tendencies by effort; the characteristics that will be *dominant* and those that will be *recessive* and so on and so forth. Strictly speaking, all yogas are combinations of planets but all combinations cannot be Yogas. Only specific combinations can be styled as Yogas. In this book, I have made an attempt to carefully select only such important combinations that could be raised to the dignity of Yogas and that could indicate certain definite physical or mental traits, or degree of wealth, fortune, or misfortune. To collect combinations at random is easy but to select notable ones illustrative of a variety of life events is not only difficult but even risky.

I should call this book a research project in the sense the material used forms part of the vast scheme of investigations I have in view. Modern astrologers seem to have overlooked an exceptionally fertile field of investigation in their indifference to study of Yogas which forms, as it were, the essence of Indian Predictive Astrology. Most modern writers are silent on the subject of the Yogas except perhaps for some odd remarks upon a few common Raja Yogas or Arishta Yogas. For this reason, there has been for several years a demand for a book devoted specially to the predictive significance of Yogas and the present work has been undertaken to meet this demand. Long back this want was supplied by my grandfather. Prof. B. Suryanarain Rao whose excellent book *Satayogamanjari* deals with some of the most important Yogas on the subject. But I felt that a more systematised account of all the important Yogas should be brought out so that, illustrated by a number of practical horoscopes, the work may stand as a foundation upon which future research may be developed.

Therefore *Three Hundred Important Combinations* is intended to provide a working knowledge of the Yogas which indicate *specific* horoscopic trends. The astrological mathematics required for this purpose is very elementary. Numerous examples especially designed to illustrate points arising in the elucidation of the Yogas have been inserted and as these are worked out fully, readers should have no difficulty in following the principles clearly. Points of a controversial nature have not been shelved or glossed over. They have been approached from the point of view of their practical applicability.

All planetary combinations may be divided into two broad groups, *viz.*, *Yogas and Arishtas.* Though by the word Yoga is meant a combination, in actual practice Yoga is always considered to imply a fortunate combination. Arishtas generally deal with misfortunes though they are also included in the generic term Yoga. The Yogas may be *Raja Yogas* (political power), *Dhana Yogas* (combination for wealth) or *Gnana Yogas* (combinations for real higher knowledge and spirituality).

The subject of interpretation of Yogas is briefly dealt with in the first few pages of the book. This branch is to be specially studied by the student of astrology in as much as it enables him to evaluate the exact implication of a particular Yoga. Special Yogas, including what are called Nabhasa Yogas, have been dealt with, with suitable illustrations wherever necessary. The difficulty arising when two or more Yogas coincide such as would be the case in respect of say Asraya and Akriti

Yogas (see page 102) have been suitably clarified with proper explanations.

In a way, the latter part of the book is more important, for it deals with such outstanding combinations as Raja Yogas, Arishta Yogas and Neechabhanga Raja Yogas about which, of late so much fuss is being made by a section of astrological students. The last pages give a summary of the entire subject, matter. The example horoscope, with which the book is closed, should be of particular interest to readers, for it shows how, in the face of many Yogas existing in a particular case, only a few can operate. It also demonstrates that in respect of certain Yogas, the indications become effective throughout life while in regard to certain other Yogas, the results can happen only during specific periods and not always.

For such a work as this which largely rests upon the principles furnished by classical astrology no originality can be claimed. But I feel I can certainly claim credit for being the first to bring together all scattered information, present it systematically, and prove its practical worth and utility. The truth of this becomes evident when it is remembered that this book carries nearly 150 practical illustrations most of them being gathered from actual lives.

I have as my readers scholars, intellectuals, students and practitioners. Therefore, to meet such different tastes and angles presents difficult problems of authorship, especially that a book dealing with the practical aspect of astrology should not merely aim at an uncritical exposition of the subject-matter. The only way to gratify the readers and at the same time preserve the theme is to present the apparently dreary principles in a graduated form and give the book a simple readability by interspersing the difficult sections with remarks which will not only elucidate the difficult points but encourage the casual reader to take a more positive interest in the study of the subject.

It is hoped that the exposition of Yogas presented in this book will stimulate readers to pursue the subject further.

BANGALORE
21st July 1947.

B. V. RAMAN.

Yogas (see page 162) have been suitably clarified with proper explanations.

In a way, the latter part of the book is more important, for it deals with such outstanding combinations as Raja Yogas, Arishta Yogas and Neechabhanga Raja Yogas about which of late so much fuss is being made by a section of astrological students. The last pages give a summary of the entire subject matter. The example horoscope, with which the book is closed, should be of particular interest to readers, for it shows how, the fact of many Yogas existing in a particular chart, only a few can operate. It also demonstrates that in respect of certain Yogas, the indications become effective throughout life while in regard to certain other Yogas, the results can happen only during specific periods [illegible]

[illegible]

[illegible] theme is to present [illegible] in a [illegible] form and [illegible] the book [illegible] the difficult sections [illegible] which will not only [illegible] the difficult points [illegible] position [illegible] the study [illegible]

It is hoped that the exposition of Yogas presented in this book will enable readers to pursue the subject further.

[illegible]

B. V. RAMAN

CONTENTS

CHAPTER I

General Introduction

THIS book is intended to place before my readers *Three Hundred Important Planetary Combinations* comprising a comprehensive list of human transactions including fortunes, misfortunes, death and various physical and mental worries and elations, financial troubles and successes and all other events connected with human life. Man wants to know something of everything connected with his career and the lives of those who are dear and near to him. These three hundred combinations include a large variety of his life transactions and a previous knowledge of these happenings will be of immense benefit to him so that he may not only take remedies to avert the evils indicated by the planets from time to time but also adjust his affairs where the remedies prove ineffectual.

Human life falls under two grand divisions—Yogas and Arishtas, or fortunes and misfortunes. *Yogas* include success in every line—health, personality, success in politics, financial gains, good education, mental strength, bodily health; good wife, dutiful children, sympathetic friends and relations, righteous conduct and other sources of pleasure and enjoyment which generally go under the name of fortunes.

Arishtas or misfortunes include all sorts and sources of sorrows, worries, miseries, troubles, distractions, bodily and mental disturbances such as ill-health, physical and mental deformities, financial losses, ugly and bad children, quarrelsome wife, hateful relations and friends, evil temper, sinful nature and other unpleasant sources in life which go under the name of evils or misfortunes. Therefore these three hundred combinations will be specially useful to astrological readers and students. I shall try and give the necessary explanations and notes where they are needed to make the meaning of the combinations clear.

General Observations

I am dealing in this book with three hundred important yogas or special combinations bearing on the twelve houses which signify certain definite indications in the horoscopes as different from the general combinations enunciated in astrological text-books. The word 'yoga' is rather difficult to define. Yoga means combination but in common parlance *yoga* means a certain definite or special combination which adds strength to the horoscope or removes the vitality from it.

If you go through standard books on astrology you will find that each ascendant has certain planets disposed towards it as *yogakarakas*. In the treatment of special combinations in this book, we have nothing to do with such planets. Again the combination of trinal and quadrangular lords is supposed to give rise to Rajayoga. We are concerned with this combination to the extent that it qualifies or modifies a certain special yoga. For example take the horoscope

Rahu		Moon Saturn	
Lagna	RASI		Sun
			Mars Venus Mercury
	Jupiter		Kethu

given herewith. The disposition of the Moon and Jupiter in kendras or quadrants has given rise to Gajakesari Yoga. The Moon and Jupiter who have generated this yoga are lords of the 6th and the 11th and consequently they are not as beneficial as they would have been were they lords of the 4th and 9th. In other words, the evil due to ownership has modified to some extent the strength of Gajakesari. What is the method of interpreting a yoga and how and when do the results manifest or make themselves felt ? Let us try to answer these important questions.

Strength of a Yoga

A yoga is formed by more than one planet. The nature of a planet is of three types, *viz.*, benefic, malefic and neutral.

According to the natural classification benefics are Jupiter, Venus, well-associated Mercury and waxing Moon and malefics are the Sun, Mars, Saturn, evil-associated Mercury and waning Moon. But in this book our reference to malefics and benefics unless otherwise stated are in the sense of malefic lords and benefic lords.

The benefics or benefic lords are (1) lord of Lagna, (2) lords of the 5th and 9th, and (3) lords of kendras or quadrants, when they are natural malefics. The malefics are (1) the lords of the 3rd, 6th and 11th, and (2) lords of kendras when they are natural benefics.

The lords of the 2nd and 12th may be termed neutral because they give good or bad results according to their other conjunctions. The 8th lord is a malefic according to *Jathaka Chandrika* but for all practical purposes he may be taken as a neutral. The above can be classified thus :

Benefics. Lord of 1, lords of 5 and 9, and lords of 4, 7 and 10 if they are natural malefics.

Malefics. Lords of 3, 6 and 11. Lords of 4, 7 and 10 if they are natural benefics.

Neutrals. Lords of 2, 8 and 12.

Of course, the 8th lord is supposed to be evil unless he be the Sun or the Moon. We shall avoid controversies and assume that the 8th lord is a neutral for the purpose of interpreting yogas.

Here an observation has to be made.

In the above list of benefics, malefics and neutrals we have completely omitted to take into account the influence due to a double lordship. Thus for Aquarius, Mars owning the 10th—a quadrant—is good. In addition to the 10th he owns the 3rd also which is bad. In other words, Mars a natural malefic becoming a benefic lord by virtue of owning a kendra is 'influenced' by his ownership of the 3rd house. It will be seen that excepting the Sun and the Moon all the other planets own two houses each so that whether a planet is a benefic or malefic can be judged only when both the lordships are taken into account. The nature of a lord is influenced by two factors, *viz.*, (1) the other lordship and (2) association. The other lordship varies with regard to different ascendants. When Pisces is Lagna, Mars owns the 2nd and 9th houses while he owns the 1st and 8th when Aries is Lagna. Thus the 'Ascendant' is of the utmost importance while deciding the benefic and malefic lords.

We shall now discuss the nature of the different planets.

The Sun.—He is *benefic* as lord of 1, 4, 7, 10, 5 and 9 which is possible in regard to Leo, Taurus, Aquarius, Scorpio, Aries and Sagittarius. He is neutral as lord of 2, 12 and 8 which is possible for Cancer, Virgo and Capricorn. He is malefic as lord of 3, 6 and 11, which is possible for Gemini, Pisces and Libra.

The Moon.—Benefic as lord of 1, 5 and 9 which is possible for Cancer, Pisces and Scorpio. *Neutral* as lord of 2, 12 and 8 which is possible for Gemini, Leo and Sagittarius ; and *malefic* as lord of 3, 6, 11, 4, 7 and 10 which is possible in regard to Taurus, Aquarius, Virgo, Aries, Capricorn and Libra.

Mars.—He is *benefic* as a lord of 1 and 8 (Aries), 2 and 7 (Libra), 2 and 9 (Pisces), 3 and 10 (Aquarius), 4 and 9 (Leo), 5 and 10 (Cancer), 5 and 12 (Sagittarius), and 7 and 12 (Taurus).

Here we have taken into account the 'modified influence' due to the second lordship. Thus if you take Sagittarius Mars is benefic as lord of a trine 5 and neutral as lord of 12. But his trinal lordship is so powerful as to overcome the 12th lordship so that he becomes a benefic.

Mars is *neutral* as lord of 1 and 6 (Scorpio) and *malefic* as lord of 3 and 8 (Virgo), 4 and 11 (Capricorn), and 6 and 11 (Gemini).

Mercury.—Benefic as lord of 2 and 5 (Taurus), 9 and 6 (Capricorn) and 9 and 12 (Libra); *neutral* as lord of 1 and 4 (Gemini), 1 and 10 (Virgo), and 5 and 8 (Aquarius); *malefic* as lord of 3 and 12 (Cancer), 4 and 7 (Pisces), 7 and 10 (Sagittarius), 8 and 11 (Scorpio), 2 and 11 (Leo), and 3 and 6 (Aries).

Jupiter.—Benefic as lord of 2 and 5 (Scorpio), 6 and 9 (Cancer) and 9 and 12 (Aries); *neutral* as lord of 1 and 4 (Sagittarius), 1 and 10 (Pisces), and 5 and 8 (Leo); and *malefic* as lord of 2 and 11 (Aquarius), 3 and 6 (Libra), 3 and 12 (Capricorn), 4 and 7 (Virgo), 7 and 10 (Gemini), and 8 and 11 (Taurus).

Venus.—Benefic as lord of 1 and 8 (Libra), 2 and 9 (Virgo), 4 and 9 (Aquarius), 5 and 10 (Capricorn), and 5 and 12 (Gemini); *neutral* as lord of 1 and 6 (Taurus); and *malefic* as lord of 2 and 7 (Aries), 3 and 8 (Pisces), 3 and 10 (Leo), 4 and 11 (Cancer), 6 and 11 (Sagittarius), and 7 and 12 (Scorpio).

Saturn.—Benefic as lord of 1 and 2 (Capricorn), 1 and 12 (Aquarius), 4 and 5 (Libra), and 9 and 10 (Taurus); *neutral* as lord of 3 and 4 (Scorpio), 5 and 6 (Virgo), 6 and 7 (Leo), and 7 and 8 (Cancer); and *malefic* as lord of 2 and 3 (Sagittarius), 11 and 12 (Pisces), 8 and 9 (Gemini), and 10 and 11 (Aries).

With the aid of this schedule the benefic and malefic planets (do not confuse this with the good and evil planets according to natural classification) for any horoscope can be easily ascertained.

In this example horoscope Lagna is Aquarius and the following are the benefics, neutrals and malefics.

Benefics.—Sun (lord of 7), Mars (lord of 3 and 10), Venus (lord of 4 and 9) and Saturn (lord of 1 and 12).

Rahu		Saturn Moon	
Lagna			Sun
			Mars Mercury Venus
	Jupiter		Kethu

Neutrals.—Mercury (lord of 5 and 8).

Malefics.—Moon (lord of 6) and Jupiter (lord of 2 and 11).

Interpretation of Yogas

Before attempting to interpret yogas properly the strengths of the various planets have to be noted. There are two methods of ascertaining the strengths which I shall name as the 'approximate' and the 'accurate'. The accurate method is the one described in my *Graha and Bhava Balas* which enables one to calculate the six sources of strength and weakness of planets. The majority of readers will probably find it difficult to work out the shadbalas so that for purposes of interpreting yogas they can rely on the 'approximate' method. This consists in ascertaining the *Saptavargaja bala* which has been fully described in my *Graha and Bhava Balas* and which I do not propose to discuss here. It must be specially noted that one should resort to this 'approximate' method only when he is quite unable to apply the 'accurate' method. Saptavargaja bala means the strength a planet gets by virtue of its disposition in a friendly, neutral or inimical Rasi, Hora, Drekkana, Sapthamsa, Navamsa, Dwadasamsa and Thrimsamsa. An objection may be raised that in case a planet is strongly disposed according to the 'approximate method' but powerless according to shadbala method, which should be accepted? The answer is, always give preference to shadbala method. We call such strengths of planets as 'inherent strength'. The next step is to ascertain what may be called the residential strength which reveals the percentage of results a planet is capable of giving by vertue of occupation of a house. This requires the determination of Bhavas (house longitudes), Bhava sandhis (junctional points) and the lengths of Bhavas. All the processes involved in ascertaining these details are given in my *Manual of Hindu Astrology*. Thus we require the following details for purposes of interpreting yogas:

1. The good and evil lords in a horoscope.
2. The inherent strengths of planets.
3. The residential strengths of planets.

A yoga is formed by at least two planets. Ascertain whether the planets forming a yoga are benefic lords or malefic lords. If benefic, they get one positive unit of strength ; if malefic, assign a negative unit of strength. Ascertain if the two planets causing the yoga are in association with or aspected by other benefic and malefic lords. Assign one positive unit for benefic aspect* or association and a negative unit for the association or aspect of a malefic. See also if the yogakarakas are in exaltation or debilitation, in friendly or inimical houses and assign positive and negative units for the same. Summarising :— positive units of strength are contributed thus :

(*a*) If Yogakaraka is a benefic lord .... 1 unit
(*b*) Yogakaraka with a benefic lord .... 1 „
(*c*) Yogakaraka receiving the aspect of a benefic lord .... 1 „
(*d*) Yogakaraka in exaltation or friendly sign .... 1 „

And negative units of strength are contributed thus :

(*a*) If Yogakaraka is a malefic lord .... 1 unit
(*b*) Yogakaraka with a malefic lord .... 1 „
(*c*) Yogakaraka receiving the aspect of a malefic lord .... 1 „
(*d*) Yogakaraka in debilitation or inimical sign .... 1 „

If the positive units predominate, the yogakaraka will confer predominantly beneficial results in respect of a beneficial yoga ; and no evil results will be given by him in regard to a beneficial yoga if the negative

---

* $\frac{1}{4}$, $\frac{1}{2}$ and $\frac{3}{4}$ aspects may also be taken into account.

units predominate. Out of the two planets causing a yoga, the planet whose inherent strength is more will fulfil the larger part of the indications of the yoga in his Dasa while the planet whose shadbala strength is less will fulfil his part as a sub-lord to a lesser extent. The nature of the results of the yoga corresponds to the nature of the house in which the yoga occurs or to which the yoga has reference and the extent of the results depends upon the residential strength of the yogakarakas. The above method of interpretation has been developed and applied by me, the germ of the method, having been taken from standard astrological works. I shall illustrate the above with a suitable example.

Chart No. 1.—*Born on 8-8-1912 at 7-35 p.m. (I.S.T.) Lat. 13° N., Long. 77° 34' E.*

Rahu		Saturn Moon	
Lagna	RASI		Sun
			Mars Merc. Venus
	Jupiter		Kethu

	Saturn	Venus	
Sun Rahu	NAVAMSA		
Lagna			Moon Mercury Kethu
	Jupiter	Mars	

Inherent strengths		*Residential strengths*	
Sun	6.2	Sun	24 Per cent
Moon	8.9	Moon	40 Per cent
Mars	6.4	Mars	31 Per cent
Mercury	6.3	Mercury	80 Per cent
Jupiter	6.9	Jupiter	90 Per cent

Inherent strengths		*Residential strengths*	
Venus	5.0	Venus	37 Per cent
Saturn	6.8	Saturn	95 Per cent

Benefics ana Malefics.—As Aquarius or Kumbha is Lagna the *benefics* are Venus, the Sun, Saturn and Mars; Mercury is *neutral*; and *malefics* are Jupiter and the Moon. Gajakesari Yoga is formed in the above horoscope by the disposition of the Moon and Jupiter in mutual kendras.

Yogakarakas.—The planets causing the Gajakesari are the Moon and Jupiter.

The Moon is a malefic lord	.... − 1	unit
The Moon is associated with Saturn, a benefic lord	.... + 1	,,
The Moon is exalted	.... + 1	,,
The Moon's aspect strength	.... − ½	,,
Total	.... + ½	unit

Jupiter is a malefic lord	.... − 1	unit
Jupiter occupies a friendly sign	.... + 1	,,
Jupiter is aspected by Saturn a benefic lord	.... + 1	,,
Aspected by Mars a benefic lord and others*	.... + 1¼	,,
Total	.... + 2¼	units

Thus the Moon is benefic and Jupiter is more benefic. The Moon's shadbala strength is greater than that of Jupiter. Hence the Moon should fulfil the larger part of the yoga pertaining to the 4th house while Jupiter gives the results pertaining to

* See "Aspect Table" for details.

the 10th house. The native cannot enjoy the Moon's Dasa and hence the Moon can produce the results of the yoga only as sub-lord and that too to the extent of only 40%. Jupiter on the other hand can give 90% of the results due by him in reference to the 10th house and gives good results of the 2nd and 11th houses.

Therefore :

(1) The yoga will be enjoyed throughout Jupiter's Dasa subject to the influences of sub-lords.

(2) The Moon's Bhukthi in Jupiter's Dasa would have been excellent so far as this particular yoga is concerned but as the Moon can give only 40% of the results of the 4th house, much importance need not be attached.

(3) During the Moon's sub-period in all Dasas the yoga will manifest to a small proportion.

(4) During Jupiter's Bhukthi in all Dasas the yoga will be felt to a fairly good proportion, subject of course to the disposition of the other major lords under whom Jupiter acts as sub-lord.

The method suggested above should be studied and applied very carefully. It has been offered with a view to enabling the readers to make further investigations. By an extension of the same principle it will no doubt be possible to interpret any kind of yoga.

In giving the combinations below no particular order has been followed but only such yogas (several of which are indeed rare) have been included which are to be met with in the generality of horoscopes and which can be easily deciphered by the astrological students.

1. Gajakesari Yoga

Definition.—If Jupiter is in a kendra from the Moon the combination goes under the name Gajakesari.

Results.—Many relations, polite and generous, builder of villages and towns or magistrate over them ; will have a lasting reputation even long after death.

Remarks.—Here as well as elsewhere great difference in the enjoyment of results should be pronounced. The original writers say that the person born in this yoga will build villages and towns. A literal interpretation of the results leads one nowhere. They have to be adapted to suit modern conditions and climes. One born in this yoga may become a member of Municipality and engineer or if the yoga is really powerful, a mayor. The results ascribed to a yoga are subject to qualification or modification according as the yogakarakas are strong or weak. There are magistrates from the village to the district with different powers. From a builder of a small shrine or choultry to the builder of a large and rich temple there is much difference. Combinations are given but the results of the same conjunction will vary with the strength of the planets, bhavas and the constellations. I would give here two typical horoscopes illustrative of the different variations in Gajakesari.

Chart No. 2.—*Born on 13-8-1894, at 2-30 p m (L.M.T.) Lat. 23° N. ; Long. 75° E.*

Rahu	Mars		Jup.
	RASI		Venus Merc. Sun
	4-175		
Moon	Lagna		Kethu Saturn

Lagna Sun	Kethu		Mars
	NAVAMSA		Venus
Jup.	Moon	Mercury Rahu	Saturn

Balance of Venus Dasa at birth : years 2-4-24.

Chart No. 3.—*Born on 9-8-1911, at 6-7 a m. (I.S.T.) Lat. 29° 1' N., Long, 77° 41' E.*

	Saturn Mars Rahu		
	RASI		Lagna Sun
Moon	4-156		Merc.
		Jupiter Kethu	Venus

Lagna	Moon		
Sun Jupit. Venus Kethu	NAVAMSA		
			Rahu
Saturn	Mars	Mercury	

Balance of Moon's Dasa at birth : years 8-8-21.

Above are given two charts—illustrative of Gajakesari Yoga.

Chart No. 2.—Yogakarakas are Jupiter and the Moon. Lagna is Scorpio, hence *benefic* lords are the Moon, the Sun and Jupiter. *Malefics* are Mercury and Venus. *Neutrals* are Mars and Saturn.

MOON

(*a*) The Moon is a benefic lord	....	1 unit
(*b*) The Moon occupies a friendly sign	...	1 ,,
(*c*) The Moon's aspect strength	....	$\frac{5}{8}$,,
(*d*) The Moon is not associated	....	0 ,,
Total		$2\frac{5}{8}$ units

JUPITER

(*a*) Jupiter is a benefic lord	....	1 unit
(*b*) Jupiter has no association	....	0 ,,
(*c*) Jupiter's aspect strength	....	1 ,,
(*d*) Jupiter is in a neutral sign	....	$\frac{3}{4}$,,
Total		$2\frac{3}{4}$ units

Both the Moon and Jupiter are beneficially disposed and as Jupiter gets more units he will fulfil the larger part of the blessings of the yoga. As the native enjoys Venus Dasa at birth (about 2 years) the Moon in his Dasa (8 to 18 age) gives rise to the results of the yoga to some extent while the larger part of it (particularly regarding finance and fortune) will be realised in Jupiter's Dasa to begin from the 43rd year. The extent of the results depends upon the residential strength.

Chart No. 3.—The ascendant is Cancer. Therefore *benefics* are Mars and Jupiter; *malefics* are

Venus and Mercury; and *neutrals* are the Sun, the Moon and Saturn.

THE MOON

(*a*) The Moon is a neutral	....	$\frac{1}{2}$ unit
(*b*) The Moon is not associated	....	0 ,,
(*c*) The Moon's aspect strength	....	$\frac{3}{4}$,,
(*d*) The Moon is in enemy's house	....	—1 ,,
Total		$\frac{1}{4}$ unit

JUPITER

(*a*) Jupiter is a benefic	...	1 unit
(*b*) Jupiter is with Kethu	....	—1 ,,
(*c*) Jupiter's aspect strength	....	$1\frac{1}{8}$,,
(*d*) Jupiter is in an unfriendly sign	....	—1 ,,
Total		$\frac{1}{8}$ unit

Jupiter and the Moon are feebly benefic. The Moon will give rise to a larger part of the yoga results than Jupiter. The Moon can fulfil his part of the results as major lord and sub-lord particularly in Jupiter's Dasa. The yoga is practically neutralised if the positive and negative units of strength obtained by both the planets are equal.

2. Sunapha Yoga

Definition.— If there are planets (excepting the Sun) in the second house from the Moon, Sunapha is caused.

Results.—Self-earned property, king, ruler or his equal, intelligent, wealthy and good reputation.

Remarks.—The Moon plays a very large part in this as well as in the following two yogas. The second house must be occupied by planets excepting the Sun. The second may be occupied by Mars, Mercury, Jupiter, Venus and Saturn either singly or collectively. Again the nature of the yoga depends to a large extent upon the nature of the lord or lords occupying the second. Thus take Taurus as the Moon's Rasi and Mercury, Jupiter and Venus being placed in Gemini. This is a powerful Sunapha Yoga capable of giving rise to much wealth. The intensity of the yoga will be heightened if Lagna happens to be Leo as in this case the yoga will have reference to the 10th and 11th houses. As usual the results will find expression in the Dasas and Bhukthis of the planets responsible for causing the yoga.

Chart No. 4 is a peculiar horoscope. Note the concentration of five planets in the 2nd from the Moon causing a Sunapha Yoga. The yoga is practically defunct because all the evil forces have been focussed on it. The Sun is in debility with Kethu aspected by Saturn and Rahu. The yoga has produced no results and the native is a non-entity. Compare this horoscope with Chart No. 5, where Sunapha is present as Venus occupies the second from the Moon. Venus is a yogakaraka from the Moon and his having caused Sunapha has fortified the financial position of the native. Note that Sunapha has much influence on the financial prosperity or adversity of a person.

Chart No. 4.—*Born on 31-10-1910 at 1-21-13 p.m. (L.M.T.) Lat. 13° N.; Long. 77°. 34'. E.*

	Saturn Rahu		
Lagna 2 17	RASI		
	1.57		
		Jupiter Kethu Mer Sun Venus Mars	Moon

Sun			Kethu
	NAVAMSA		Saturn
Rahu Jupiter Venus Merc.	Mars	Lagna	Moon

Balance of Mars Dasa at birth : years 4–7–10.

Chart No. 5.—*Born on 28-5-1903 at 1-19 a.m. (L.M.T.) Lat. 9° N.; Long. 77° 42' E.*

Kethu Lagna 1 55		Sun Moon Mercury	Venus
Jupiter	RASI		
Saturn	111.8		
			Mars Rahu

Mars	Sun	Venus	Jupiter Saturn
	NAVAMSA		Lagna Rahu
Kethu			Moon Mercury

Balance of Mars Dasa at birth : years 5-3-25.

3. Anapha Yoga

Definition.—If there are planets in the 12th from the Moon, Anapha Yoga is formed.

Results.—Well-formed organs, mejestic appearance, good reputation, polite, generous, self-respect, fond of dress and sense pleasures. In later life, renunciation and austerity.

Remarks.—In Anapha also the Sun is not taken into account. The remarks made for Sunapha apply to this also with slight variation.

Chart No. 6.—*Born on 20-8-1902 at 11-33 a.m. Lat. 9° 58′ N.; Long. 78° 10′ E.*

	Kethu		Mars
Moon	RASI		Venus
Jupiter Saturn	4.107		Sun Merc.
		Lagna Rahu	

Moon	Kethu	Sun	Mars Lagna Jupiter
	NAVAMSA		
Saturn			Mercury
		Rahu	Venus

Balance of Rahu Dasa at birth: years 3-7-22.

The Anapha is caused by the presence of Jupiter and Saturn in the 12th from the Moon. The yoga is feebly present inasmuch as Jupiter is debilitated—though there is Neechabhanga because of Saturn's disposition in a kendra from Lagna. Saturn's quota of the yoga will manifest in his Dasa. Note also the fact that the 12th has reference to moksha or spiritual emancipation so that the native would cultivate an outlook of detachment for worldly things in his later years.

4. Dhurdhura Yoga

Definition.—If there are planets on either side of the Moon, the combination goes under the name of Dhurdhura.

Results.—The native is bountiful. He will be blessed with much wealth and conveyances.

Remarks.—Whatever may be the results ascribed to different yogas, one important truth emerges, that is, the person gets money, power, fame and reputation of varying gradations. This, of course, does not apply to strictly *Parivraja Yogas.* Many varieties of Sunapha, Anapha and Dhurdhura are formed by permutations and combinations of the five planets and their results should be particularly noted. If Mars is in the 2nd and Mercury is in the 12th a kind of Dhurdhura is formed. Similarly Mars in the 12th and Mercury in the 2nd gives rise to another kind and Jupiter in the 2nd and Mercury in the 12th gives rise to yet another type though all these go under the name of Dhurdhura. Each conjunction in these permutations produce different results. To give a simple illustration take Mars in the 2nd in Capricorn where he is exalted and Jupiter in the 12th in Scorpio in a friendly sign. Now take Jupiter in the 2nd (debilitated) and Mars in the 12th (in his own house). Would the results in both cases be the same? All these permutations must be carefully analysed. There will be thirty-one varieties of Sunapha, and an equal number of Anapha combinations and there are something like 180 varieties of Dhurdhura. For fuller details refer to the English Translation of *Brihat Jathaka* by Prof. B. Suryanarain Rao.

Chart No. 7.—*Born on 31-7-1910 at Gh. 32-15 after Sunrise. Lat. 8° 44' N.; Long. 77° 44' E.*

	Saturn	Moon Rahu	Venus	Merc.		Moon Mars	Jupiter
	RASI		Merc. Sun	Venus Rahu	NAVAMSA		
Lagna	4.187		Mars				Kethu Lagna Saturn
	Kethu		Jupit.		Sun		

Balance of Moon's Dasa at birth: years 6-3-23.

In this horoscope the Dhurdhura Yoga formed is a typical one. The Moon is exalted in Taurus, Saturn is in the 12th and Venus is in the 2nd. Saturn is Neecha but there is Neechabhanga. From Chandra Saturn is a yogakaraka. The results of the yoga may find expression in a large measure in Sani Dasa particularly in Sukra Bhukthi.

5. Kemadruma Yoga

Definition.—When there are no planets on both sides of the Moon, Kemadruma Yoga is formed.

Results.—The person will be dirty, sorrowful, doing unrighteous deeds, poor, dependent, a rogue and a swindler.

Remarks.—Some authors say that if planets are in a kendra from birth or from the Moon or if the Moon is in conjunction with a planet there is no Kemadruma. There are yet other authors who say that these yogas arise from kendras and navamsas but these observations are not generally acceptable. Varahamihira adds emphasis by saying that when persons born in royal families are subjected to such degradations much more of these unfortunate results must be predicted than in the case of persons born in ordinary families. Sorrows mean physical as well as mental. The word *Neecha* is used in the original and this refers to such acts as are prohibited by the religious, moral and social codes and are therefore held to be disgraceful.

Chart No. 8 is a typical Kemadruma Yoga horoscope. No planets are placed on either side of Chandra and no planets are to be found in kendras either from Lagna or from the Moon.

In Chart No. 9 you will see that Kemadruma is present because the houses on either side of the Moon are vacant. But there is distinct cancellation of the Kemadruma because (*a*) the kendras from the

Moon are occupied and (*b*) kendras from the Lagna are also occupied.

Chart No. 8.—*Born on 28-7-1896 at Gh. 10 after Sunrise. Lat. 13° N.; Long. 77° 34' E.*

	Mars		
Moon Rahu	RASI		Jupit. Venus Merc. Sun
	4.163 a		Kethu
		Saturn	Lagna

	Lagna Saturn	Moon Kethu	
Jupit.	NAVAMSA		
Mars Venus	Rahu Sun	Mercury	

Balance of Jupiter's Dasa at birth: years 10-9-4.

Chart No. 9.—*Born on 26-2-1908 at 2-56 p.m. (L.M.T.) Lat. 18° 55' N.; Long. 72° 54' E.*

Venus Saturn	Mars		Rahu
Mercury Sun	RASI		Jupit. Lagna
	4.246		
Kethu Moon			

	Mercury Moon Rahu		
Sun	NAVAMSA		Mars Lagna
Venus			Saturn
	Jupiter	Kethu	

Balance of Kethu Dasa at birth: years 6-3-15.

6. Chandra Mangala Yoga

Definition.—If Mars conjoins the Moon this yoga is formed.

Results.—Earnings through unscrupulous means, a seller of women, treating mother harshly and doing mischief to her and other relatives.

Remarks.—The results given above are those ascribed by ancient writers. With due respect to the ancient masters in the science I have to observe that *Chandra Mangala Yoga* acts as a powerful factor in establishing one's financial worth. The earnings will generally be through such occupations as toddy contract, beer shop, bar, etc. One has to cater to the baser needs of men, but when the Moon and Mars are well disposed, the earnings will be through other approved means. The yoga is said to arise by the association of Mars and the Moon but I feel that the yoga will also be formed if the Moon and Mars are in mutual aspect. Take the Moon in Taurus and Mars in Scorpio. Take the Moon in Cancer and Mars in Capricorn. These are excellent positions. The combination can be productive of good if it occurs in the 2nd, 9th, 10th or 11th house.

Chart No. 10.—*Born on 24-8-1890 at Gh. 37-10 after Sunrise. Lat. 13° N ; Long. 77°34′ E.*

Lagna		Rahu	
	RASI		
Jupiter	11.31		Sun Sat.
	Moon Mars Kethu		Merc. Venus

Kethu	Jupiter		
Lagna Moon Merc.	NAVAMSA		Sun
Mars			Venus Saturn
			Rahu

Balance of Mercury's Dasa at birth : years 7-3-24.

In the above chart Chandra Mangala Yoga has taken place in Scorpio the 9th from Lagna. Mars is in his own house and the Moon is in debilitation. Because the Moon is waxing and Mars occupies his own sign, this yoga has received some vitality. The Dasa of Mars will be the best.

When Chandra Mangala Yoga occurs in unfavourable houses, the native will have debased character. He may even sell his wife, his sister, etc., and make money out of unholy transactions.

7. Adhi Yoga

Definition.—If benefics are situated in the 6th, 7th and 8th from the Moon, the combination goes under the name of *Adhi Yoga*.

Results.—The person will be polite and trustworthy, will have an enjoyable and happy life, surrounded by luxuries and affluence, will inflict defeats on his enemies, will be healthy and will live long.

Remarks.—Adhi Yoga is one of the most important combinations. Astrological authorities classify this *Adhi Yoga* as *Papadhi Yoga* and *Shubhadhi Yoga*. But Varahamihira and that section of astrologers do not seem to favour such a classification. Bhattotpala, the erudite commentator of the writings of Varahamihira suggests the existence of *Papadhi Yoga*. Varahamihira distinctly observes *Soumyehi*—implying clearly only the *benefics*, *viz*., Mercury, Jupiter and Venus. All these benefics may be in the 6th, 7th or 8th or in two houses or all of them may be in any one of these houses. If there is one planet in full strength in any one of these signs, that person becomes a leader. If there are two, he will be a minister and if there are three, he will occupy an eminent station in life. If all the three benefics, devoid of strength, are in the three signs above mentioned, then also Adhi Yoga will be present but the influence it exerts would indeed be feeble. Adhi Yoga may be considered as a Raja Yoga or almost its equivalent.

The Adhi Yoga is fairly powerful in Chart No. 11, because Jupiter is exalted in the 7th and Mercury is in the 8th from the Moon. Jupiter's Dasa was an excellent one as it enabled him to attain a good position in life. Note also the presence of *Gajakesari* as Jupiter is exalted in a kendra from the Moon. Jupiter has given rise to two yogas.

Chart No. 11.—*Born on 24-9-1871 at Gh. 7 after Sunrise. Lat. 10° N.; Long. 77° 34′ E.*

			Rahu
	RASI		Jupit.
Moon	1.125		Merc.
Saturn Kethu	Mars	Lagna	Sun Venus

Sun	Venus Moon Lagna	Kethu	
	NAVAMSA		Saturn
			Jupiter
Merc.	Rahu		Mars

Balance of Moon's Dasa at birth: years 8-8-7.

Chart No. 12.—*Born on 7-8-1887 at 1-30 p.m. (L.M.T.) Lat. 11° N.; Long. 77° 2′ E.*

Moon			Mars
	RASI		Sun Merc. Sat. Rahu
Kethu	K. S.		
	Lagna	Jupiter	Venus

Rahu		Mars	
Venus Sun	NAVAMSA		Moon
Jupit.	Lagna	Mercury	Kethu Saturn

Balance of Jupiter's Dasa at birth: year 0-7-6.

In Chart No. 12. also the Adhi Yoga is fairly powerful, Venus and Jupiter occupying the 7th and 8th from the Moon. Evidently Venus is more powerful as, though he is Neecha, he is in a friendly Navamsa, while Jupiter is in an inimical house. The native's Sukra Dasa had been brilliant and he was a leading figure in the Indian political scene.

8. Chatussagara Yoga

Definition.—Chatussagara Yoga is caused when all the kendras are occupied by planets.

Results.—The person will earn good reputation, be an equal to a ruler, have a long and prosperous life, be blessed with good children and health and his name will travel to the confines of the four oceans.

Remarks.—According to the dictum *Kendrasthatibalassuhuhu* planets disposed in kendras add great strength to the horoscope. The four angles in a horoscope are like the four walls of a building.

Chart No. 13.—*Born on 19-7-1816 at Gh. 15¾ after Sunrise. Lat. 17° N.; Long. 5h 10m. 20s. E.*

	Moon	Rahu	Merc.
	RASI B.G.R.		Sun Venus
Saturn			Mars
	Kethu	Lagna Jupiter	

	Mars		
Kethu	NAVAMSA		
Jupit.			Sun Venus Rahu Saturn
	Moon	Lagna	

The results should not be applied literally. Planets in the 10th kendra are more powerful than those in the 7th ; those in the 7th are more powerful than those in the 4th. Those in the 4th, in turn, are more powerful than those in the 1st though Lagna Kendra is an exception. In ascribing results to the Dasas, the usual considerations such as a planet being a benefic or malefic lord, etc., have to be taken into account. Chatussagara Yoga contributes to considerable financial soundness and good name to the person irrespective of the fact whether or not one is a ruler.

Chart No. 13 is the horoscope of the father of late Professor B. Suryanarain Rao. Note all the kendras are occupied. He was a man of great self-respect, held a decent position as a Dewan, a great yogee and knew well eight languages.

9. Vasumathi Yoga

Definition.—If benefics occupy the upachayas (3, 6, 10 and 11) either from the ascendant or from the Moon, the combination goes under the name of Vasumathi Yoga.

Results.—The person will not be a dependent but will always command plenty of wealth.

Remarks.—Vasumathi Yoga has more to do with wealth than with anything else. The Vasumathi resulting from the Lagna seems to have more influence than the one formed with reference to the Moon. By implication it also means that two benefics will give less wealth while only one benefic will give ordinary wealth. If the upachayas happen to be exaltation places, the yoga becomes extremely powerful while the reverse holds good in case the upachayas happen to be debilitation places. When counted from the Moon all the four upachayas cannot be occupied because there will be only three benefics left. The authorities are silent on the matter and they simply say that the upachayas should be occupied. Varahamihira seems to go so far as to assert that predictions made according to ordinary combinations may sometimes fail but the results predicted by *Vasumathi Yoga* do not fail. In all such planetary combinations, one must be very careful in assessing the real strength of a yoga and see if its results have already been comprehended by some other more powerful yogas. It will be seen that purely *Vasumathi Yogas* are a rare occurrence. You will find very few examples in which benefics are in *all the upachayas*. Even when benefics are in upachayas, they will be found to be associated with or aspected by malefics and due allowance must be made for such evil dispositions.

Chart No. 14.—*Born on 31st October 1915 at 7 p.m., Lat. 31° 27′ N.; Long. 74° 26′ E.*

		Lagna	Sat.
Jupiter	RASI		Kethu Moon Mars
Rahu			
		Sun Venus	Merc.

	Lagna	Saturn	Jupiter Venus
Sun	NAVAMSA		Rahu
Moon Kethu Mars			
			Mercury

Balance of Mercury's Dasa at birth: years 12-8-7.

In Chart No. 14, the 3rd, 6th and 10th are occupied respectively by the Moon, Venus and Jupiter suggesting the presence of Vasumathi Yoga. Of the three planets that have caused the Yoga, Venus is the most powerful and hence most of the indications of the Yoga will fructify in Venus period or sub-periods. A purely beneficial Vasumathi Yoga cannot occur inasmuch as, in very rare instances, all the four upachayas can be occupied.

10. Rajalakshana Yoga

Definition.—Jupiter, Venus, Mercury and the Moon should be in Lagna or they should be placed in kendra.

Results.—The native will possess an attractive appearance and he will be endowed with all the good qualities of high personages.

Remarks.—The weak Moon or badly associated Mercury cannot make a person possess a beautiful appearance. However, the yoga seems to contribute *Adrishta* or luck in such a way that the person can command respect, dignity and regard. One need not necessarily be a king to inherit all the virtues, for all kings are not virtuous. Personalities or strokes of luck which many will not have and which many covet.

Chart No. 1 (page 10) may be cited as an example for Rajalakshana inasmuch as Jupiter, Venus, Mercury and the Moon are all in kendras. But owing to the association of the Moon with Saturn and the predominance of Saturnine influence both on the Moon and the Lagna except for the physical appearance, the blessings of this yoga have fully manifested otherwise.

11. Vanchana Chora Bheethi Yoga

Definition.—The Lagna is occupied by a malefic with Gulika in a trine: or Gulika is associated with the lords of Kendras and Thrikonas; or the lord of Lagna is combined with Rahu, Saturn or Kethu.

Results.—The native will always entertain feelings of suspicion towards others around him. He is afraid of being cheated, swindled and robbed.

Remarks.—Here three sets of combinations can be noted. They are :—

(*a*) The ascendant must have an evil planet with Gulika disposed in the 5th or 9th.

(*b*) Gulika should be associated with the lords of 1, 4, 7, 10, 5 and 9.

(*c*) Lord of Lagna should join Rahu or Saturn or Kethu.

In all these cases, the person will not only have fears from cheats, rogues and thieves but he will also have huge material losses. The combinations pertaining to this Yoga are found in almost all horoscopes, so that we are all guilty of cheating and being cheated one another in some form or the other. It is a tragedy of our social life that a merchant minting millions at the cost of the poor is left scot-free while the poor, committing theft in the face of poverty and want, are booked by law. Cheating is practised in a variety of ways. Fertile brains find countless methods to cheat their associates. The merchants have various ways of cheating their clients. The lawyer is equally successful. The medical man commands many ways to defraud his patients.

Gulika is considered the son of Saturn and his position is to be carefully fixed in the Zodiac. The Yoga given above refers to persons who will be the victims of fraud but the same combination can also be extended to apply to those who perpetrate the deeds.

Chart No. 15.—*Born on 29-7-1909 at Gh. 1-15 after sunrise. Lat. 17° N. ; Long. 77° E.*

Mars	Saturn	Rahu	
	RASI		Sun Merc. Lagna
			Jup. Venus
	Moon Kethu		

	Saturn		Venus
Moon	NAVAMSA		Rahu
Kethu			
Lagna	Sun	Mars Jupiter	Mercury

Balance of Mercury's Dasa at birth : years 6-6-16.

In Chart No. 15. you will see that lord of Lagna is Neecha and he is with Kethu aspected by Rahu. The Lagna is occupied by the Sun. The native is always afraid that he will be cheated and defrauded. Naturally he is nervous and extremely sensitive, miserly and very cautious. He adopts towards others the same suspicious behaviour, that he thinks others adopt towards him. This is a typical horoscope.

12. Sakata Yoga

Definition.—The Moon in the 12th, 6th or 8th from Jupiter gives rise to Sakata Yoga.

Results.—The native loses fortune and may regain it. He will be ordinary and insignificant. He will suffer from poverty, privation and misery. He will be stubborn and hated by relatives.

Remarks.—While the generality of astrological writers hold that Sakata Yoga is productive of evil results, there is difference of opinion as regards the definition of this Yoga. The great Parasara and Varahamihira say that when all the planets are in the 1st and 7th, Sakata is caused. Prof. Rao opines that this definition leaves room for doubt as to why it should be the 7th. On the contrary, the definition given above appears more reasonable inasmuch as the Yoga is generated by the Moon occupying the three Dusthanas from the greatest benefic Jupiter thus obstructing the free flow of fortune; but it is also open to objection as will be seen from the following observations:—

In the large number of horoscopes examined by me I have been able to mark that Sakata Yoga has not really made the natives poor and wretched but often the degree of poverty and wretchedness has been nominal. I have a work entitled *Sukranadi* which says that one born in Sakata will have his fortune obstructed now and then. The exact words used are "Sakatayogajatasya Yogobhangam Padepade". The periods of misfortune will accord with the times of transits in malefic Rasis, *viz.*, 6th, 8th and 12th. In other words, every time the Moon transits the 6th, 8th and 12th from the radical Jupiter, the effects of Sakata are realised.

According to the definition given above, Sakata is caused by the Moon being placed in the 6th or 8th or 12th from Jupiter. When one planet is in the 8th from the other, naturally the other will be in the 6th.

13. Amala Yoga

Definition.—The 10th from the Moon or Lagna should be occupied by a benefic planet.

Results.—The person will achieve lasting fame and reputation. His character will be spotless and he will lead a prosperous life.

Remarks.—As in interpreting every combination, due consideration should be given to the strength of the lord causing the *Amala* and the aspects and associations he receives. Some benefic planets must occupy the 10th from Lagna or the Moon to cause Amala. If no benefic is present, then Amala is not caused. But yet on the strength of the dictum "Udayat Indutovapi Yegrahadasamasthithaha Te sarve arthapradagneya swa dasasu yatoditha" which means that *any planet* in the 10th from Lagna or Chandra would give, during his Dasa, much wealth, a malefic also is not ruled out. *Amala* means pure and when the Yoga is present, prosperity and affluence will be achieved through fair means while a *malefic*, whilst giving wealth, may make the means questionable. After all, the end justifies the means according to some and, therefore, Amala makes one scrupulous as to the means he employs for earning while a malefic in the 10th while no doubt good in its own way, as causing wealth to come, would not make one famous or a man of character.

Chart No. 16.—*Born on 12-2-1856 at 12-21 p.m. (L.M.T.) Lat. 18° N.; Long. 84° E.*

	Rahu Moon	Lagna	Sat.
Sun Mercury Jupiter	RASI		
Venus		Mars Kethu	

Jupit.		Lagna	Rahu
	NAVAMSA		
Merc			
Kethu		Moon Sun Mars Saturn Venus	

Balance of Venus Dasa at birth: years 6-11-3.

In this chart, one can easily detect the presence of Amala because of the situation of Jupiter and Mercury in the 10th from Lagna.

Chart No. 17.—*Born on 7-9-1904 at 1-55 p.m. (L.M.T.) Lat. 18°. 54' N; Long. 62°. 46' E.*

	Jupiter		
Kethu	RASI		Mars Moon
Saturn			Sun Rahu
Lagna			Merc. Venus

Merc. Venus			Jupiter Kethu
Mars	NAVAMSA		
			Lagna Saturn
Moon Rahu		Sun	

Balance of Mercury's Dasa at birth: years 14-5-27.

Amala is prominently marked by the presence of Venus and Mercury in the 10th from Lagna and Jupiter in the 10th from the Moon. The subject is a high civilian officer, confident, imaginative and a good judge of human nature. Venus as Karaka of Amala Yoga proved very beneficial to the native.

14. Parvata Yoga

Definition.—Benefics being disposed in Kendras, the 6th and 8th houses should either be unoccupied or occupied by benefic planets. This combination goes under the name of Parvata Yoga.

Results.—The person will become wealthy, prosperous, liberal, charitable, humorous and head of a town or village. He will be passionate also.

Remarks.—According to some, Parvata is also caused if the lords of Lagna and the 12th are in mutual Kendras. Thus, three sets of combinations are comprehended :—

(*a*) Benefics should be in Kendras, and 6th and 8th must be free.

(*b*) Benefics should be in Kendras, and 6th and 8th should be occupied by benefics.

(*c*) The lords of Lagna and the 12th should be in mutual Kendras.

Strangely enough, for Kumbha Lagna, the definition mentioned in item (*c*) *supra* cannot hold good inasmuch as the lord of the 12th and the Lagna happen to be Saturn. Instead of the 6th and 8th being occupied by benefics, it is better they are entirely free in which case, the native will be free from machinations of enemies and debts. In my humble opinion, *Parvata Yoga* cannot be so powerful as to minimise the strength of other important yogas. Its presence, no doubt, adds to making the person an entity within a limited circle. The Yoga does not seem to contribute much to political power. One may become a District Board member or a Municipal Commissioner. But it seems to have capacity enough to add financial stability.

15. Kahala Yoga

Definition.—Lords of the fourth and ninth houses should be in Kendras from each other and the lord of Lagna should be strongly disposed.

Results.—The native will be stubborn, not well informed, daring, head of a small army and a few villages.

Remarks.—No yogas should be interpreted *verbatim* if the results are to hold good to modern life and conditions. An appropriate and intelligent interpretation of Kahala Yoga should suggest that the person concerned will eke out his existence as a member of the army or police or in the capacity of a Collector or Tahsildar and the like.

Kahala Yoga is also caused when the 4th lord is exalted or in his own house being conjoined with or aspected by the lord of the 10th. Both the definitions of Kahala Yoga mentioned above assume the strength of Lagna, the 4th and the 9th. For Kumbha Lagna Venus happens to be the lord of the 4th and 9th. Therefore, Kahala Yoga is applicable to Kumbha Lagna *only* according to the second definition, which means that Venus should be in Pisces or Taurus or Libra in conjunction with or aspected by Mars. Naturally, Venus in Pisces and Mars in Sagittarius will be an ideal Kahala Yoga.

In Chart No. 1 lord of the 4th and 9th happens to be Venus. He is in Kendra and the lord of Lagna is in the 4th fairly strongly disposed. But Jupiter aspecting lord of Lagna takes away much of the evil aspect of the Yoga.

16. Vesi Yoga

Definition.—If planets other than the Moon occupy the 2nd from the Sun, Vesi Yoga is formed.

Results.—The person will be fortunate, happy, virtuous, famous and aristocratic.

Remarks.—Excepting the Moon and Rahu and Kethu, any other planet or planets may cause Vesi Yoga. If malefics occupy the second from the Sun, *papavesi* is caused while *subhavesi* is given rise to by the presence of benefic planets. The degree of the yoga to do good or bad depends to a large extent upon the Sun and the planets causing the Yoga. The results given above are for Subhavesi Yoga. Obviously quite the reverse holds good in case of papavesi. If the Sun is exalted, Lagna being Cancer and the subhavesi is caused by the presence of Venus in Taurus and both the Sun and Venus are inherently strong, then in spite of the fact that both the Sun and Venus are natural enemies the Yoga becomes supremely powerful and almost all the good results attributed to it would find full play when the Dasa and Bhukthi of the two planets operate. Obviously, if more than one planet causes the Yoga, one of the planets being a malefic, say Saturn, the good influences have to be sufficiently moderated. Thus it will be seen that proper interpretation of a Yoga is not a joke. It demands on the part of the astrologer great analytical powers and a thorough acquaintance with the technicalities of the subject.

Chart No. 18.—*Born on 8-8-1912 A.D. at 7-23 p.m. (L.M.T) Lat. 13° N. ; Long. 77° 34′ E.*

Rahu		Saturn Moon	
Lagna	RASI		Sun
			Mars Merc. Venus
	Jupiter		Kethu

	Saturn	Venus	
Rahu Sun	NAVAMSA		
Lagna			Kethu Moon Mercury
	Jupiter	Mars	

Balance of Mars Dasa at birth : years 6-0-10.

In Chart No. 18 Vesi Yoga is caused by the presence of Mars, Mercury and Venus in the 2nd from the Sun, the Lagna being Aquarius. Out of the

Yogakarakas, Mars in the least powerful inasmuch as he is removed from the Sun by nearly 29 degrees while Mercury and Venus alone can function as Yogakarakas. The Yoga having been primarily caused by the owner and the residents of the 7th house, the results will pertain to the Bhava in question, so that the person will be generally fortunate in respect of all the functions of the seventh house subject, of course, to the inherent strength of the house concerned.

17. Vasi Yoga

Definition.—Planets other than the Moon occupying the 12th from the Sun give rise to Vasi Yoga.

Results.—The subject will be happy, prosperous, liberal and the favourite of the ruling classes.

Remarks.—Here again, the definition and results are in reference to subhavasi. If malefics are present in the 12th, the results will be quite the reverse. The explanations given for the previous Yoga apply to this as well as to the next Yoga.

18. Obhayachari Yoga

Definition.—If planets other than the Moon are present on either side of the Sun, Obhayachari is caused.

Results. – The person will be an eloquent speaker. He will have well-proportioned limbs, will take delight in everything, will be liked by all, wealthy and famous.

Remarks.—One or more of the above three Yogas caused by the Sun would be present in almost every horoscope. Mercury is always confined within a certain elongation from the Sun unless the Sun is in the last part of a sign and Mercury has attained his greatest elongation, in which case, he will be in the 3rd or 11th house from the Sun's position, Veṣi or Vasi Yoga will invariably be present. Obviously, these Solar Yogas cannot be compared in their eminence to Rajayogas. They indicate more or less the 'ego' development of the individual concerned. Sometimes the Solar Yogas may be merged into other more important Dhana or Raja Yogas with the result their interpretation is always subject to a closer analysis of the more powerful combinations obtaining in the horoscope.

19. Hamsa Yoga

Definition.—Jupiter should occupy a Kendra which should be his own house or exaltation sign.

Results.—His legs will have the markings of a conch, lotus, fish and ankusa. He will possess a handsome body; he will be liked by others; he will be righteous in disposition and pure in mind.

Remarks.—This and the following four Yogas go under the special distinction of *Panchamahapurusha Yogas* producing five kinds of great men. Varahamihira has extolled these five combinations in his *Brihat Samhita*. Hamsa Yoga is caused if Jupiter is in a Kendra which should be identical with his own sign (Swakshetra) or the sign in which he gets exalted. In other words, Hamsa Yoga is possible in respect of all common and the movable signs Aries, Cancer, Libra and Capricorn. The assumption here is that Lagna is also a Kendra or quadrant. Those born in fixed signs (Taurus, Leo, Scorpio and Aquarius) cannot possess Hamsa Yoga inasmuch as neither Jupiter's exaltation sign nor own house can be identical with his situation in a Kendra. The strength of the Yoga is dependent as usual on the strength of Lagna and Jupiter and in which Kendra he is disposed. Obviously, the tenth Kendra is the most powerful. The ownership of Kendra by Jupiter is not desirable but when Hamsa Yoga is present, the general principle loses its significance. As between the situation of Jupiter in a Kendra identical with Swakshetra and a Kendra identical with his uccha, Hamsa Yoga caused by the latter is preferable inasmuch as even the trace of evil due to Jupiter's quadrangular ownership disappears. Hamsa Yoga should be very carefully interpreted, as it is supposed to produce a man of sterling character and immense moral fibre.

Chart No 19.—*Born on 12-5-1916 at Gh. 39-15 after Sunrise. Lat. 13° N.; Long. 77° 35' E.*

Jupiter		Sun Mercury	Venus Sat.
	RASI		Kethu
Rahu			Mars Moon
Lagna			

Jupit.	Rahu Mars Saturn		
Venus	NAVAMSA		Lagna Mercury
Sun			
Moon		Kethu	

Balance of Sun's Dasa at birth : years 5-11-3.

The Lagna is Sagittarius and Jupiter is in Pisces—a kendra causing Hamsa Yoga. But still the native is neither a King nor a high personality. The reason is obvious. Jupiter is powerfully aspected by Saturn and Mars. But still, Jupiter is capable of giving rise to the results of Hamsa Yoga to a good extent in his Dasa. The native has a good personality, is good-tempered and liked by his associates. The above horoscope is illustrated with a view to showing the restrictive effects of a Hamsa Yoga when Jupiter is subject to malefic aspects and associations.

Chart No. 20.—*Born on 11-4-1880 at Gh. 12 after Sunrise. Lat. 18° N.; Long. 32° 4' E.*

Sun Venus Jupiter Saturn Mercury	Moon		Kethu Mars Lagna
	RASI		
Rahu			

Kethu Sat. Lagna	Sun		
	NAVAMSA		
			Venus
Mars		Jupiter Mercury	Moon Rahu

Balance of Venus' Dasa at birth: years 11-6-27.

In Chart No. 20 Hamsa Yoga has resulted on account of the disposition of Jupiter in his own sign in 10th from Lagna. The 10th is the most powerful Kendra and Jupiter is in conjunction with lords of Lagna, 5th and 9th and hence fortified. Still the Yoga is not completely unadulterated with the result the native is not a King. He was a well-known figure in Indian Politics and Journalism, self-made and earned good reputation for his sober and balanced views.

Chart No. 21.—*Born on 14-12-1895 at 3-5 a.m. Lat. 51° N.; Long. 0° 5′ E.*

Rahu	RASI		Jupit.
			Kethu
Sun	Moon Mars Mercury	Lagna Venus Saturn	

Merc. Rahu	Sun	Saturn	
Venus	NAVAMSA		
			Moon
Jupit. Lagna		Mars	Kethu

Balance of Saturn's Dasa at birth : years 17-10-27.

Chart No. 21 is a typical example of Hamsa Yoga in its full swing. The Lagna is Libra and Jupiter is in a Kendra in exaltation in the 10th house. Naturally, the Yoga has manifested in regard to the 10th house. In addition to Hamsa Yoga, Malavya and Sasa Yogas are also present inasmuch as Venus and Saturn are respectively in Kendras identical with their Swakshetra and Swauccha. No wonder the horoscope belongs to a great King. Sasa Yoga rendered the native covetous of other's possessions. Consequently he was the head of the greatest imperial possession, an anachronism with modern concepts of democracy and freedom.

20. Malavya Yoga

Definition.—Venus should occupy a quadrant which should be his own or exaltation sign.

Results.—The person will have a well-developed physique, will be strong-minded, wealthy, happy with children and wife, will command vehicles, endowed with clean sense-organs and renowned and learned.

Remarks.—Malavya Yoga can come into existence if Venus is exalted in a Kendra or occupies a Kendra which should be his own house. Malavya Yoga cannot occur with reference to every sign of the zodiac. Consistent with the nature of Venus, Malavya Yoga will make one resolute, immensely rich and give him happiness from wife and children and fame and name. Venus is the indicator of conveyances, sensual pleasures, music, dancing, fine arts, luxury and material comforts. Naturally Malavya Yoga renders one inclined towards all the indications of Venus, with the result his spiritual advancement and outlook will be in inverse ratio to his material comforts and pleasures. In other words, while both Hamsa and Malavya are Raja Yogas, the former makes one more idealistic, spiritual, broad-minded and selfless, while the latter indicates love of pleasure, and a predominantly materialistic outlook of life. Malavya Yoga can manifest in reference to the various Bhavas as given hereunder for persons born in different Lagnas.

Taurus, Libra and Pisces .... First house
Aries, Scorpio and Virgo .... Seventh house
Gemini, Leo and Capricorn .... Tenth house
Sagittarius, Aquarius and Cancer ... Fourth house

Chart No. 20 on page 46 may be taken as an example of Malavya Yoga as Venus is exalted in the 10th house which is a Kendra. It may be noted that all the five Yogas, going under the special distinction of Panchamaha Yogas, can occur unblemished only in exceptional cases and with regard to the generality of horoscopes, these Yogas will not be of much political value.

21. Sasa Yoga

Definition.—Sasa Yoga is given rise to if Saturn occupies a Kendra which should be his own or exaltation sign.

Results.—One born in this Yoga will command good servants. His character will be questionable. He will be head of a village or a town or even a King, will covet other's riches and will be wicked in disposition.

Remarks.—Here Saturn comes into the picture. He should be exalted in a Kendra or occupy a Kendra being his own house. Birth in movable or fixed signs can give rise to Sasa Yoga by a certain disposition of Saturn. Naturally, common signs are exempted. Saturn's inherent nature seems to play a large part in giving rise to the Yoga. Saturn is cruel, mean, undignified and sinful and consistent with these characteristics, the results of Sasa Yoga should be depicted. The man no doubt becomes famous and happy but his sexual outlook would be perverse. He would be sporting with other men's wives and he would employ every unscrupulous means to gain other's money. Most of our 'war contractors' would perhaps be having Sasa Yoga ; otherwise they could not have minted millions at the cost of the poor man.

In interpreting the Sasa Yoga, due consideration should be bestowed on the disposition of the Moon. If this luminary is free from affliction, then the person having 'Sasa Yoga' will not covet other's wealth nor will he be unscrupulous. Where the Moon is not afflicted, the evil results attributed to Sasa Yoga can have anonly 'restricted play'.

Chart No. 22.—*Born on 31-1-1896 at 4-40 a.m. Lat. 22° 20′ N. ; Long. 73° E.*

Mercury Rahu	RASI		Moon Jupit.
Sun			Kethu
Lagna Mars Venus		Saturn	

Moon			Sun Saturn
Rahu	NAVAMSA		Venus
			Kethu Moon
	Mercury	Jupiter	Lagna

Balance of Mercury's Dasa at birth : years 2-3-1

Saturn is in the 4th Kendra from Moon in exaltation. The Moon is not free from affliction. But Jupiter's exaltation has immensely improved the Moon's situation with the result the native cannot entertain unholy thoughts. The Sasa Yoga is powerful inasmuch as it has occurred in the 4th or house of lands, houses, etc. This will make the native more or less equal to a King and his earnings would be by lakhs. Saturn makes the native a great industrialist.

22. Ruchaka Yoga

Definition.—Mars should be exalted in a Kendra or occupy a Kendra which should be his own sign.

Results.—The person born in Ruchaka will have a strong physique, famous, well-versed in ancient lore, King or an equal to a King, conforming to traditions and customs. He will have a ruddy complexion, attractive body, charitable disposition, wealthy, long-lived and leader of an army.

Remarks.—The Panchamahapurusha Yogas can be said to exist only when the planets concerned are strong and are full of vitality. The meaning implies five types of great men. Naturally a really powerful Yoga would be a rare phenomenon. Emphasis is laid on the word *balishta* so that if a planet is weak by debilitation, association or aspect the Yoga does not operate in its real sense, though nominally, it may exist. Here importance is attached to the *de facto* rather than *de jure* presence of the Yoga. Out of the several horoscopes given above illustrating the Panchamahapurusha Yogas, excepting Nos. 20 and 21 the rest are of no practical value inasmuch as their strength is either nominal or completely negligible.

Ruchaka Yoga is caused by the strong disposition of Mars in a Kendra identical with his own or exalted sign. Ruchaka Yoga makes one martial, a leader of men, a great Commander, an aggressive but a patriotic ruler or an equal.

Chart No. 23.—*Born on 20-4-1889 at 6-30 p.m. Lat. 48° N.; Long. 13° E.*

	Sun Mars Venus Mercury		Rahu
	RASI		Saturn
Moon Jupiter Kethu		Lagna	

		Mercury Rahu	Sun
	NAVAMSA		
Saturn			Moon
	Mars Lagna Kethu Venus		Jupiter

Balance of Venus' Dasa at birth: years 16-4-6.

In Chart No. 23 Mars is in the 7th, a Kendra in his own house. Mars is rendered extremely powerful by conjunction with the Sun, lord of the 11th, Saturn a Yogakaraka, and Mercury lord of the 9th. Mars is no doubt very powerful but highly malefic. So Ruchaka Yoga is present in all its strength but because Mars is subject to the other evil rays, there is an element of destructiveness in this Yoga. Ruchaka

Yoga made the native daring, extremely aggressive, arrogant, a great leader and the greatest ruler and tyrant of modern times leading his country to abysmal depths of destruction. Though born in humble circumstances, he became ruler of a most powerful country and a whole continent trembled before his mite and power of destruction.

23. Bhadra Yoga

Definition.—Bhadra Yoga is caused by the disposition of Mercury in a Kendra which should be identical with his own or exaltation sign.

Results.—The person born in Bhadra Yoga will be strong, will have a lion-like face, well-developed chest, well-proportioned limbs, will be taciturn, will help relatives and will live upto a good old age.

Remarks.—Mercury is the planet of intellect and in consonance with the inherent nature of Mercury, Bhadra Yoga will manifest. Mercury must be very powerful as otherwise the presence of the combination will be simply *de jure*.

In Chart No. 24 Mercury is in the 10th in his own house having caused Bhadra Yoga. Mercury is not subjected to any evil influences. The physical features of the person have partaken of the characteristic of the Lagna while in the matter of intellectual development, learning, wealth and generous instincts, Bhadra Yoga has been fully illustrated.

Chart No. 24 —*Born on 23-10-1883 at Gh. 10-45 after Sunrise. Lat. 12° N.; Long. 77° 34' E.*

	Kethu	Saturn	
	RASI		Moon Mars Jupit.
Lagna		Rahu Venus Sun	Merc.

Venus			Saturn Lagna
	NAVAMSA		Kethu Mercury
Rahu			
Sun	Mars	Moon Jupiter	

Balance of Mercury's Dasa at birth: years 7-3-23.

24. Budha-Aditya Yoga

Definition.—If Mercury combines with the Sun, the combination goes under the name of Budha-Aditya Yoga.

Results.—Highly intelligent, skilful in all works, good reputation, personal respect and surrounded by all comforts and happiness.

Remarks.—Generally, any planet in association with the Sun becomes combust or *Astha* and loses its power to do good. perhaps Mercury is an exception. It should not be taken for granted that irrespective of the distance between the Sun and Mercury, *Budha-Aditya Yoga* would be present. On the contrary, Mercury should not be within 10° of the Sun to give rise to Budha-Aditya Yoga. This combination is not, of course, rare.

25. Mahabhagya Yoga

Definition.—In the case of a man, when the birth is during daytime the Sun, the Moon and the Lagna should be in odd signs. In the case of women, when the birth is during night, the Sun, the Moon and Lagna must be in even signs.

Results.—A male born under this Yoga will have good character, will be a source of pleasure to others, will be liberal, generous, famous, a ruler or an equal to him and lives to a good old age. A female born in this combination will be blessed with long-lived children and wealth and she will be of good conduct.

Remarks.—Mahabhagya means good fortune. Obviously, one born in this combination will be really fortunate. The Lagna, the Sun and the Moon form the tripod of life ruling as they do the body, the soul and the mind respectively and when these three elements are disposed in odd or masculine signs, the person will be an ideal one.

Chart No. 25.—*Born on 1-9-1897 at 8-35 p.m. (L.M.T.) Lat. 11° N.; Long. 78° 40' E.*

	Lagna		
	RASI		Venus Kethu
Rahu			Sun Jupit.
	Saturn	Moon	Merc. Mars

Moon	Lagna Rahu	Mercury Mars	
	NAVAMSA		
			Saturn
Jupit		Kethu	Sun Venus

Balance of Rahu Dasa at birth : years 3-5-17.

In this horoscope, the Lagna is Aries, the Sun is in Leo and the Moon is in Libra – all odd signs, consequently Mahabhagya Yoga is fully present. But since however the Lagnadhipathi is bereft of Jupiter's influence, the native is miserly though in very affluent circumstances. Has risen by sheer merit.

26. Pushkala Yoga

Definition.—The lord of the sign occupied by the Moon (who should be associated with lord of Lagna) should be in a Kendra or in the house of an intimate friend aspecting Lagna and at the same time, Lagna should be occupied by a powerful planet.

Results.—Wealthy, sweet speech, famous, honoured by the King and a lord.

Remarks.—The Yoga is somewhat complicated. First of all, the lord of Lagna should be with the Moon. Lord of the sign occupied by the Moon should be in a very friendly sign or in Kendra aspecting the Lagna and the Lagna should have a strongly disposed planet. Pushkala Yoga in actual practice is full of significance inasmuch as it comprehends that Lagna, the lord of Lagna, the Moon and lord of Chandra Lagna should all be powerful.

In Chart No. 26, lord of Lagna Saturn is with the Moon; lord of Chandra Lagna is in a Kendra aspecting Lagna. But there is no planet in Lagna. Subject to the absence of the third condition, Pushkala Yoga may be said to be present. The native has been enjoying all the blessings of this Yoga. An absolutely favourable Yoga is an impossibility.

Chart No. 26.—*Born on 8-8-1912 at 7-23 p.m. (L.M.T.) Lat. 13° N.; Long. 77° 34' E.*

Rahu		Saturn Moon	
Lagna	RASI		Sun
			Mars Merc. Venus
	Jupiter		Kethu

	Saturn	Venus	
Sun Rahu	NAVAMSA		
Lagna			Kethu Moon Merc.
	Jupiter	Mars	

Balance of Mars' Dasa at birth: years 6-0-10.

27. Lakshmi Yoga

Definition.—If the lord of Lagna is powerful and the lord of the 9th occupies own or exaltation sign identical with a Kendra or Thrikona, Lakshmi Yoga is caused.

Results.—The person will be wealthy, noble, learned, a man of high integrity and reputation, handsome appearance, a good ruler, and enjoying all the pleasures and comforts of life.

Remarks.—Different definitions are given for Lakshmi Yoga. I mention a few versions for the readers' information. Lakshmi Yoga is said to arise (*a*) by the mutual association of lords of Lagna and the 9th ; (*b*) by the lord of the 9th occupying Kendra, Thrikona, or exaltation, and the lord of Lagna being disposed powerfully ; and (*c*) by the lord of the 9th and Venus being posited in own or exaltation places which should be Kendras or Thrikonas.

Obviously, Lakshmi Yoga presumes the strength of lord of Lagna, Venus, and the lord of the 9th. Lakshmi has predominantly to do with wealth and one born in this combination will be wealthy, the degree of wealth varying with regard to the degree of strength or weakness of the planets causing the Yoga. The definition given in para (*c*) *supra* will produce the most powerful type of Lakshmi Yoga indicating immense wealth, while the mutual association of or aspect between the lords of Lagna and the 9th in houses other than 3, 6 and 8 would also result in an ordinary type of Lakshmi Yoga which might be fortified by the presence of other Dhana Yogas.

Chart No. 27.—*Born on 14-7 1887 at 9-15* a.m. *(L.M.T.) Lat. 13° N ; Long. 77° 34' E.*

	Moon		Sun Mars
	RASI		Merc. Saturn Rahu
Kethu			Venus Lagna
		Jupiter	

Rahu			Sun
	NAVAMSA		Moon
Mars Merc.			Venus Saturn
Lagna	Jupiter		Kethu

Balance of Kethu's Dasa at birth : years 1-5-19.

Lakshmi Yoga is present in the above horoscope by the association of lord of Lagna (the Sun) and the lord of the 9th (Mars) both being posited in the 11th. Mars' Dasa was very bright and it gave the native much wealth, name and reputation.

Where a really strong Lakshmi Yoga is present, and this is indeed a rare phenomenon, the results will manifest fully.

But in almost every horoscope of any pretence to wealth, Lakshmi Yoga in some form or other is likely to be found.

Chart No. 28.—*Born on 26-9-1874 at 10 p.m. Lat. 13° N.; Long. 77° 34'. E.*

Moon	Rahu	Lagna	
	RASI		
Saturn			Mars
		Venus Kethu	Sun Merc. Jupit.

	Sun		Saturn Jupiter Venus Rahu
Moon	NAVAMSA		Lagna
			Mars
Kethu			Mercury

Balance of Mercury's Dasa at birth : years 7-10-26.

In Chart No. 28 lord of the 9th is in a Thrikona in his own house. But Venus though in his own house is not in a thrikona or kendra. Lakshmi Yoga is present. Besides this, the Dhana Yoga is excellent because lord of the 2nd Mercury is in the 5th exalted and in association with the 4th lord Sun. The native was the ruler of a small but independent State and he commanded much wealth.

28. Gauri Yoga

Definition.—The lord of the Navamsa occupied by the lord of the 10th should join the 10th in exaltation and combined with the lord of Lagna.

Results.—The person belongs to a respectable family, owns several lands, charitable, performs religious rites, his sons will be of good character and he will be praised by all.

Remarks.—Here again two definitions are to be found. Apart from what is given above, another school of Astrologers hold that Gauri Yoga is produced if the lord of the 9th and the Moon be posited in their own or exaltation signs identical with a trine or quadrant. The view held by certain orthodox Pandits that Gauri Yoga will manifest only between the ages of 36 and 48, does not seem to be reasonable inasmuch as there is no special injunction warranting such a belief. We shall stick to the definition we have first propounded and deem that in order to cause Gauri Yoga, the lord of the Navamsa occupied by the 10th lord be in the 10th exalted. Such a definition does not exclude the possibility of some other planet occupying the 10th house.

Chart No. 29.—*Born on 1-8-1908 at Gh. 15-30 after Sunrise. Lat. 11° N.; Long. 78° 40′ E.*

Saturn			Merc. Rahu Venus
	RASI		Jupit. Sun Mars
Kethu		Lagna	Moon

Jupit. Lagna Moon			Mercury
Venus Mars	NAVAMSA		Kethu
Rahu			
Saturn Sun			

Balance of Sun's Dasa at birth: years 4-1-10.

In Chart No. 29 (*see page 61*), lord of the 10th is the Moon. He is in Pisces in Navamsa. The lord of this Navamsa is Jupiter and he is exalted in the 10th. This is a typical horoscope illustrating the presence of Gauri Yoga. The native is in the Indian Civil Service and has all the characteristics of Gauri Yoga.

29. Bharathi Yoga

Definition.—The lord of the Navamsa occupied by the lords of the 2nd, 5th and 11th should be exalted and combined with the 9th lord.

Results.—World famous, a reputed scholar, fond of music, romantic, handsome, attractive, religiously inclined and bewitching eyes.

Remarks.—Three Yogas are given rise to inasmuch as the 9th lord cannot be in simultaneous conjunction with all the three Navamsa lords. Therefore Bharathi Yoga may be said to exist (*a*) if the lord of Navamsa occupied by the 2nd lord is exalted and in conjunction with the 9th lord, (*b*) if the lord of the Navamsa occupied by the 5th lord is exalted and combines with the 9th lord, and (*c*) if the lord of the Navamsa occupied by the 11th lord is similarly disposed. Bharathi Yoga is not quite a common combination.

In Chart No. 30 the lord of the 5th Venus is in the Navamsa of Gemini, the lord of which, *viz.*, Mercury is exalted in the 4th and in association with the lord of the 9th. This chart is a typical example of Bharathi Yoga. On account of other evil combinations, the significance of the Yoga in question is practically non-existent.

Chart No. 30.—*Born on 28-8-1863, at Gh. 52-0 after Sunrise. Lat. 13° N.; Long. 77° 34' E.*

		Kethu	Lagna
Moon	RASI		
	R. H. 79		Sun Mars
	Rahu	Jupiter	Merc. Saturn Venus

	Kethu	Saturn	Lagna Venus
Merc. Moon	NAVAMSA		
			Sun
	Mars Jupiter	Rahu	

Balance of Rahu Dasa at birth: years 6-11-21.

30. Chapa Yoga

Definition.—If the Ascendant lord is exalted and the 4th and 10th lords have interchanged houses, Chapa Yoga is caused.

Results.—The person will grace a King's Council, be wealthy and full of strength and an Exchequer or a Comptroller of treasury.

Remarks.—My observations extending over nearly twenty years lead me to conclude that Chapa Yoga makes one control the wealth of others rather than make him rich. Horoscopes of bank cashiers, financial secretaries and exchequers could be advantageously studied.

31. Sreenatha Yoga

Definition.—If the exalted lord of the 7th occupies the 10th and the lord of the 10th is with the 9th lord, Sreenatha Yoga is caused.

Results.—The native will have on his body the insignia of Vishnu, *viz.*, the conch, the wheel, etc., be an agreeable speaker, godly, have a good wife and children and be loved by all.

Remarks.—Sreenatha Yoga may be said to be one of the important Raja Yogas inasmuch as a point of contact is established between the 7th, 9th and 10th houses. It is held to give rise to power as well as wealth. The lord of the 7th should be invariably exalted in the 10th, the lord of which, in turn, must be with the 9th lord. Obviously Sreenatha Yoga can occur only in respect of Sagittarius in which case Mercury, lord of the 7th, could remain exalted in the 10th. For no other Lagna can the 7th lord remain exalted in the 10th. Since the original writers have laid emphasis on the fact that the 7th lord should be in the 10th* exalted, we have to conclude that the Yoga is a rare one and that it cannot arise with regard to any other sign of the zodiac than Sagittarius If the definition could be extended to mean that the

* Kamesware Karmagate Swatunge

exalted 7th lord could also aspect the 10th, then Cancer and Libra could be included. Whether such a departure is permissible, I cannot yet say as the materials at my disposal are too inadequate to admit of a definite opinion.

32 to 43. Malika Yogas

Definition.—If all the seven planets occupy the seven houses contiguously, reckoned from Lagna or any particular Bhava, the appropriate Malika Yoga is caused.

Results.—*Lagna Malika*—King, Ruler or Commander, wealthy; *Dhana Malika*—very wealthy, dutiful, resolute and unsympathetic; *Vikrama Malika*—ruler, rich, sickly, surrounded by brave men; *Sukha Malika*—charitable and wealthy; *Putra Malika*—highly religious and famous; *Satru Malika*—greedy and somewhat poor; *Kalatra Malika*—coveted by women and influential; *Randhra Malika*—poor and hen-pecked; *Bhagya Malika*—religious, well-to-do, mighty and good; *Karma Malika*—respected and virtuous; *Labha Malika*—skilful and lovely women; and *Vraya Malika*—honoured, liberal and respected.

Remarks.—Twelve types of Malika Yogas, one for each Bhava, are caused. Thus the Yoga beginning from the first is Lagna Malika, the one beginning from the fifth, Putra Malika and so on. The seven planets (excluding of course Rahu and Kethu) should occupy the seven houses contiguously from a Bhava in question. While the generality of Astrologers hold the view suggested above as regards the twelve kinds of Malika Yogas, *Bhavartha Rathnakara* makes a departure and suggests that the Malika Yoga should always commence from Lagna and be disposed within five to nine houses from Lagna. According to this view, evidently no contiguity is implied.

44. Sankha Yoga

Definition.—The lords of the 5th and 6th should be in mutual Kendras and the lord of Lagna must be powerful.

Results.—Fond of pleasures, humanitarian, blessed with wife, children and lands, righteously inclined, doing good deeds, learned in sciences and living upto a good old age.

Remarks.—Where the planet or the house is not powerful, all the results attributed to a particular Yoga cannot happen but only traces of them will be present. Where Sankha Yoga is present, the sixth lord also becomes beneficial inasmuch as by causing the Yoga, he must also be capable of producing the good results of the Yoga in his Dasa or Bhukthi. But still the blemish due to the sixth lordship must express itself by way of the native suffering from the machinations of debts, diseases or enemies.

Chart No. 31.—*Born on 8-8-1912 at 7-23 p.m. (L.M.T.) Lat. 13° N.; Long 5h. 10m. 20s. E.*

Rahu		Saturn Moon	
Lagna	RASI		Sun
			Mars Merc. Venus
	Jupiter		Kethu

	Saturn	Venus	
Rahu Sun	NAVAMSA		
Lagna			Mercury Moon Kethu
	Jupiter	Mars	

Balance of Mars' Dasa at birth: years 6-0-10.

In Chart No. 31, lord of the 5th Mercury is in a Kendra from the Moon, lord of the 6th, and lord of Lagna Saturn is powerful by being placed in the 4th in a friendly house aspecting Lagna.

45. Bheri Yoga

Definition.—If Venus, lord of Lagna and Jupiter are in mutual Kendras and the lord of the 9th is powerfully disposed, Bheri Yoga is caused.

Results.—Long-lived, free from desease, ruler, various sources of income, happiness from wife and children, exalted soul, generous instincts and religiously inclined.

Chart No. 32.— *Born on 23-2-1896 at Gh. 38-30 at 13° N.; 77° 35′ E.*

			Moon
Sun Rahu	RASI		Jupit.
Mars Venus Mercury			Kethu
		Lagna Saturn	

Venus			Mercury Saturn
Sun	NAVAMSA		Kethu
Rahu Mars			
Lagna	Moon		Jupiter

Balance of Mars' Dasa at birth: years 2-1-28.

R*emarks*.—The sum and substance of Bheri Yoga is that it will make the native lead a happy and comfortable life.

In Chart No. 32 Venus is lord of Lagna and he is in a Kendra from Jupiter and Mercury lord of the 9th is powerfully disposed. The native is a high Educational Officer and is enjoying all the blessings of the Yoga subject of course to other evil dispositions of planets.

46. Mridanga Yoga

Definition.—The lord of the Navamsa occupied by an exalted planet should be posited in a trine or quadrant identical with friendly or exalted sign, and the lord of Lagna should be strongly disposed.

Results.—Respected by rulers, famous, attractive and commanding much influence.

Remarks.—The definition of the Yoga is somewhat confusing. Some planet is exalted and he occupies some Navamsa. The lord of the said Navamsa should occupy a Kendra, or Thrikona which should be either his own or exaltation or friendly house. In addition to this, the lord of Lagna should also be powerful.

In Chart No. 33 Jupiter, an exalted planet, is in Sagittarius Navamsa. The lord of this is Jupiter himself and he is in a Kendra identical with his own exaltation. Even taking Venus lord of Amsa in which Saturn (another exalted planet) is placed, we find that he is in a Kendra identical with his own house while lord of Lagna is also Venus. Mridanga Yoga is present. The native was the ruler of a vast Empire.

Chart No. 33.—*Born on 14-12-1895 at 3-5 a.m. (L. M. T.) Lat. 51° 31′ N. ; Long. 0° 6′ W.*

Rahu	RASI		Jupit.
			Kethu
Sun	Moon Mars Mercury	Lagna Venus Saturn	

Rahu Merc.	Sun	Saturn	
Venus	NAVAMSA		
			Moon
Jupit. Lagna		Mars	Kethu

Balance of Saturn's Dasa at birth : years 17-10-27.

47. Parijatha Yoga

Definition.—The lord of the sign in which the lord of the house occupied by the Ascendant lord, or the lord of Navamsa occupied by the lord of the Rasi in which the Ascendant lord is posited, shall join a quadrant, a trine or his own or exaltation places.

Results.—Happy in the middle and last parts of life, receiving the homage of Kings and Rulers, fond of wars, possessing elephants and horses, conforming to traditions and customs, generous and famous.

Remarks.—Parijatha Yoga may be held to be equivalent to a powerful Raja Yoga. Where it is interspersed with Parivraja Yoga or the latter Yoga is also present in addition to Parijatha, the native

Chart No. 34.—*Born on 11-3-1858 at 9 p.m. Lat. 13° N.; Long. 77° 34' E.*

Sun Venus	Jupiter		
Mercury Rahu	RASI		Sat.
Moon			Kethu
	Mars	Lagna	

Merc.	Jupiter	Moon	Rahu
	NAVAMSA		Venus Saturn Sun
Lagna			
Kethu			Mars

Balance of Moon's Dasa at birth: years 7-2-8.

becomes a religious head commanding all the King's paraphernalia and holding spiritual authority over millions of people.

In Chart No. 34 is the horoscope of a brilliant and learned man advanced in Yoga. Lord of Lagna is Venus. He is in Pisces ; lord of this sign, *viz.*, Jupiter occupies Aries and the lord of this sign Mars is in his own house, causing Parijatha Yoga. The native of the horoscope was one of the most learned men of his times and was a highly advanced Yogee. Being the head of millions of Hindus, several Rajas and Maharajas used to prostrate before his feet. He commanded all the privileges and paraphernalia of a secular ruler even though his authority was purely religious.

48. Gaja Yoga

Definition.—The lord of the 9th from the 11th should occupy the 11th in conjunction with the Moon and aspected by the lord of the 11th.

Results.—Will command cattle, elephants and horses ; will be happy and rich throughout life.

Remarks.—The Yoga is said to operate between the ages of 20 and 29. Obviously, this injunction is inconsistent with the statement that the native would be happy throughout life. The 9th from the 11th would be the 7th so that the lord of the 7th should occupy the 11th with the Moon and be aspected by the lord of the 11th. The native may be generally happy throughout life but the exact period during which the Yoga may hold sway would be in proportion to the strength of the various planets causing the Yoga and their Dasa and Bhukthi periods. The underlying idea seems to be that when Gaja Yoga is powerful, the native would always gain in his dealings with others.

It is difficult to get examples of Gaja Yoga. In Chart No. 35 lord of the 7th (or 9th from 11th) is the Moon. He is in the 11th aspected by Mars, lord of the 11th so that Gaja Yoga is illustrated. Since the lord of the 7th himself is the Moon, the question of his association with the Moon does not arise at all.

Chart No. 35.—*Born on 6-9-1943 at 3-15 p.m. (L.M.T.) at 18° 58′ N.; 72° 49′ E.*

		Mars	Sat.
	RASI		Jupit. Rahu
Lagna Kethu			Sun Venus
	Moon 6° 20′		Merc.

		Mars Mercury	
	NAVAMSA		Kethu
Jupit. Rahu Lagna			
		Sun Saturn Venus	Moon

Balance of Saturn's Dasa at birth: years 12-9-18.

49. Kalanidhi Yoga

Definition.—Jupiter must join or be aspected by Mercury and Venus either in the 2nd or in the 5th house ; Jupiter must occupy the 2nd or 5th identical with the swakshetra of Mercury or Venus.

Results.—Highly passionate, good-natured, revered by kings, commanding different kinds of conveyances and all sorts of aristocratic paraphernalia and immune from disease.

Remarks.—Kalanidhi Yoga, based on our own humble observations, seems to arise not so much by the disposition of Jupiter with Mercury or Venus in their signs as by the conjunction of Mercury, Jupiter and Venus in the 2nd or 5th. Moreover, where Kalanidhi Yoga is really powerful, the subject seems to enjoy alternate periods of adversity and prosperity. There is no suggestion to this effect in any of the ancient writings but I am venturing an opinion based on my own observations. This is a pucca Raja Yoga because of the conjunction of three benefics in the house of wealth or fortune. I have also been able to observe that Kalanidhi Yoga could result if Jupiter is either with Mercury or with Venus or with both Mercury and Venus not only in the 2nd and the 5th but in the 9th also inasmuch as the 9th is the house of fortune. I am giving a typical horoscope illustrating what a really powerful Kalanidhi Yoga can do.

Chart No. 36 is the horoscope of a great administrator, a brilliant lawyer and an astute statesman. Lagna is Capricorn and the 2nd is occupied by Jupiter, Mercury and Venus (in addition to the Sun and Moon) thus causing a powerful Kalanidhi Yoga. The native was Dewan of a leading Indian State, served in the Viceroy's Executive

Chart No. 36.—*Born on 20/21-2-1879 at 4-50 a.m. (L.M.T.) Lat. 10° 43' N.; Long. 76° 48' E.*

Saturn			
Sun Venus Moon Mercury Jupiter	RASI		Kethu
Lagna Rahu	A. 5		
Mars			

	Rahu		Venus Lagna
	NAVAMSA		
Sun			
Moon		Saturn Mercury Jupiter Kethu Mars	

Balance of Rahu Dasa at birth: years 14-6-29.

Council and was a capable politician and an authority on constitutional law. He was not only honoured by the rulers but was highly independent and to a certain extent, autocratic. The horoscope fully illustrates what a powerful Kalanidhi Yoga can do.

50. Amsavatara Yoga

Definition.—Venus and Jupiter should be in Kendras, the Lagna must fall in a movable sign and Saturn must be exalted in a Kendra.

Results.—Unsullied name and fame, versatile learning, fond of sex pleasures, passions under control, an authority of philosophy, a ruler or an equal to him.

Remarks.—Emphasis is laid on the unsullied or pure nature of reputation. One born in this yoga cannot be unscrupulous. Of course in a horoscope, where so many other influences are present, one's character analysis should not be made on the strength of a mere yoga however powerful it may be.

Chart No. 37.—*Born on 14-12-1895 at 3-5 a.m. (L.M.T.) Lat. 51° 31' N.; Long. 0° 6' W.*

Rahu	RASI		Jupit.
			Kethu
Sun	Moon Mars Mercury	Lagna Venus Saturn	

Rahu Merc.	Sun	Saturn	
Venus	NAVAMSA		
			Moon
Jupit. Lagna		Mars	Kethu

Balance of Saturn's Dasa at birth : years 17-10-27.

In Chart No. 37 Jupiter and Venus are in Kendras and Saturn is exalted in a Kendra so that

Amsavatara Yoga is present. The native was the ruler of a full-blown Empire.

51. Harihara Brahma Yoga

Definition.—If benefics are in the 8th or 12th from the 2nd lord ; or if Jupiter, the Moon and Mercury are in the 4th, 9th and 8th from the 7th lord ; or if the Sun, Venus and Mars are in the 4th, 10th and 11th from the lord of Lagna, the above Yoga is caused.

Results.—One born in this Yoga will be an eminent scholar in Vedas, truthful, surrounded by all pleasures, a pleasing speaker, fond of sex pleasures, conqueror of enemies, helpful to others and engaged in virtuous deeds.

Remarks.—This seems to be a somewhat complicated Yoga. Three combinations are comprehended, *viz.*, (*a*) benefics should occupy the 8th and 12th from the 2nd lord ; (*b*) Jupiter, Moon and Mercury must be in the 4th, 9th and 8th respectively from the 7th lord ; or (*c*) the Sun, Venus and Mars must be in the 4th, 10th and 11th from the lord of Lagna. The Yoga to be effective must be strong and be disposed as suggested above. Thus, pride of place has been given to Lagna, the 2nd and 7th lords. There seems to be some good reason for considering these three factors. Lagna represents the birth or creation of the individual. The 2nd represents the wealth which is so very essential for protection or preservation while the 7th being the house of Maraka signifies destruction. These three activities of creation, protection and destruction are carried on by the Hindu Trinity, *viz.*, Brahma, Vishnu or Hari and Maheshwara or Hara and hence the combination is termed Harihara Brahma Yoga.

52. Kusuma Yoga

Definition.—If Jupiter is in Lagna, the Moon in the 7th and the Sun in the 8th from the Moon, Kusuma Yoga is caused.

Results.—The person will be a King or equal to a King, protector of kith and kin, founder of a town or a headman, and possessed of unsullied reputation.

Remarks.—Jupiter in Lagna is a highly beneficial combination and when the Moon is in the 7th from Jupiter, Gajakesari Yoga is caused. The Sun's situation in the 8th from the Moon, which means the same as being in the 2nd, results in Subhavasi Yoga as Jupiter will be in the 12th. Thus Kusuma Yoga has resulted by the mingling of Gajakesari and Vasi Yogas. In such cases where two or more Yogas are merged together, the most powerful of the lot is to be taken into account. Magistrates, munsiffs, village headmen, mayors and municipal commissioners may be born when Kusuma Yoga is strongly formed.

Chart No. 38. (See page 78) is a typical horoscope illustrating Kusuma Yoga. Jupiter is in Lagna, the Moon in the 7th and the Sun in the 2nd. But all the three planets who have caused the Yoga are subject to evil influences because the Moon is with Kethu, Jupiter is subject to Rahu's influence and the Sun is of course associated with Saturn and other malefics. Chart No. 38, whilst illustrative of the theory of the Yoga, has not given rise to more than 20 or 25% of the results because of its restrictive nature.

Chart No. 38.—*Born on 15-12-1899 at 5-42 a.m. (L.M.T) Lat. 10° 45' N.; Long. 19° 4' E.*

		Moon Kethu	
	RASI		
Saturn Sun Mars Venus	Mercury Jupiter Lagna Rahu		

Rahu Moon	Sun	Saturn	Mars
Lagna	NAVAMSA		
	Venus Mercury		Jupiter Kethu

Balance of Sun's Dasa at birth : years 1-2-12.

Prof. Rao gives another definition in his *Satayoga Manjari* according to which Venus should occupy a fixed sign in a Kendra, weak Moon in a trine and the Sun in the 10th house to cause Kusuma Yoga. Obviously Venus cannot occupy any other Kendra than the 10th house in case the Sun is also to be in the 10th for Venus and the Sun cannot be apart from each other beyond 47°. This will therefore mean that the weak Moon should occupy a trine and the Sun and Venus must be in the 10th. In higher latitudes, however, where often there is merging of two signs in a Bhava, Venus can occupy either Lagna or the 7th house and the Sun can join the 10th, depending upon whether Venus is heading towards inferior or superior conjunction. As almost all Yogas seem to have been based upon certain mutual angular dispositions of planets, Rasis are implied and not Bhavas, because if the Yoga-formation is based on Bhava reckoning, the distance between the planets forming a particular Yoga will be varying with reference to each individual horoscope. Thus for instance in Kusuma Yoga, the Sun is to be in the 10th. This according to Rasi reckoning means an aspectal angle of 270° while according to Bhava reckoning, it may mean just the distance between the Lagna and the 10th Bhava which varies with regard to each horoscope. Without straining the combinations too much, it seems safe to assume that Yogas are based on the disposition of planets in certain Rasis from each other.

53. Matsya Yoga

Definition.—If Lagna and 9th are joined by malefics the 5th by both malefics and benefics and the 4th and 8th by malefics, Matsya Yoga is formed.

Results.—The person will be an ocean of love, a reader of times, good-natured, strong character, famous, religious and learned.

Remarks.--This seems to be a peculiar combination because the two most important houses, *viz.*, Lagna and the ninth should be occupied by evil planets, the fifth should contain a mixture of good and evil planets while malefics alone should occupy the 4th and 8th. Such Yogas, though not impossible of occurrence, are indeed rare because if Mercury and the Moon become beneficial by good association and waxing respectively, only three malefics are left out (excluding Rahu and Kethu) to cause the Yoga. If Rahu and Kethu are also included, then all the malefics cannot occupy the 1st, 9th, 4th and 8th inasmuch as Rahu and Kethu must always be 180° apart. The presence of Matsya Yoga in a horoscope may be admitted if Lagna, 4th, 8th and 9th, or at least Lagna and 9th have malefics and the fifth both benefics and malefics. In Sanskrit *Matsya* means a fish and this Yoga is supposed to be a very favourable one. The high place given to it is equalled by its conspicuous rarity in actual horoscopes. If we include the aspects of planets also, then the Yoga can occur in a number of horoscopes.

54. Kurma Yoga

Definition.—When benefics occupy the 5th, 6th and 7th and join their exaltation, own or friendly Navamsas; or when benefics occupy the 1st, 3rd and 11th identical with their exaltation, own or friendly signs, there results what is called Kurma Yoga.

Results.—World famous, princely enjoyments, righteous, courageous, happy, helpful to others, leader of men and a man of mild temperament.

Remarks.—Opinion is divided as regards the exact interpretation of the word *mitramsakarasiyatah* which may mean a friendly sign or a friendly Navamsa. Some authorities suggest that as in the second part of the stanza the word *mitrochasamsthah* has been used, it is more reasonable to interpret that the reference is to friendly Rasis. It is of course somewhat difficult to conceive of a planet occupying a particular house identical with a friendly Navamsa since two sets of combinations are given. I am inclined to accept the views of Prof. Rao, that the first set of combinations would be partly in reference to the Navamsa disposition while the second one is to be applied solely to the usual Rasi dispositions. In other words, Kurma Yoga is said to arise (*a*) if benefics occupy the 5th, 6th and 7th houses and join own, exalted and friendly Navamsas or (*b*) if benefics occupy the 1st, 3rd and 11th identical with their exalted, own or friendly places. I have my own doubts as to the correctness or otherwise of the interpretation given above. Therefore readers must accept my remarks with a certain amount of reservation. So far as the results are concerned, Kurma Yoga seems to indicate reputation, fame and influence but not much wealth.

Chart No. 39.—*Born on 1-9-1897 at 8-35 p.m. (L.M.T.) at 10° 58' N. ; 79° 29' E.*

	Lagna		
	RASI		Venus Kethu
Rahu			Sun Jupit.
	Saturn	Moon	Merc. Mars

Moon	Lagna Rahu	Mercury	
	NAVAMSA		Mars
			Saturn
Jupit.		Kethu	Sun Venus

Balance of Rahu Dasa at birth : years 3-8-8.

In Chart No. 39 the 5th, 6th and 7th are occupied by Jupiter, Mercury and the Moon respectively. Jupiter is in his own Amsa and the Moon and Mercury in friendly Amsas so that Kurma Yoga is formed. But much of the efficacy is carried away because of the presence of malefics in the 5th and 6th. The subject has risen from humble circumstances but is somewhat unscrupulous.

55. Devendra Yoga

Definition.—When Lagna is a fixed sign, the lords of the Lagna and the eleventh interchange their houses and the lord of the 2nd is in the 10th and *vice versa*, the combination is called Devendra Yoga.

Results.—Handsome appearance, romantic, unsullied reputation, builder of fortifications, commander of armies and good longevity.

Remarks.—Devendra is supposed to be the king of all celestials and the Yoga named after him is expected to usher into this world a man of sterling character, ruler or an equal to him, successful commander and a powerful monarch. Though all these results may not be produced, at least some of them must be present. The requirements are the Lagna must always be a fixed sign and its lord should be in 11th, while the 11th lord should be in Lagna and the 2nd and 10th lords should exchange their houses. Two Parivarthana Yogas are therefore implied. It must be noted that mere exchange of houses is not enough to produce the Yoga. The lords must be really powerful.

56. Makuta Yoga

Definition.—If Jupiter is in the 9th from the 9th lord, a benefic is in the 9th from Jupiter and Saturn is in the 10th, Makuta is caused.

Results.—A king or head of forest tribes or hunters, powerful, evil-minded and a successful sportsman.

Remarks.—My Research Department, which is engaged in the statistical analysis of thousands of horoscopes, has been able to discern that Makuta Yoga is a feature in 6 to 7 out of every 10 horoscopes belonging to petty chiefs, conservators of forests, and leaders of forest tribes and gangs. In order to control such unruly gangs, one will have to be cruel and hence seems to be the suggestion that Saturn be in the 10th or house of actions.

57. Chandika Yoga

Definition.—If the lord of the Navamsa occupied by the lord of the 6th and the lord of the Navamsa occupied by the lord of the 9th combine with the Sun and if the Lagna being a fixed sign is aspected by the lord of the 6th, Chandika Yoga is caused.

Results. –The person will be aggressive, charitable, wealthy, minister or an equal to him, will have a long and happy life and fame.

Remarks.—The definition is somewhat complicated. Both lords of the Navamsas occupied by the lord of the 6th and 9th should be associated with the Sun, the Lagna should receive the aspect of the 6th lord and the Lagna must be a fixed sign. Here a conglomeration of good and evil forces are blended so that the net result is a good Yoga. The evil attendant upon the 6th lordship seems to lose its effect in the face of the Navamsa lord association. The native will be highly war-like and aggressive because of the element of the 6th lordship. Chandika can happen with reference to only four signs, *viz.*, Taurus, Leo, Scorpio and Aquarius. Movable and common signs have nothing to do with this Yoga. Chandika Yoga seems to make for political power.

58 Jaya Yoga

Definition.—When the lord of the 6th is debilitated and the lord of the 10th is deeply exalted Jaya Yoga will arise.

Results.—The native will be happy, victorious over his enemies, successful in all his ventures and long-lived.

Remarks.—As the name implies, Jaya Yoga gives success in all undertakings. If the Yoga is really powerful, the person will hardly meet with failures or disappointments. The 6th is a Dusthana and when the lord is debilitated, then all the indications of the sixth house, *viz.*, debts, disease and enemies will be at a discount so that all the obstructive forces in the way of the person's prosperity will have been removed. The lord of the 10th or house of effort, occupation and deeds will have to be in deep exaltation. Otherwise, the yoga cannot have its full value.

Chart No. 40.—*Born on 21-4-1867 at 9-30 p.m. Lat. 13° N.; Long. 77° 34' E.*

Kethu Merc. Venus	Sun		
Jupiter	RASI		Mars
	Lagna Moon Saturn		Rahu

Lagna	NAVAMSA		Venus Saturn Kethu Sun
Jupit. Rahu			
	Mercury	Moon	Mars

In Chart No. 40 the lord of the 6th Mars is debilitated and the lord of the 10th Sun is in deep exaltation. Hence this is a distinct case of Jaya Yoga. But the Yoga has lost much of the effect because the Sun's exaltation has occurred in the sixth and both the Lagna and the Moon are associated with Saturn. The 6th lord is no doubt Neecha, but since he happens to be lord of Lagna also, the disposition is not desirable.

In Chart No. 41, the lord of the 6th Mercury is debilitated while the lord of the 10th Saturn is exalted, definitely causing Jaya Yoga. The horoscope is that of a great religious leader and prophet who influenced the world in no ordinary way. He is one of the most extraordinary characters in the stage of the world's religious drama. He had to deal with very rough and uncontrollable elements and the Jaya Yoga seems to have gone a long way in enabling him to enlist the sympathies of millions of people for his cause. There are of course other strong elements in the horoscope.

Chart No. 41—*Born on 25-2-1894 at about 8-55 a.m. Lat. 18° 32′ N.; Long. 73° 53′ E.*

Mercury Rahu	Lagna	Jupiter	
Sun Venus	RASI		
	M.B.		
Mars		Moon Saturn	Kethu

Moon	Lagna		
Sun	NAVAMSA		Kethu
Rahu Jupit.			Mercury
	Saturn	Venus	Mars

Balance of Rahu Dasa at birth: years 1-1-15.

59. Vidyut Yoga

Definition.—When the 11th lord is in deep exaltation and joins Venus in a Kendra from the lord of Lagna, Vidyut Yoga is caused.

Results.—Charitable, pleasure-loving, a treasurer or controller of wealth and a great king or an equal to him.

Remarks.—Depending upon the exact strength of the two lords causing the yoga, the person will either be a king or an equal to him. He will control wealth and he will be a man of generous instincts. Here Venus, the 11th lord and lord of Lagna are required to be disposed in a particular manner. Venus is the planet of pleasure and comforts, whereas the lord of the 11th indicates gains. Naturally when the Lagna is strong and the house of gains and lord of comforts and luxuries is equally strong one is bound to be well off in life.

60. Gandharva Yoga

Definition.—If the 10th lord is in a Kama Thrikona, the lord of Lagna and Jupiter are in association, the Sun being strong, is exalted and the Moon occupies the 9th, Gandharva Yoga arises.

Results.—The person will attain unparalleled skill in fine arts, will be strong, will be pleasure-loving, will be well-dressed, will become famous and will live upto 68 years.

Remarks.—Gandharva Yoga as the name implies makes one a connoisseur in fine arts such as music, dancing, painting, etc. Kama Thrikona means the trinal houses from the 7th, *viz.*, 7th, 11th and 3rd. The 10th lord must occupy one of these houses in conjunction with Jupiter, the Sun being strong should be exalted and the Moon should remain in the 9th house. If all these conditions are present, then the Yoga will be in full swing. Otherwise, a trace of the Yoga may be present rendering the person take some interest in these arts, but not make him an adept.

61. Siva Yoga

Definition.—If the lord of the 5th is in the 9th, the lord of the 9th is in the 10th and the lord of the 10th is in the 5th, Siva Yoga is caused.

Results.—The person will be a big trader, a conqueror and commander of armies ; he will possess divine wisdom and will lead a virtuous life.

Remarks.—The combination seems to be simple but full of significance. The 5th and 9th are powerful trikonas and the 10th is a powerful kendra. Disposition of the lords of these three in a particular order as adumbrated in this combination fortifies the houses of fortune and Karma so that the person is supposed to become a beneficiary in respect of fortune, trade, philosophical knowledge and other activities. In estimating the strength of this yoga, due importance must be given to the mutual relations of the lords of the 9th, 5th and 10th. Thus, in respect of Mesha Lagna, Siva Yoga can be caused by the presence of the 5th lord (Sun) ·in the 9th, and Saturn in the 10th or 5th, because of the ownership of the two adjoining houses by Saturn. The Sun being placed in the 9th, and Saturn in the 10th, is a stronger Siva Yoga than the Sun and Saturn exchanging their houses. In the latter circumstance whilst no doubt Siva Yoga is caused by the Sun (lord of the 5th) occupying the 10th (a house of Saturn) and Saturn (lord of the 10th) occupying the 5th, both the planets are such bitter enemies that the combination, though on account of Parivarthana between the 5th and 10th lords some kind of Yoga is generated, is full of evil indications. In other words, Siva Yoga, as far as this writer's study goes, is not of much consequence in respect of Mesha Lagna unless both the Sun and Saturn have acquired sufficient Moolathrikonadi Bala.

62. Vishnu Yoga

Definition.—If the lord of Navamsa in which the 9th lord is placed, and the 10th lord joins the 2nd house in conjunction with the 9th lord, Vishnu Yoga is caused.

Results.—The person will lead an enjoyable life, acquire fortunes from various countries, earn in lakhs, will be strong, well-versed in discussions, witty in conversations, a worshipper of Vishnu, praised by the rulers and will live upto one hundred years free from disease.

Remarks.—All the results attributed to the Yoga may not happen. But the native will enjoy most of the blessings of Vishnu Yoga. The Navamsa in which the 9th lord is placed plays an important part in the formation of this yoga. If per chance such a lord of the Navamsa happens to be the strongest planet, having obtained the requisite quantity of shadbala, then the Yoga will operate practically throughout life. I know an instance of Vishnu Yoga operating powerfully in the horoscope of a close associate of mine. But unfortunately, the lord of the Amsa occupied by the 9th lord happened to be Saturn and his shadbala strength was not much. Consequently, the Yoga could operate with certain restrictions, the various results happening on a moderate scale.

In all such cases, where big results are attributed to yogas, the astrologer should be very careful in assessing the real strength of the main lord causing the Yoga. The combination of the 9th and 10th lords constitutes in itself a powerful Raja Yoga and this occurring in the 2nd, combined with the Amsa lord, is indeed a powerful Dhana Yoga so that there is a blending of Raja and Dhana Yogas. The combination implies that the 2nd house must be occupied by at least three planets and hence not of very frequent occurrence.

Chart No. 42.—*Born on 1-10-1901 at 6-48 a.m. (L.M.T.) at 13° N ; 77° 35′ E.*

	Moon Kethu		
	RASI		
Jupiter Saturn		Venus Mercury Mars Rahu	Lagna Sun

		Rahu Sun Venus	Mars
	NAVAMSA		
			Jupiter Lagna
Merc.	Kethu Moon		Saturn

Balance of Venus Dasa at birth : years 1-7-6.

In Chart No. 42 the lord of the 9th Venus is in Taurus Amsa. The lord of this Amsa is again Venus.

He is in the second along with the 10th lord and he himself happens to be the 9th lord. Hence Vishnu Yoga is present though it cannot have full play because of Rahu's presence also in the 2nd. The horoscope is that of an influential man of high rank.

Chart No. 43.—*Born on 21-2-1879 at 4-58 a.m. (L.M.T.) at 13° 0' N.; 77° 35' E.*

Saturn			
Sun Moon Mercury Jupiter Venus	RASI		Kethu
Lagna Rahu			
Mars			

	Rahu		Venus Lagna
	NAVAMSA		
Sun			
Moon		Mercury Jupiter Kethu	Mars Saturn

Balance of Rahu Dasa at birth: years 15-10-19.

In Chart No. 43, Vishnu Yoga is more pronounced. Venus happens not only to be the lord of the 10th but also lord of the Amsa occupied by the 9th lord Mercury. Both Mercury and Venus are in the 2nd. The native enjoyed almost all the blessings of this Yoga. He earned in lakhs. He was in the good books of some of the Indian princes and the British Government, was highly learned, a brilliant statesman and a capable lawyer.

63. Brahma Yoga

Definition.—If Jupiter and Venus are in Kendras respectively from the lords of the 9th and 11th, and Mercury is in a similar position from the lord of either Lagna or the 10th, Brahma Yoga is caused.

Results.—The person will enjoy luxurious foods, will be respected by Brahmins and learned men, will be highly learned, long-lived, charitable and always bent on doing good deeds.

Remarks.—The Yoga in question seems to bestow highly beneficial results implying that the native would command health, wealth, fame and above all instincts for serving others. It will be seen that in the formation of this Yoga, all the natural benefics are involved. Even here, the exact strength and signification of the Yoga rests to a large extent upon a number of other horoscopic factors. For Mesha Lagna, for example this yoga cannot be deemed to be formed in all its aspects inasmuch as lord of the 9th is Jupiter so that Jupiter's disposition in a Kendra from the 9th lord is entirely ruled out.

Similarly when Cancer is the Lagna, two conditions of the yoga would be absent as lords of the 9th and 11th respectively become Jupiter and Venus. Again if Lagna is Virgo or Sagittarius the yoga cannot be full, because in regard to Virgo. Mercury becomes lord of the 10th while in regard to Sagittarius, Mercury and Venus become lords of the 10th and 11th so that the disposition of Venus and Mercury respectively in kendras from the lords of the 11th and 10th is not possible. So far as Dhanus is concerned, in the place of the 10th lord, lord of Lagna may be considered. Therefore we may assume that Brahma Yoga is possible to the full extent in respect of all the signs except Aries, Cancer and Virgo. However, it does not seem erroneous to assume that even in respect of Aries, Cancer and Virgo, this yoga could be deemed to be present with a slight modification. If, say, three factors are necessary to make up a certain yoga, the presence of even one or two cannot but suggest that the yoga does operate, may be feeble.

Chart No. 44.—*Born on 7-5-1886 at 2-30 p.m. Lat. 40° 24' N.; Long. 3h. 41m. W.*

Venus Mercury	Sun		Moon Sat.
Kethu	RASI		
	R. 4P. 47		Mars Rahu
			Lagna Jupit.

Merc.	Kethu		
Moon Lagna Jupit. Saturn	NAVAMSA		
	Sun	Rahu	Venus Mars

Balance of Rahu Dasa at birth : years 10-4-22.

In Chart No. 44, Jupiter is in a kendra from the lord of the 9th, *viz.*, Venus. Venus is in a kendra from the lord of the 11th, *viz.*, the Moon. The third combination cannot obtain because Virgo is Lagna. Therefore Brahma Yoga is present with a slight variation.

The native of the horoscope was a ruler of an Indian State and enjoyed all the results attributed to this yoga. This may be taken as a rare combination occurring in a very small number of horoscopes.

64. Indra Yoga

Definition.—If the lords of the 5th and 11th interchange their houses and the Moon is in the 5th, Indra Yoga is caused.

Results.—Highly courageous, lasting fame, a King of Kings, good enjoyments and living upto 36 years.

Remarks.—Unless the house of longevity is powerful, one has to assume that Indra Yoga does not confer longevity. Professor Rao has offered very suggestive remarks on his *Sata Yoga Manjari* in suggesting that Christ, Shankara and Alexander are examples of short life but of lasting name and I would refer the readers to these notes. Though classical writers have attributed highly favourable results to this Yoga, I have my own doubts.

65. Ravi Yoga

Definition.—The Sun should join the 10th and the lord of the 10th must be in the 3rd in conjunction with Saturn.

Results.—Respected by rulers, well-versed in sciences, becoming famous after the 15th year, highly passionate, liking simple food, possessing lotus-like eyes and well-developed chest.

Remarks.—Each rule has an exception. Whilst Saturn's association with any favourable horoscopic element is not desirable, under this Yoga, the 10th lord should occupy the third in conjunction with Saturn. In the course of his Dasa, Saturn, under such a combination, would be capable of giving highly favourable results. Ravi Yoga comprehends a point of contact between the Sun, Saturn, the 10th and 3rd houses. The Sun should occupy the 10th, while the 10th lord should be in the third with Saturn. For Mesha, Vrishabha and Vrischika Lagnas, Ravi Yoga cannot at all be said to exist in its real sense.

For Dhanus, Makara, Simha and Kanya Lagnas, Ravi Yoga would be almost impossible because in these cases the 10th lord happens to be either Mercury or Venus; when the Sun is in the 10th, Mercury or Venus cannot be in the 3rd from Lagna as it implies a distance of nearly 150 to 180 degrees from the Sun which is astronomically impossible. In view of the above explanations, one can easily see that Ravi Yoga is indeed of rare occurrence.

Chart No. 45.—*Born on 21-3-1921 at 12 noon (L.M.T.) Lat. 10° N.; Long. 77° 34′ E.*

Sun	Venus Mars Kethu		Lagna
Mercury	RASI		
			Saturn Jupit. Moon
		Rahu	

		Moon Mars	Kethu
Lagna	NAVAMSA		
Merc.			Venus
Rahu Saturn		Jupiter	Sun

Balance of Kethu's Dasa at birth : years 4-9-10.

In Chart No. 45, the 10th is occupied by the Sun, the 10th lord Jupiter is in the 3rd, *viz.*, Leo with Saturn.

This chart is therefore typically illustrative of Ravi Yoga. Of course, the merits of the chart cannot be judged merely upon this single Yoga.

66. Garuda Yoga

Definition.—The lord of Navamsa occupied by the Moon should be exalted and birth should occur during daytime when the Moon is waxing.

Results.—Respected by the pious, polished speech, feared by the enemies, strong and facing danger from poison in the 34th year.

Remarks.—Importance is given to the Moon. The lord of the Moon's Navamsa should be exalted. The Yoga cannot occur in regard to people born during night times or when the Moon is waning. Why the native should meet with danger from poison in his 34th year is not at all clear. A lot of practical experience must have guided the framers of this combination in coming to the conclusions they have done. The danger should not be predicted when the house of longevity is strong enough.

Chart No. 46.—*Born on 15-9-1861 at about 2-20 p.m.*

			Kethu
	RASI		
Lagna Moon	A.7		Saturn Jupit. Mars
Rahu		Venus	Sun Merc.

Merc. Kethu			Moon
	NAVAMSA		
Sun Lagna			
	Mars Venus	Saturn	Jupiter Rahu

Balance of Moon's Dasa at birth ; years 3-1-24.

Chart No. 46 belongs to a day birth. The birth has taken place in the bright half of the lunar month. The Moon is in Gemini Navamsa and the lord, *viz.*, Mercury is exalted. The horoscope is that of a great Indian engineer and statesman of international fame. His manners and speech were extremely polished and he had perhaps all the qualifications of the Yoga in question. In a science like astrology, a combination or Yoga should be adapted to fit into the particular horoscope as no yoga can have absolute sway.

67. Go Yoga

Definition.—Strong Jupiter should occupy his Moolathrikona with the lord of the 2nd house and the lord of Lagna should be in exaltation.

Results.—Hailing from a respectable family, a king or an equal to him, wealthy and strong.

Remarks.—Jupiter is Dhanakaraka or indicator of wealth. He should occupy his Moolathrikona with the lord of the 2nd and the ascendant lord must remain in exaltation.

The Sun, the Moon, Mars, Mercury, Jupiter, Venus and Saturn, respectively have, as their Moolathrikonas, Leo, Taurus, Aries, Virgo, Sagittarius, Libra and Aquarius. For Scorpio and Aquarius, since the second happens to be owned by Jupiter, the question of association with the second lord does not arise.

Jupiter's Moolathrikona being confined to the first thirteen degrees of Sagittarius, Go Yoga can be present only in respect of those born when Jupiter occupies his particular arc in the heavens. In other words, this yoga, unlike Gajakesari, Vasi or Vesi, is subject to a law of periodicity, coming into effect only when Jupiter occupies the constellation of Moola.

Chart No. 47.—*Born on 2-1-1901 at 8 p.m. (L.M.T.) at 12° 58′ N.; 77° 34′ E.*

		Kethu Moon	
	RASI		Lagna
			Mars
Saturn Sun Mercury Jupiter	Venus Rahu		

Kethu		Jupiter	Mercury
	NAVAMSA		Moon
Venus Lagna			
		Sun Mars	Rahu Saturn

Balance of Moon's Dasa at birth : years 2-5-21.

In Chart No. 47, Cancer is Lagna, the 2nd lord Sun is in Sagittarius with Jupiter who, being placed in Moola, occupies his own Moolathrikona. Lord of Lagna, *viz.*, the Moon is exalted. Hence Go Yoga is present in the horoscope. Of course, the Moon's conjunction with Kethu and Saturn's presence in Sagittarius have produced an adverse influence so that the yoga cannot be effective. The example is only illustrative of the presence of the particular yoga.

68. Gola Yoga

Definition.—If the Full Moon is in the 9th in conjunction with Jupiter and Venus, and Mercury joins Navamsa Lagna, Gola Yoga is produced.

Results.—Polite, learned, Magistrate or head of a village, long-lived and eating wholesome food.

Remarks.—The yoga can come into effect provided the Moon is full and not otherwise. Mercury must occupy Navamsa Lagna. Such a Full Moon should be in the 9th with Jupiter and Venus. In other words, even Gajakesari Yoga gets merged into Gola, inasmuch as when Jupiter and the Moon are in conjunction, they would be supposed to be in a kendra from each other.

69. Thrilochana Yoga

Definition.—The Sun, the Moon and Mars should be in trines from each other.

Results.—Great wealth, a terror to his enemies, highly intelligent and good longevity.

Remarks.—Irrespective of the presence of any particular kind of Yoga, dispositions of planets in mutual trines is always held to be highly favourable. One born in such a combination will have a smooth career and will not have to contend against unfavourable forces.

70. Kulavardhana Yoga

Definition.—All planets should be in the 5th from Lagna, the Sun and the Moon.

Results.—Unbroken line of successors, wealthy, healthy and long-lived.

Remarks.—As the name implies, one born when the benefics are disposed in 5th from Lagna, the Sun and the Moon will have plenty of children and the family traditions will be perpetuated by his children, grand-children and so on in an unbroken fashion. The fifth house becomes the focal point. The man will also be capable of producing a large number of children.

71 to 102. Nabhasa Yogas

Varaha Mihira has dealt with these various yogas in his immortal *Brihat Jataka* and the English rendering of this work by the late Prof. B. Suryanarain Rao would be of inestimable help to students of astrology. The Yavanas have treated *Nabhasa Yogas* extensively.

The Nabhasa Yogas consist of four groups, *viz.*,

Akriti Yogas	....	20
Sankhya Yogas	....	7
Asraya Yogas	....	3
Dala Yogas	....	2
		32

According to Varaha Mihira, the effects of Nabhasa Yogas are said to be felt throughout one's life and not merely during the Dasa and Bhukthi periods of the planets causing the Yoga.

71. Yupa Yoga
72. Ishu Yoga
73. Sakti Yoga
74. Danda Yoga

Definition.—When all the planets occupy four signs contiguously from the Lagna and other kendras respectively Yupa, Ishu, Sakti and Danda Yogas are caused.

Results.—One born in *Yupa* becomes liberal, self-possessed and noted for charitable deeds. *Ishu* makes one successful as a superintendent or head of a jail, concentration camp, etc., *Sakti* renders the native lazy, slothful, devoid of riches, and generally disliked by people and *Danda* suggests that the person will lack happiness due from wife and children.

Remarks.—These four yogas arise by virtue of the seven planets being disposed in four contiguous houses as reckoned from the Ascendant and other kendras. Thus if all the planets are placed in Lagna, 2nd, 3rd and 4th houses, Yupa is caused; in 4th, 5th, 9th and 7th, Ishu or Sara is produced; in 7th, 8th, 9th and 10th, Sakti is caused and in the 10th, 11th, 12th and 1st Danda is caused.

Personally, we are of opinion that all these various Akriti Yogas do not contribute much to the making of the horoscope. In fact they seem to give rise to clues as regards the means of livelihood one is likely to have. Thus, for instance, Ishu Yoga, said to be caused by the seven planets occupying the 4th, 5th, 6th and 7th houses, is common in the horoscopes of persons, who may have anything to do with prisons, lock-ups, concentration camps, etc. Of course these deductions are based on our own observations and readers have to view them with due reserve.

In Chart No. 48, all the planets have occupied the four signs contiguously from Lagna kendra causing Yupa Yoga while in Chart No. 49, the disposition of planets in the 4th, 5th, 6th and 7th in a contiguous manner suggests the presence of Ishu Yoga. Whether the various Nabhasa Yogas can have an independent effect on the horoscope or whether they get mixed up with other Yogas, we shall discuss on a subsequent occasion. Now suffice it to say that they will have important bearings on certain aspects of one's life depending upon the stress that is laid on particular bhavas by the dispositions of planets in or around them.

Chart No. 48.—*Born on 1-10-1945 at 1 a.m. (I.S.T.) Lat. 18° 52' N.; Long. 72° 35' E.*

			Mars Rahu Lagna
	RASI		Sat. Moon
	H. 677		Venus
Kethu			Sun Merc. Jupit.

	Mars	Sun Mercury Jupiter	Lagna
	NAVAMSA		Saturn Kethu
Rahu			Venus
	Moon		

Balance of Saturn's Dasa at birth : years 3-8-5.

Chart No. 49.—*Born on 28-8-1921 at 8-30 p.m. (L.M.T.) Lat. 6° N.; Long. 80° 10′ E.*

Kethu Lagna			Moon
	RASI		Mars Venus
			Sun Merc.
			Jupit. Sat. Rahu

Kethu			
Sat. Mars Lagna	NAVAMSA		
Moon Jupit.			Sun Venus
			Mercury Rahu

Balance of Rahu Dasa at birth : years 12-7-22.

Out of the four yogas mentioned above, Yupa and Danda are better than Ishu and Sakti because in the latter two, planets are about to culminate or about to set.

75. Nav Yoga
76. Kuta Yoga
77. Chhatra Yoga
78. Chapa Yoga

Definition.—By virtue of the disposition of the seven planets in seven contiguous houses from Lagna, 4th house, 7th house and 10th house respectively Nav, Kuta, Chhatra and Chapa Yogas are produced.

Results.—*Nav* makes one occasionally happy, famous and miserly; one born in *Kuta* becomes a liar and a jailor. *Chhatra* Yoga produces a happy individual while one born in *Chapa* becomes brave and happy in the first and last periods of his life.

Remarks.—The above definitions are simple. The seven planets should occupy the seven houses without a break from Lagna, 4th house, 7th and 10th houses respectively to produce the four kinds of yogas. Apart from the results ascribed by the classical writers, we may make a few observations.

In regard to Nav Yoga (75), all the planets will be in the invisible sphere of the heavens. It seems to be generally productive of good and to have a bearing on the native having to do with water, watery places and aquatic substances.

In regard to Kuta, when all the planets will be in the seven houses from the fourth, it will be more or less an equal distribution of planets in the visible halves of the zodiac. The native may frequent caves, mountains, etc., and he will be addicted to evil habits. Robbers, drunkards, cheats and others may have this combination. In Chhatra Yoga, all the planets will be in the visible half and hence may be deemed to be favourable. The native will be happy in the beginning and end of his life. He will possess great strength of mind and will earn much wealth. In Chapa Yoga all the planets will be in the 10th and subsequent houses and one born in this yoga will lead a comfortable life delighting in good deeds.

79 Ardha Chandra Yoga

Definition.—All the planets should occupy the seven houses beginning from a Panapara or Apoklima.

Results.—The native will have fair features and will be happy throughout life.

Remarks.—There are four Panaparas (cadent houses) and four Apoklimas (succeedent houses). Consequently there are eight kinds of Ardha Chandra Yogas, the planets occupying (*i*) from 2nd to 8th, (*ii*) 3rd to 9th, (*iii*) 5th to 11th, (*iv*) 6th to 12th, (*v*) 8th to 2nd, (*vi*) 9th to 3rd, (*vii*) 11th to 5th and (*viii*) 12th to 6th.

80. Chandra Yoga

Definition.—All the planets should occupy the 1st, 3rd, 5th, 7th, 9th and 11th houses.

Results.—The subject will be a king or an equal to him. He will command respect and submission from others and he will earn and spend well.

Remarks.—On page 114 we have dealt with Samudra Yoga which is said to result by all the planets occupying the even houses, whereas in this regard, all the odd houses must be occupied. The combination is not a rare one. So far as the results are concerned, the Yoga cannot produce rulers or emperors, but one who has this combination would certainly become an entity amongst his own people.

81. Gada Yoga
82. Sakata Yoga
83. Vihaga Yoga

Definition.—All the planets occupying two adjacent kendras, the 1st and 7th houses, and the 4th and 10th houses respectively will produce Gada, Sakata and Vihaga Yogas.

Results.—Gada Yoga makes one highly religious and wealthy; Sakata renders one poor and unhappy in domestic life; and one born in Vihaga will be a vagrant, quarrelsome and mean.

Remarks.—A study of Nabhasa Yogas outlined in *Brihat Jataka* and the comments made by Varaha Mihira clearly reveal that attempts had been made to assess clearly the strength due to every conceivable combination.

Gada Yoga is caused when the planets occupy two successive kendras. Four varieties are to be seen in this, *viz.*, (*a*) all the planets may occupy the 1st and 4th houses, (*b*) 4th and 7th houses, (*c*) 7th and 10th houses and (*d*) 10th and 1st houses. The Yavanas consider these as four *distinct* Yogas and not merely as variations of a single combination and call them as Gada, Sanaha, Vibhuka and Dhuriya respectively. It is clear from the above that Gada Yoga and its variations are nothing but the disposition of all the planets in mutual square aspects. Of course Rahu and Kethu are omitted. The effects of Gada Yoga are assumed to be good so that the Western astrological theory, that square aspects are all evil, has no warrant in Hindu astrology.

Sakata Yoga is said to arise by the disposition of all the planets in the Lagna and the 7th. It will be seen that the 1st and 7th houses become *focii* of attraction so that there seems to be justification in attributing evil results especially pertaining to the native's body and wife. Sakata will make one derive his livelihood by manual labour; he will be sickly and his wife will be quarrelsome.

Vihaga means a bird and Vihaga Yoga is caused if all the planets are in the 4th and 10th houses. Evil results are attributed to this combination. The native is said to be a vagrant and in modern parlance the yoga must be common in the horoscopes of travelling agents or guards of trains who are required to be always moving. One who has a powerful *Vihaga Yoga* is said to become a tale-bearer also.

It is evident that the ancient writers have attributed *evil results* for opposition aspects though certain yogas such as *Gajakesari* must have been treated as exception. The results due to single yoga or a combination of yogas are always dependent upon the inherent strength of the horoscope.

In Chart No. 50. all the planets are in the 4th and 10th houses so that it is a typical illustration of Vihaga Yoga.

Chart No. 50.—*Born on 1-11-1910 at 1 p.m. Lat. 13' N.; Long. 77° 35' E.*

	Rahu Saturn		
	RASI		
Lagna			
		Sun Moon Mars Ket Ven. Mer. Jup.	

			Kethu
Sun	NAVAMSA		Saturn
Venus			
Rahu Moon Merc.	Mars Jupiter		Lagna

Balance of Rahu's Dasa at birth : years 15-3-26.

84. Vajra Yoga
85. Yava Yoga

Definition.—Benefics occupying the ascendant and the 7th house, while malefics occupying the 4th and the 10th give rise to Vajra Yoga; the reverse will be the case in Yava Yoga.

Results.—Vajra gives rise to a happy and handsome person; Yava makes one happy in his middle life.

Remarks.—The difference between Vajra and Yava Yogas is very thin. In the former, benefics will found in the ascendant and the descendant, and malefics in the meridian and the nadir while in other, the Lagna and the descendant must have malefics and the meridian and the nadir should have benefics. Even in the production of results the difference between the two yogas is hardly worth attention, for while Vajra makes one fair, brave and happy, the effects of Yava are restricted to a particular period of life, *viz.*, the middle portion. If one makes a serious attempt to study a number of horoscopes, he will not be slow in appreciating one important truth, *viz.*, that Yava Yoga is hardly conducive to the health and bodily happiness of the native or his wife, for if malefics occupy the Lagna and the 7th, their effects, unless counterbalanced by other horoscopic factors, such as more powerful yogas or inherent strength, etc., would necessarily converge on these two houses. These two yogas are not after all very important, because oftentimes their influences become merged with those of other powerful yogas.

Chart No. 51 illustrates Vajra Yoga because Lagna is occupied by Jupiter and the 7th by Venus, the 4th by the Sun and the 10th by Saturn and Mars. Chart No. 52 is a distinct case of Yava Yoga.

Chart No. 51.

	Lagna Jupiter Moon	Rahu	
	RASI		Sun
Saturn Mars			Merc.
	Kethu	Venus	

Chart No. 52.

Mars Lagna Sat.	Kethu		Venus Mercury Moon
	RASI		Sun
Jupit.		Rahu	

86. Sringhataka Yoga
87. Hala Yoga

Definition.—If all the planets occupy the ascendant and its trines Sringhataka is caused. If planets are confined to other triangular houses, Hala Yoga arises.

Results.—One born in Sringhataka becomes happy in later life while Hala Yoga makes one an agriculturist.

Remarks.—Sringhataka may mean junction of four roads or a square. Planets must invariably occupy the 1st, 5th and 9th houses. Lagna represents body, the 5th indicates progeny and the 9th suggests fortune in general. If these three houses are well fortified, then the native will have a smooth career, progeny and success in life. One born in Sringhataka is said to be happy in his later life. With due deference to the sages who have attributed this result, I have to observe that the period of happiness depends upon the stress laid on any one of the trines by virtue of a larger number of benefics being placed in it. Thus if the stress is on the Lagna, the beginning of life will be happy; if in the 5th, the middle part of life; and if in the 9th, the last part. This is a simple observation that any student of astrology could conveniently carry on.

Chart No. 53 is an example of Sringhataka Yoga.

Chart No. 53.—*Born on 28/29-4-1901, at 4-47 a.m. Lat. 32° 10' N.; Long. 74° 15' E.*

	Lagna Mercury Venus Sun	Kethu	
	RASI		
	H. 646		Moon Mars
Jupiter Saturn	Rahu		

	Mercury	Mars	Lagna
	NAVAMSA		Rahu
Kethu			Venus
	Moon Saturn	Jupiter	Sun

Balance of Venus' Dasa at birth: years 2-6-27.

Hala implies a plough. Consistent with this meaning, Hala Yoga is said to make one an agriculturist. Three variations can be seen in this Yoga, all the planets may occupy (*a*) the 2nd, 6th and 10th houses, (*b*) the 3rd, 7th and 11th houses and (*c*) the 4th, 8th and 12th houses. Hala Yoga would be helpful in deciding one's profession, for a number of horoscopes possessing this combination, belong to agriculturists, farmers, estate managers, zamindars and petty landlords.

88. Kamala Yoga
89. Vapee Yoga.

Definition.—Kamala Yoga will result when the planets are situated in the four kendras, while Vapee is caused when they are ranged in the four Panaparas or the four Apoklimas.

Chart No. 54.—*Born on 25-7-1896 at 10-52 a.m. Lat. 18° 55' N.; Long. 72° 54' E.*

	Mars		
Rahu	RASI		Sun Merc. Jupit. Venus
Moon			Kethu
		Saturn	Lagna

	Saturn	Kethu	Moon
Jupit.	NAVAMSA		
			Mercury Lagna
	Mars Venus Rahu	Sun	

Balance of Moon's Dasa at birth : years 4-4-24.

Results.—One born in Kamala will not become much wealthy, but he will command high prestige, wide fame and innumerable virtues. Vapee makes one hoarder of money.

Remarks.—Kamala Yoga is practically the same as Chathussagara Yoga though not synonymous with it. Kendras are strongholds in a horoscope and when all the four kendras are occupied, the horoscope is rendered highly powerful. Kamala Yoga lays emphasis on fame, virtue, and prestige as different from mere earning capacity. Vapee, which means a well, on the other hand, is said to make one mean, trickery and always pine for and hoard wealth. Panaparas are the 2nd, 5th, 8th, and 11th and Apoklimas are 3rd, 6th, 9th and 12th. The planets should occupy exclusively all the Panaparas or all the Apoklimas.

In Chart No. 54 all the planets are disposed in Panaparas. It is a typical example for Vapee Yoga.

90. Samadura Yoga

Definition.—All the planets must occupy the six even houses.

Results.—The native will be a ruler or live like him free from care and worry.

Remarks.—This is indeed a somewhat rare combination because all the seven planets have to occupy six alternate signs beginning from the second. All odd houses reckoned from Lagna should be free from occupation.

This is one of the several Akriti Yogas dealt with by the great Varahamihira. In our humble experience, Akriti Yogas by themselves cannot exercise any definite influences unless the horoscope has gained strength otherwise.

With this we complete the 21 Akriti Yogas, comprising the first of the 4 groups of Nabhasa Yogas. Yogas like Vajra and Yava which require the positions of the planets exclusively in kendras do not seem to have the approval of Varahamihira. He deals with them in his *Brihat Jataka* simply adopting the views of Yavana and others and feels sceptical about their possibility with the query 'How can Mercury and Venus occupy the 4th sign (Bhavana) from the Sun ?' The possibility or otherwise of Vajra, Yava and similar yogas which require mutual angular dispositions of the Sun and Mercury and Venus depends upon whether these yogas refer to the positions of planets in the *Rasi Chakra* or *Bhava Chakra.* If the former, as is clearly implied by the letter *Bhavana* used by Mihira which means a sign, then the Sun can never be in a Kendra from Mercury or Venus. If on the other hand, the reference is to Bhava Chakra as some scholars contend, then Mercury can occupy a kendra bhava from the Sun, which could be possible in very high latitudes. Therefore the ancient writers have not erred if the Vajra and Yava Yogas refer to the positions in the Bhava Chakra.

91. Vallaki Yoga

Definition.—All the planets must occupy any seven signs.

Results.—The person will have a large number of friends, fond of music and fine arts, learned, happy and famous.

Remarks —This is the first of the Sankhya Yogas or numerical combinations. Vallaki is also known as Veena Yoga. All the seven planets should be disposed of in any seven signs. It will be seen, as would be shown subsequently that sometimes Sankhya Yogas actually coincide with Akriti Yogas (already discussed above). In such cases, Sankhya Yogas lose their individuality and they should not be considered at all. There seems to be some justification in adopting this course, because in almost every horoscope since all the seven planets will have to occupy any seven, or less than seven Rasis, Sankhya Yoga must be present in some form or the other. Provided no other *Nabhasa Yoga* is present, then alone Sankhya Yogas have to be reckoned. Vallaki and the six other Yogas to follow, belong to the category of Sankhya Yogas.

Chart No. 55.— *Born on 10-8-1937 at 4-57 a.m. Lat. 7° N., Long. 79° 45′ E.*

Saturn		Kethu	Venus			Moon	
	RASI		Sun	Lagna Sun Venus	NAVAMSA		Kethu
Lagna	5.59		Merc.	Rahu			
Jupiter	Mars Rahu		Moon	Jupit.	Saturn	Mercury	Mars

Balance of Moon's Dasa at birth : years 5-10-15.

The above is a typical illustration of Vallaki or Veena Yoga for all the seven planets (Rahu and Kethu excepted) have occupied *any* seven Rasis. Whether the Yoga is able to independently function or has been absorbed by some other more powerful *Nabhasa Yoga*, the reader can easily find out.

92. Damni Yoga

Definition.—All the seven planets should occupy any six signs.

Results.—The person will be highly charitable, always helping others and a protector of cattle.

Remarks.—In ascribing results to these Yogas, classical writers have deffered from each other. For instance, the effects given above for Damini are based on Varahamihira while *Saravali* glorifies the Yoga considerably. But all writers seem almost agreed on the general good or bad nature of the results due to a yoga. Damini or Dama Yoga seems to give a man intellect, fame and wealth also. Of course, the exact nature of effects depends upon the general disposition of the chart.

Chart No. 56.—*Born on 11-10-1916 at 5-55 a.m. Lat. 13° 35' N.; Long. 77° 35' E.*

Moon		Jupiter	
	RASI		Sat. Kethu
Rahu	5.60		Venus
	Mars		Lagna Sun Merc.

		Mercury	
Rahu	NAVAMSA		Mars Jupiter Venus
Moon			Lagna Sun Kethu
			Saturn

Balance of Mercury's Dasa at birth : years 9-6-7.

Both the Charts 56 and 57 illustrate the presence of Damini Yoga. But a careful examination of the two reveals that Chart No. 57 is stronger and more potential. 56 is marred by the weakness of Lagnadhipati while Chart No. 57 is considerably fortified by the presence of Mars, a yogakaraka in the 5th and another trine lord Jupiter in the 11th. In point of fame and wealth, Chart No. 57 is decidedly more powerful. Such illustrations furnish clues as to how the same Yoga can operate in different ways in different horoscopes.

Chart No 57.—*Born on 29-12-1893 at 7 p.m. Lat. 11° N.; Long. 78° 40′ E.*

Rahu		Jupiter	
Venus	RASI		Lagna
	5.70		
Sun	Mars Mercury	Saturn	Moon Kethu

Merc.	Moon		
Rahu	NAVAMSA		
Jupit.			Lagna Kethu
		Venus Saturn	Sun Mars

Balance of Moon's Dasa at birth : years 8-1-15.

93. Pasa Yoga

Definition.—The planets should occupy any five signs.

Results.—The person will acquire wealth through right means and he will always be surrounded by friends, servants and relatives.

Remarks.—Saravali suggests that one born in Pasa Yoga will suffer from incarceration. This statement should not be taken in its face value. Pasa Yoga in itself cannot make one a prisoner unless there are other combinations indicating the same event. The presence of Lagna, and the lord of Lagna in the 6th and 8th in *Pasa Drekkanas* would be a powerful combination for imprisonment.

Chart No. 58.—*Born on 4-3-1886 at 11-30 p.m. Lat. 16° 40' N.; Long. 81° E.*

Mercury			Sat.
Kethu Venus Sun Moon	RASI		
	5.24		Rahu Mars
	Lagna		Jupit.

	Sun Jupiter	Kethu	
	NAVAMSA		Mercury
Moon Saturn			
	Mars Rahu	Venus	Lagna

Balance of Rahu's Dasa at birth : years 12-5-1.

Charts No. 58 and 59 are examples of Pasa Yoga. Chart No. 58 belongs to an ex-Speaker of Provincial Legislative Assembly who has suffered incarceration a number of times as would be evident by Rahu-Mars combination in the 10th aspected by Saturn. The tenth house has received no other benefic aspect. The disposition of Pasa Yoga may have also contributed its share of evil in making the subject undergo imprisonment. In Chart No. 59, on the other hand, the 10th is considerably strengthened by the presence of Mercury and Venus while the birth is forified by the aspect of its own lord, in this case Jupiter. The native of the horoscope was a Joint-Secretary in the Government of India and had been getting on very well. These illustrations are provided with a view to driving home to the reader that great care must be exercised in sifting the evidence furnished by different combinations. In both the horoscopes the benefic aspects of Pasa Yoga have manifested considerably.

Chart No. 59.—*Born on 7-9-1904 at 1-50 p.m. (I.S.T.) Lat. 18° 52' N.; Long. 72° 35' E.*

	Jupiter		
Kethu	RASI		Moon Mars
Saturn			Sun Rahu
Lagna			Merc. Venus

Merc. Venus			Jupiter Kethu
Mars	NAVAMSA		
			Lagna Saturn
Moon Rahu		Sun	

Balance of Mercury's Dasa at birth : years 15-0-24.

94. Kedara Yoga

Definition.—All the planets must be ranged in any four signs.

Results.—The person will earn his livelihood by agriculture and be highly helpful to others.

Remarks.—A comparative study of a large number of horoscopes possessing Akriti Yogas leads me to the perception that these yogas could furnish helpful hints for guessing one's profession which has always been a hard nut to crack. Hala Yoga (*vide* Page No. 111) makes one pursue agriculture. Similarly Kedara also is said to make one an agriculturist. *Saravali* points out that one having Kedara Yoga will have a bull intellect or poor comprehensive power.

95. Sula Yoga
96. Yuga Yoga
97. Gola Yoga

Definition.—Sula Yoga, Yuga and Gola are given rise to by the seven planets occupying respectively, any three signs, two signs or single sign.

Results.—Sula makes one devoid of wealth, courageous, cruel and possess marks of wounds received in battle; Yuga renders one poor, ostracised by society, heretical and a drunkard. Gola gives rise to a poor, dirty, unnamed, ignorant and indolent individual.

Remarks.—All the above three yogas are said to cause poverty, render the person unfit for company by his wrathsome conduct and habits and make him miserable. Probably the joining together of all the seven planets within a space of 90 degrees would release a conglomeration of evil forces that the rays of benefics would lose their lustre and merge with those of the evil planets. As, however, no Yoga can exclusively manifest itself, the results due to it should not be applied in their entirety. Sula Yoga may be present in a horoscope. The native may be poor, and may have sustained injuries in fights yet, on account of the strength of Lagna or the Moon he may be a man of sterling character. Therefore judgment in astrology has a number of pitfalls which a clever student has to avoid.

In Chart No. 60 Sula Yoga is present, as all the planets have occupied three signs. It pertains to a Commander in the British Royal Air Force. Some of the results attributed to Sula Yoga are to be found in the native. But he is neither poor nor cruel.

Chart No. 60.—*Born on 8-12-1921 at 12-15 a.m. Long. 0° 5' W.; Lat. 51° 30' N.*

Kethu			
Moon	RASI		
	U. 264		
	Sun Mercury Venus		Rahu Lagna Mars Jupiter Saturn

		Saturn	Moon
Kethu Sun	NAVAMSA		Jupiter
Lagna			Rahu
		Mercury	Venus Mars

Balance of Jupiter's Dasa at birth: years 5-1-18.

Yuga Yoga is brought out in Chart No. 61 as all the planets are situated in two signs. But as the horoscope has a number of other relieving features, viewed from Chandra Lagna, the effects of Yuga Yoga have been considerably restricted.

Chart No. 61.—*Born on 9-10-1923 at 6-38 p.m. (I.S.T.) Lat, 10° 58′ N. ; Long. 79° 25′ E.*

	Lagna		
Kethu	RASI		
	U. 125		Rahu
		Venus	Mars Merc. Moon Sun Jupiter Saturn

Kethu Merc.		Moon	
	NAVAMSA		Lagna
Mars			Sun
		Venus Saturn	Jupiter Rahu

Balance of Moon's Dasa at birth : years 7-0-0.

Gola Yoga is indeed a rare combination, as it requires the presence of all the planets in a single sign.

98. Rajju Yoga
99. Musala Yoga
100. Nala Yoga

Definition.—If all the planets exclusively occupy movable, fixed or common signs respectively, Rajju, Musala and Nala Yogas are caused.

Results.—The person born in Rajju will be fond of travel, handsome, searching for wealth in foreign countries, somewhat cruel and envious. One born in Musala will be endowed with self-respect, wealth, learning a steady mind, engaged in many works, famous and proud. Nala Yoga makes one deformed, shrewd, and defected.

Chart No. 62.—*Born on 1-11-1910 at 1 p.m. Lat. 13° N.; Long. 77° 35′ E.*

	Rahu Saturn		
	RASI		
Lagna			
		Moon Kethu Venus Mercury Jupiter Sun Mars	

Sun			Kethu
	NAVAMSA		Saturn
Venus			
Rahu Moon Merc.	Mars Jupiter		Lagna

Balance of Rahu's Dasa at birth: years 15-6-17.

Chart No. 62 has all the planets in moveable signs and therefore illustrates Rajju Yoga.

Remarks.—The above three yogas constitute the Asraya group being one of the sub-divisions of Nabhasa Yogas. All the planets must occupy *exclusively* movable signs, or *exclusively* fixed signs or *exclusively* common signs to give rise to these three yogas. Here, no reference is made to the situation of Lagna or the disposition of the planets in the cardinal, fixed or common signs with reference to the Lagna. Some commentators are of the opinion that in order to cause Asraya Yogas, all the four movable, all the four fixed and all the four common signs should be occupied. But Garga refutes this view and thereby implies that the only condition is that when the movable—all or any of the four—signs are occupied, the fixed and the common signs should be vacant for causing Rajju Yoga. Similarly with regard to

Musala and Nala. As Rajju has reference to movable signs, one born under its influence would always be wandering about in quest of wealth and fame. when all the planets are in immovable signs, the native is expected to be fixed in determination. Whereas, planets confined to common signs are held to make the person depressed and disappointed.

101. Srik Yoga
102. Sarpa Yoga

Definition.—If all the benefics occupy kendras, Srik Yoga is caused. If all the malefics occupy kendras Sarpa Yoga is produced.

Results.—The person born in Srik Yoga will live in comfort, will possess conveyance and will have many enjoyments. Sarpa Yoga renders one miserable in many ways, cruel and stupid.

Remarks.– Srik (also known as Mala) and Sarpa Yogas are the two Dala Yogas mentioned by Parasara. The Kendras must be exclusively occupied by benefics or malefics. It must be noted that so far as this yoga is concerned, the Moon is completely left out of account so that there remain only three benefics and three malefics. We have formulated above in a fairly exhaustive manner all the Nabhasa Yogas mentioned by Varahamihira. In locating these yogas, there are certain factors to be considered. By carefully remembering the definition of Asraya Yogas, Akirti Yogas, Dala Yogas and Sankhya Yogas it would occur to any student of Astrology that sometimes Asraya Yogas become identical with Akriti Yogas;

Sankhya Yogas become identical with Akriti Yogas; Asraya Yogas coincide with Sankhya Yogas and Dala Yogas coincide with Sankhya Yogas. When such identification of two yogas belonging to two different groups of the Nabhasa Yogas happens, one of the two will cease to operate. Mihira answers this point clearly and succinctly.

It will be seen that three Asraya Yogas (Rajju, Musala and Nala) are practically the same as Yava, Abja, Vajra, Andaja or Pakshi, Gola, Gada and Sakata, among the Akriti Yogas and Sula and Kedara among the Sankhya Yogas, while the two Dala Yogas (Srik and Sarpa) give results similar to those of benefics and malefics occupying kendras (Vajra and Yava). Elaborating the comparison further let us suppose that in a horoscope Cancer and Libra (movable signs) have been occupied by all the planets, thereby causing Rajju Yoga. Two adjacent angles are occupied. If the ascendant is either Cancer or Libra, then Gada is caused with the result it becomes identical with Rajju. Similarly if the planets occupy Cancer and Capricorn and the Lagna is Cancer or Capricorn, both Rajju and Sakata Yogas merge together. Nala and Sakata coincide if we switch on to Gemini and Sagittarius provided one of these two signs is raising. Thus, if the ascendant falls elsewhere then both the yogas will be present. Similarly examples for coincidence of Asraya or Dala Yogas with other Akriti and Sankhya Yogas can be given. These coincidences do not include all possible instances of Asraya and Dala Yogas in the Akriti and Sankhya Yogas. Therefore, in order to show that

Asraya and Dala Yogas are also Nabhasa Yogas, Varahamihira has treated of them saparately. We have now to consider another point. When Sankhya Yogas coincide with Akriti Yogas, the latter alone prevail. When Asraya Yogas coincide with other yogas (Akriti) the former cease to function. When Dala Yogas coincide with Sankhya Yogas the latter become defunct. And if Asraya Yogas coincide with Sankhya, *i.e.*, Kedara, Sula and Yuga, the former alone will prevail and finally if an Asraya Yoga coincides with Gola Yoga, the Asraya Yoga becomes defunct. Thus it will be seen that the differences between some of the yogas are very thin and call forth on the part of the astrologer keen perception and analytical power.

103. Duryoga

Definition.—If the lord of the 10th is situated in the 6th, 8th or 12th, Duryoga is caused.

Results.—The person will not derive the fruits of his own bodily exertion; he will be looked down by others; highly selfiish and always intent upon deceiving others, he will live in a foreign place.

Remarks.—The 10th is the pivot of the horoscope and its lord should be strong if one's life is to be tolerably happy. When the 10th lord is in Dusthanas he will lose his vitality and is therefore said to confer on the native just those qualities which render him insignificant in the eyes of the public. Harming others, selfishness and gluttony are not qualities conducive to making one virtuous. One who has Duryoga is supposed not to derive the benefits of his own bodily exertions. Duryoga seems to indicate that one would earn his livelihood by manual labour. Of the three Dusthanas, the 12th seems to be the least malefic so far as this Yoga is concerned, because whilst depriving one of the fruits of his labours, it will at least give him noble qualities and therefore a certain amount of respect in society.

104. Daridra Yoga

Definition.—The lord of the 11th in the 6th, 8th or 12th will give rise to Daridra Yoga.

Results.—The native will contact huge debts, will be very poor, will suffer from auditory troubles, will be mean and will commit sinful and criminal deeds.

Remarks.—The yoga is a simple one and is quite common. Therefore one should not rush to ascribe all these results to a horoscope in which Daridra Yoga is present. When the Lagna is strong and the 11th lord is in the 6th, Daridra Yoga exists nominally. Because, such a disposition whilst rendering the person mean and inclined to pursue sinful activities, will not make him very *poor*. Criminal intentions are not the sole monopoly of the poor. The rich are equally culpable to such a tendency because the richer a person the more avaricious he becomes to gain his selfish ends. Generous instincts and the tendency to worship mammon are indeed poles apart.

105. Harsha Yoga
106. Sarala Yoga
107. Vimala Yoga

Definition.—The lords of the 6th, 8th and 12th occupying the 6th, 8th and 12th will give rise to Harsha, Sarala and Vimala Yogas respectively.

Results.—Harsha makes one fortunate, happy, invincible, physically strong, wealthy, famous and afraid of sinful deeds. One born in *Sarala* becomes long-lived, fearless, learned, a terror to enemies, celebrated and prosperous. *Vimala* renders the person frugal, happy, independent and possessed of ennobling qualities.

Remarks.—These three yogas furnish us with a clue as to how lords of Dusthanas by occupying Dusthanas can overcome the evil due to such malefic ownership. Even though the author of the above yogas has ascribed very pleasant results to these three combinations, yet in actual practice, quite the contrary have been the results. Parasara and Lomasa do not seem to favour the conception that the sting arising from an evil lordship can disappear entirely as a result of the lord occupying another Dusthana. On the other hand, the intensity will be *somewhat* modified. This is evident from the fact that according to Parasara, when the 6th lord is in the 6th, the native's relatives become enemies while he would befriend outsiders and when the 6th lord is in the 8th or 12th, "the person becomes sickly, hates learned men, goes after others' women and takes pleasure in causing violence". Therefore in interpreting the three yogas given above, one should have an eye on the intrinsic evil nature of the ownership.

108. Sareera Soukhya Yoga

Definition.—The lord of Lagna, Jupiter or Venus should occupy a quadrant.

Results.—The subject will be endowed with long life, wealth and political favours.

Remarks.—If all the three factors above referred to, *viz.*, the ascendant lord, Jupiter and Venus are in kendras, the Yoga would be rendered highly powerful with the result all the blessings of the Yoga will manifest. The Yoga is fairly common but hardly noticed.

109. Dehapushti Yoga

Definition.—The ascendant lord in a movable sign aspected by a benefic gives rise to this Yoga.

Results.—The native will be happy, will possess a well-developed body, will become rich and will enjoy life.

Remarks.—Leading a happy life is different from having amenities needed for it. Lord of Lagna must be in a movable sign and some benefic must aspect him. Some people are indifferent to bodily care and comforts while there are others who, in spite of meagre earnings, will look after their body with the utmost care.

110. Dehakashta Yoga

Definition.—The lord of Lagna must join a malefic or occupy the 8th house.

Results.—The subject will be devoid of bodily comforts.

Remarks.—As the name implies, Dehakashta Yoga means difficulty for the body. Most of the manual workers belong to this category. The Yoga is said to become defunct if a benefic aspects the ascendant lord.

111. Rogagrastha Yoga

Definition.—(*a*) If the lord of Lagna occupies the ascendant in conjunction with the lord of the 6th, 8th or 12th; or (*b*) if the weak lord of Lagna joins a trine or a quadrant, Rogagrastha Yoga is caused.

Results.—The native will possess a weak constitution and be sickly.

Remarks.—The Yoga comprehends to combinations, *viz.*, (1) the ascendant lord being placed in the ascendant and joined by the lord of the 6th, 8th or 12th; and (2) the *weak ascendant lord* occcupying a trine or a quadrant. It is a general astrological precept that when the ascendant lord joins a trine or a quadrant he acquires vitality When he is weak, by which term is implied that his *shadbala pinda* (sum total of strength) falls short of the requisite quantity, the distinction attached to location in a kendra or thrikona is lost. It is found in actual practice that the lordship of the 12th is less malefic than that of the 6th or 8th and hence when the lords of the Lagna and 12th join, the affliction expresses itself more in the nature of financial stress than in terms of Dehakashṭa or Rogagrastha Yogas. One born under this combination will not have a healthy constitution. It will lack the requisite power of resistancc so that the native falls an easy prey to disease.

112 and 113. Krisanga Yogas

Definition.—The ascendant lord should occupy a a dry sign or the sign owned by a 'dry' planet (112).

The Navamsa Lagna should be owned by a 'dry' planet and malefics should join the Lagna (113).

Results.—The subject will have an emaciated or lean body and will suffer from bodily pains.

Remarks.—Dry signs are Aries, Taurus, Gemini, Leo, Virgo and Sagittarius. Dry planets are the Sun, Mars and Saturn. Mercury may also be held to be a dry planet for all practical purposes. The same result can be judged if the Lagna and the lord have acquired a large number of dry vargas or divisions such as Rasi, Hora, etc.

Chart No. 63—*Born on 8-8-1912 at 7-23 p.m. (L.M.T.) Lat. 13° N.; Long. 77° 34 E.*

Rahu		Moon Saturn	
Lagna	RASI		Sun
			Mars Merc. Venus
	Jupiter		Kethu

	Saturn	Venus	
Rahu Sun	NAVAMSA		
Lagna			Moon Mercury Kethu
	Jupiter	Mars	

Balance of Mars' Dasa at birth: years 6-0-10.

Here the Amsa Lagna belongs to a dry planet and it is aspected by a first rate malefic, *viz.*, Mars. The result is obvious, *viz.*, the native has a lean and emaciated physical appearance.

114 to 116. Dehasthoulya Yogas

Definition.--Lord of Lagna and the planet, in whose Navamsa the lord of Lagna is placed, should occupy watery signs (114).

The Lagna must be occupied by Jupiter or he must aspect the Lagna from a watery sign (115).

The ascendant must fall in a watery sign in conjunction with benefics or the ascendant lord must be a watery planet (116).

Remarks.—Possessing a strong body is different from having an unwieldy and corpulent appearance. In the above three combinations,by *dehasthoulya* is meant stoutness of the body and has no reference to a well-built or strong physical appearance. Watery signs are Cancer, Aquarius, Capricorn, Pisces, Scorpio and Libra, and the watery planets are the Moon and Venus. Of course, Mercury and Jupiter are also water resorters and a predominance of the water element in regard to Lagna or lagnadhipathi would invariably make the person corpulent.

Chart No. 64.—*Born on 29-7-1909 at Gh. 1-15 after sunrise ; Lat. 13° N ; Long. 77° 34' E.*

Mars	Saturn	Rahu			Saturn		Venus
	RASI		Sun Merc. Lagna	Moon	NAVAMSA		Rahu
	11-23		Jupit. Venus	Kethu Lagna			
	Moon Kethu				Sun	Mars Jupiter	Mercury

Balance of Mercury's Dasa at birth: years 6-5-23.

In Chart No. 64, Cancer, a watery sign, is rising and the Moon, a watery planet, is in Scorpio another watery sign. The Moon (lord of the ascendant) is in Aquarius (a watery sign) in Navamsa aspected by Jupiter. The subject has a stout body.

117. Sada Sanchara Yoga

Definition.—The lord of either Lagna or the sign occupied by Lagna lord must be in a movable sign.

Results.—The native will almost always be a wanderer.

Remarks.—The combination referred to above is very common in the horoscopes of travelling agents, diplomats and globe-trotters. If both the Lagna and the Navamsa Lagna are in movable signs, the subject would hardly confine himself to any particular locality. On the contrary, he will always be moving about.

118 to 122. Dhana Yogas

Definition.—If the 5th from the Ascendant happens to be a sign of Venus, and if Venus and Saturn are situated in the 5th and 11th respectively, Dhana Yoga is caused—118.

Mercury should occupy his own sign which should be the 5th from Lagna and the Moon and Mars should be in the 11th—119.

Saturn should occupy his own sign which should be the 5th from Lagna, and Mercury and Mars should be posited in the 11th—120.

The Sun must occupy the 5th identical with his own sign and Jupiter and the Moon should be in the 11th—121.

If the 5th from Lagna happens to be a house of Jupiter with Jupiter there and Mars and the Moon in the 11th, Dhana Yoga arises—122.

Results.—In all the above cases, the native will acquire much wealth.

Remarks.—The above five Yogas caused by the disposition of certain planets in the 5th and 11th houses are really significant as they indicate great riches. In the first case, the Lagna must invariably be Capricorn or Gemini. When Makara is the Ascendant Saturn will have to be in Scorpio, the 11th. Lord of Lagna in the 11th is indeed a fine combination. Similarly when Gemini is Lagna, Saturn will have to be in Aries. This cannot be as powerful as in the first instance unless Saturn gets Neechabhanga.

In 119 Lagna must fall either in Aquarius or in Taurus. In regard to Aquarius, the combination in the 11th will be due to the lord of the 10th and 6th while for Taurus, the location in the 11th would be of the lords of the 3rd and 7th. The degree of wealth would be the same but the sources of getting it would be different.

Combination 120 has reference to Virgo and Libra. If Virgo is Lagna, then Mercury lord of the 10th will be in the 11th. If Libra is Lagna, then the 9th lord will be in the 11th. Both the dispositions are highly favourable though, in the first instance, Mercury being lord of Lagna also in addition to the lordship of the 10th would certainly have greater significance.

Combination 121 is applicable only to Aries in which case the Sun as lord of the 5th would be in the

5th and the Moon lord of the 4th and Jupiter lord of the 9th would be in the 11th. Moon—Jupiter combination itself comprehends two powerful Raja Yogas, because firstly they are lords of a kendra and thrikona respectively, and secondly, Gajakesari would be formed—all occurring in the 11th house. 121 would indeed be a powerful Dhana Yoga.

If Jupiter could be in the 5th identical with his own sign (as required in combination 122) in respect of Scorpio and Leo, the Yoga could be expected to be more powerful in respect of Scorpio, because when Mars and the Moon occupy the 11th, they do so as lords of 1 and 9 and hence of considerable significance.

It will be seen that all the five combinations given above have reference to the fortification of the 5th and 11th houses.

Chart No. 65.—*Born on 30-6-1897 at 7-20 p.m. (L.M.T.) Lat. 8° N. ; Long. 79° 45' E.*

		Venus	Moon Sun Merc.
	RASI		Kethu
Rahu Lagna			Mars Jupit.
	Saturn		

Sun	Moon	Mars Rahu	
	NAVAMSA		
Lagna Venus			Jupiter Saturn
	Kethu	Mercury	

Balance of Jupiter's Dasa at birth: years 12-1-13.

In Chart No. 65 the 5th from Lagna is owned by Venus, and Venus and Saturn occupy, respectively, the 5th and 11th houses, hence illustrating combination 118. Saturn's Dasa proved highly beneficial from the point of view of of finance, prosperity having set in, as soon as Venus' sub-period commenced.

Chart No. 66.—*Born on 5-9-1906 at 9-16 a.m. (L.M.T.) Lat. 25° N.; Long. 84° E.*

Moon			Jupit.
Saturn	RASI		Rahu
Kethu			Sun Mars Merc.
		Lagna Venus	

	Saturn	Mars Mercury	Kethu
Jupit.	NAVAMSA		
Lagna Rahu	Moon Venus	Sun	

Balance of Saturn's Dasa at birth: year 0-0-9.

Chart No. 66 is a typical example for combination 120. Saturn owns and occupies the 5th and Mars (lord of the 2nd) and Mercury (lord of the 9th) are in the 11th in association with the Sun, the lord of the 11th. The peculiarity in this case is that during Mercury's Dasa the native's father became extremely wealthy, probably due to the fact that Mercury having caused Dhana Yoga is associated with the Pitrukaraka Sun.

Chart No. 67 illustrates combination 121. The Sun occupies the 5th which is his own sign while the Moon and Jupiter are together in the 11th. It will be seen that the Moon and Jupiter have caused two yogas, *viz*., Gajakesari and another Raja Yoga thus fortifying the house of gains considerably.

Chart No. 67.—*Born on 20-8-1891 at 10 p.m. Lat. 19° N.; Long. 72° 35' E.*

	Lagna	Rahu	
Moon Jupiter	RASI		Mars Venus
			Sun Sat.
	Kethu		Merc.

Venus Moon Mars	Rahu	Sun Jupiter	
Merc.	NAVAMSA		
			Lagna
	Saturn	Kethu	

Balance of Rahu's Dasa at birth : years 2-6-15.

Chart No. 68.—*Born on 30-8-1927 at 12-30 p.m. (L.M.T.) Lat. 12° N.; Long. 72° 50' E.*

Jupiter			Rahu
	RASI		
			Sun Merc.
Kethu	Lagna Saturn		Mars Moon Venus

	Kethu		Moon
	NAVAMSA		Mercury
Venus Mars			Sun
	Lagna	Saturn Rahu	Jupiter

Balance of Moon's Dasa at birth : years 3-8-21.

Chart No. 68 is an example for combination 122 which requires the presence of Jupiter in the 5th (in his own sign) and Moon and Mars in the 11th. A powerful Chandramangala Yoga occurs in the 11th. As Mars and the Moon are lords of the 1st and 9th respectively a powerful Raja Yoga is also caused.

123 to 128. Dhana Yogas *(Contd.)*

Definition.—If the Sun is in Lagna identical with Leo, and aspected or joined by Mars and Jupiter, Dhana Yoga is formed—123.

If the Moon is in Lagna identical with Cancer and aspected by Jupiter and Mars, Dhana Yoga is caused—124.

Mars should be in Lagna identical with Aries or Scorpio and joined or aspected by the Moon, Venus and Saturn—125.

Mercury should be in Lagna identical with his own sign and joined or aspected by Saturn and Venus —126.

Jupiter should be in Lagna identical with his own sign and joined or aspected by Mercury and Mars—127.

Venus should be in Lagna identical with his own sign and joined or aspected by Saturn and Mercury —128.

Results.—In all the above cases, the subject acquires immense wealth.

Remarks.—In the above six combinations, planets from the Sun to Venus are to occupy Lagna which should be the own sign of the planet concerned and it should be conjoined or aspected by certain other planets as per details given below :—

Planet	*Ascendant*	*Conjunction or Aspect of*
Sun	Leo	Mars, Jupiter
Moon	Cancer	Mars, Jupiter
Mars	Aries and Scorpio	Moon, Venus, Saturn
Mercury	Gemini and Virgo	Venus, Saturn
Jupiter	Sagittarius and Pisces	Mars, Mercury
Venus	Taurus and Libra	Mercury, Saturn

It will be seen that except *Capricorn* and *Aquarius*, the rest of the signs have been taken into account. In all the above cases, the lord of Lagna must be in his own sign identical with Lagna and aspected by or associated with certain favourable lords.

Each of the above combinations can have a number of variations as could be seen from the following explanation. Take for example the Sun. Leo is Lagna, and the Sun is there.

The Dhana Yoga in question may be caused by:

(a) Jupiter and Mars being in Lagna.

(b) Jupiter being in Sagittarius and Mars in Capricorn.

(c) Jupiter being in Sagittarius and Mars in Aquarius.

(d) Jupiter and Mars being in Aquarius.

(e) Jupiter being in Aries and Mars in Taurus.

The same variations can be seen in regard to the Dhana Yoga arising out of other planets also.

Chart No. 69.—*Born on 15-5-1909 at 6 a.m. (L.M.T.) Lat. 13° N.; Long. 77° 35' E.*

Moon Saturn		Lagna Sun Rahu Venus Mercury	
Mars	RASI		
			Jupit.
	Kethu		

Lagna Venus Kethu Saturn			
	NAVAMSA		Moon
Sun			Mercury Jupiter
		Mars	Rahu

Balance of Jupiter's Dasa at birth : years 3-1-16.

Combination 128 is shown by Chart No. 69. The Lagna is Taurus and lord Venus is in Lagna in conjunction with Mercury and aspected by Saturn.

Chart No. 70—*Born on 29-1-1940 at 7-06 a. m. (I.S.T.) Lat. 30° 12' N.; Long. 67° 02' E.*

Kethu	Saturn Jupiter		Moon Venus
	RASI		
			Lagna Sun Merc. Mars
			Rahu

Moon			Venus Mercury
	NAVAMSA		Rahu
Kethu			Sun Mars
	Jupiter	Saturn	Lagna

Balance of Rahu Dasa at birth : years 1-7-05.

Chart No. 70 is an example for combination 123. Lagna is Leo and the Sun is in Leo with Mars and is aspected by Jupiter.

129. Bahudravyarjana Yoga

Definition.—Lord of the Lagna in the 2nd, lord of the 2nd in the 11th and the lord of the 11th in Lagna will give rise to this Yoga.

Results.—The subject will earn lot of money and will amass a good fortune.

Remarks.—A point of contact is established between the Lagna, 2nd and 11th houses—the lords of these three houses interchanging their respective positions. Here again, the real value of the Yoga depends upon the strength of the lords concerned and how they are disposed in regard to the general scheme of the horoscope.

Chart No. 71.—*Born on 2-6-1892 at 10-16 a.m. Lat. 13° N.; Long. 77° 35' E.*

Jupiter	Rahu	Sun Mercury	
	RASI		Lagna Venus
Mars			Moon
		Kethu	Saturn

		Kethu	
Lagna Jupit.	NAVAMSA		Sun Venus Mars
Merc. Saturn			
	Rahu		Moon

Balance of Venus' Dasa at birth: years 11-6-9.

In Chart No. 71 lord of Lagna is in the 2nd, the lord of the 2nd is in the 11th and the lord of the 11th in Lagna thus showing the presence of a very powerful Dhana Yoga.

130 to 132. Swaveeryaddhana Yogas

Definition.—The Lord of Lagna, being the strongest planet, should occupy a kendra in conjunction with Jupiter and the 2nd lord should join Vaiseshikamsa—130.

The lord of the sign in which the lord of the Navamsa occupied by the Ascendant lord is, should be strong, and join a quadrant or a trine from the 2nd lord or should occupy his own or exaltation sign —131.

The 2nd lord should occupy a quadrant or trine from the 1st lord or the 2nd lord being a benefic should be either in deep exaltation or in conjunction with an exalted planet—132.

Results.—The subject will earn money by his own efforts and exertions.

Remarks.—Inherited wealth cannot last long nor is it made use of properly. Generally such wealth is squandered away on pleasures and valueless purposes. The person concerned will have no experience as to how difficult it is to earn money by fair means. On the other hand, wealth acquired through personal effort would be rightly spent or at least not wasted because of the exertions put forth in making the money. The above three combinations are quite clear and need no clarification.

According to 130, the ascendant lord must be the strongest planet in the horoscope and he should be in a kendra in conjunction with Jupiter and 2nd lord in Vaiseshikamsa.

131 is somewhat confusing. Lord of Lagna is in some Navamsa. The lord of that Navamsa occupies some sign. Its lord must be disposed in a kendra or thrikona from the 2nd lord. Suppose Lagna is Kanya and the lord is in Makara Navamsa. The lord of Makara is Saturn and suppose he occupies (in Rasi) Mesha. Then the lord of this sign, *viz.*, Mars should be in a kendra from Venus, lord of the 2nd.

Chart No. 72.—*Born on 8-3-1912 at 7-23 p.m. (L.M.T.) Lat. 13° N.; Long. 77° 34′ E.*

Rahu		Moon Saturn	
Lagna	RASI		Sun
			Venus Mars Merc.
	Jupiter		Kethu

	Saturn	Venus	
Sun Rahu	NAVAMSA		
Lagna			Moon Mercury Kethu
	Jupiter	Mars	

Balance of Mars' Dasa at birth: years 6-0-10.

In Chart No. 72, lord of Lagna, Saturn, is in Mesha Navamsa; the lord of which, *viz.*, Mars is in Leo. Its lord Sun is in a trine from Jupiter lord of the 2nd. The native started life with no financial facilities but earned decently by his own exertions. 132 is quite simple.

133. Madhya Vayasi Dhana Yoga

Definition.—The 2nd lord possessing Kalabala must join the lords of Lagna and the 11th in a quadrant or a trine and be aspected by benefics.

Results.—The person will acquire money by self-effort towards the middle part of his life.

Remarks.—Kalabala or temporal strength is one of the six sources of planetary strength enumerated at length in my *Graha and Bhava Balas*. Kalabala consists of various sub-divisions based upon the lunar phases, weekday, time, solstice and planetary fights. Generally speaking, planets are said to acquire Kalabala in their weekdays, months and years. The Moon, Mars and Saturn are powerful during the night. The Sun, Jupiter and Venus are powerful during the day. Mercury is always powerful. Malefics and benefics are powerful during the dark half and bright half of the lunar month respectively.

In order to make one get wealth in the middle part of his life lord of the 2nd having acquired Kalabala should be in a kendra or a thrikona in conjunction with the lords of Lagna and the 11th.

A perusal of astrological literature bearing upon 'Wealth' reveals clearly that in order to become rich, one should have in his horoscope combinations which comprehend a point of contact between lords of Lagna, 2nd, 11th, 5th and 9th. Permutations and combinations of these lords give rise to a stupendous number of Dhana Yogas.

134. Anthya Vayasi Dhana Yoga

Definition.—The planets owning the sign in which the lords of the 2nd and 1st together with a natural benefic are placed, should be strongly disposed in Lagna.

Results.—The subject will acquire finance through various means towards the last part of his life.

Remarks.—There are some who eke out a miserable existence almost throughout their lives but all of a sudden, just at the fag end of their lives fortune dawns on them. Such instances are not rare. The combination requires that lords of Lagna and the 2nd should be in conjunction with a benefic and the lord of this sign should be strong and occupy Lagna. The combination is not of frequent occurrence.

135. Balya Dhana Yoga

Definition.—The lords of the 2nd and 10th should be in conjunction in a kendra aspected by the lord of the Navamsa occupied by the ascendant lord.

Results.—The person acquries immense riches in the early part of life.

Remarks.—The Yoga is a round about one. Three conditions have to be fulfilled for its presence, *viz.*, (*a*) the 2nd and 10th lords should be in conjunction; (*b*) they must occupy a kendra from Lagna, and (*c*) they must be aspected by the planet who owns the Navamsa in which the lord of Lagna is located.

The following horoscope illustrates combination No. 135.

Chart No. 73.—*Born on 25-4-1945 at 4-7 p.m. I.S.T. Lat. 18° 52' N.; Long. 72° 35' E.*

Mars Mercury Venus	Sun		Sat. Rahu
	RASI		
	885		Jupit.
Kethu			Moon Lagna

Lagna Venus	Rahu		
Merc. Sat.	NAVAMSA		Moon Sun Mars
	Jupiter	Kethu	

Balance of Moon's Dasa at birth : years 1-5-16.

136 and 137. Bhratrumooladdhanaprapti Yoga

Definition.—The lords of Lagna and the 2nd should join the 3rd aspected by benefics—136.

The lord of the 3rd should be in the 2nd with Jupiter and aspected by or conjoined with the lord of Lagna who should have attained Vaiseshikamsa —137.

Results.—The native gets money through brothers and relatives.

Remarks.—Predicting the source of income astrologically is a difficult job. The above two combinations give a hint that one can earn money through brothers by a certain disposition of the 2nd and 3rd lords.

138. Matrumooladdhana Yoga

Definition.—If the lord of the 2nd joins the 4th lord or is aspected by him the above yoga will be caused.

Results.—One earns money with the help of one's mother.

Remarks.—The combination may also be interpreted to mean that depending upon the nature of the 4th lord, the source of earning could also vary. Thus if the 4th lord is Mars, agriculture may be the source.

139. Putramooladdhana Yoga

Definition.—If the strong lord of the 2nd is in conjunction with the 5th lord or Jupiter and if the lord of Lagna is in Vaiseshikamsa, the above yoga arises.

Results.—The person gets wealth through his sons.

Remarks.—There are several instances of persons living from hand to mouth but becoming rich after their sons come to age and assist them in founding and developing some business or otherwise extending them financial facilities. The Lagna must be in Vaiseshikamsa and the strong 2nd lord should be associated with the 5th lord.

In Chart No. 74, the 2nd lord is Jupiter and he is in conjunction with 5th lord Mercury. The Lagna lord is not in Vaiseshikamsa but he is decidedly strong. Till the age of 50, the native had never seen the bright side of life but beginning from the 51st year, father and son jointly floated a small business which steadily developed into a substantial concern. When the Yoga is present, it does not necessarily imply that the son would help the father with money. It may mean that after the birth of a son the father would become rich. In such a case the son only brings invisible luck to the father.

Chart No. 74.—*Born on 1-6-1895 at Gh. 45-12 after Sunrise at 13° N.; 77° 34' E.*

		Sun	Merc. Jupit.
Lagna Rahu	RASI		Mars Venus
	11.6		Kethu
		Saturn	Moon

Jupit.		Rahu	Sun
Moon	NAVAMSA		Mars Venus
Sat.			
Merc. Lagna	Kethu		

Balance of Sun's Dasa at birth : years 1-6-13.

140. Satrumooladdhana Yoga

Definition.—The strong lord of the 2nd should join the lord of the 6th or Mars and the powerful lord of Lagna should be in Vaiseshikamsa.

Results.—The native earns money through his enemies.

Remarks.—In all these Yogas, stress is evidently laid on the strength of the 2nd lord and the powerful disposition of Lagnadhipathi in Vaiseshikamsa. To give the results suggested in the above Yoga, the 2nd lord may either join the 6th lord or Mars or be aspected by one of them.

141. Kalatramooladdhana Yoga

Definition.—The strong lord of the 2nd should join or be aspected by the 7th lord and Venus and the lord of Lagna must be powerful.

Results.—The subject will earn money through wife.

Remarks.—If the 2nd lord, whose inherent strength is of course assumed, is associated with the 7th lord and Venus, one would become rich on account of one's wife.

142. Amaranantha Dhana Yoga

Definition.—If a number of planets occupy the 2nd house and the wealth-giving ones are strong or occupy own or exaltation signs, the above Yoga is caused.

Results.—The native will enjoy wealth throughout life.

Remarks.—The 2nd should be occupied by a number of planets. Besides this wealth-giving ones, *viz.*, the 2nd lord and Jupiter should be strongly disposed. The Yoga given rise to in this way would enable the person concerned command riches all through life. When a horoscope is inherently strong in respect of any particular bhava, its results will manifest permanently as different from those given rise to by Yogakarakas which generally hold sway during the Dasas concerned.

143. Ayatnadhanalabha Yoga

Definition.—The lord of the Lagna and the 2nd must exchange their places.

Results.—The person earns wealth without much effort.

Remarks.—There are some who lead a miserable existence in spite of their best attempts to enrich themselves whilst there are others who without straining themselves much earn decently. We attribute this to chance or luck. Actually it is neither luck nor chance but the result of one's good previous Karma. Parivarthana between the 1st and 2nd lords is a highly desirable feature.

144 to 153. Daridra Yogas

Definition.—The lords of the 12th and Lagna should exchange their positions and be conjoined or be aspected by the lord of the 7th—144.

The lords of the 6th and Lagna interchange their positions and the Moon is aspected by the 2nd or 7th lord—145.

Kethu and the Moon should be in Lagna—146.

The lord of Lagna is in the 8th aspected by or in conjunction with the 2nd or 7th lord—147.

The lord of Lagna joins the 6th, 8th or 12th with a malefic aspected by or combined with the 2nd or 7th lord—148.

Lord of Lagna is associated with the 6th, 8th or 12th lord and subjected to malefic aspects—149.

The lord of the 5th joins the lord of the 6th, 8th or 12th without beneficial aspects or conjunctions —150.

The lord of the 5th is in the 6th or 10th aspected by lords of the 2nd, 6th, 7th, 8th or 12th—151.

Natural malefics, who do not own the 9th or 10th, should occupy Lagna and associate with or be aspected by the maraka lords—152.

The lords of the Lagna and Navamsa Lagna should occupy the 6th, 8th or 12th and have the aspect or conjunction of the lords of the 2nd and 7th—153.

Results.—All the above Yogas produce dire poverty, financial straits, wretchedness and miseries.

Remarks.—Poverty is a horrible spectre more grim-like than even death. Death puts an end to life and settles all worldly states. What happens after death, nobody knows. It is supposed to put an end to all the worldly miseries, sorrows and anxieties. Hence there are some people who prefer death to abject poverty. A poor man leads a wretched life. He is compelled to live in squalid and unhealthy houses. The children have no facilities for education, health and decent existence. The poor man is generally shunned everywhere. He is an unwelcome guest at the doors of the 'well-to-do' classes. His legitimate activities are obstructed by financial difficulties and want of sympathy. Poverty is the hot-bed of crime and vice and the impervious sensations of hunger and thirst drive the poor to disgraceful acts. Whatever philosophers may say, the pangs of poverty are difficult to bear.

In all the above combinations, reference is made in the original to the conjunction of lords of Lagna and the 5th with maraka lords. Evidently, the maraka lords are the 2nd and 7th lords. Some authors include 6th, 8th and 12th houses also as belonging to maraka category.

154 and 155. Yukthi Samanwithavagmi Yogas

Definition.—The 2nd lord should join a benefic in a kendra or thrikona, or be exalted and combined with Jupiter—154.

The lord of speech should occupy a kendra, attain paramochha and gain Parvatamsa, while Jupiter or Venus should be in Simhasanamsa—155.

Results.—The person will become an eloquent and skilled speaker.

Remarks.—The art of speaking is not an easy one. The gift of eloquence can influence men and manners. Men can succeed beyond expectation by convincing speeches. Different occasions and conditions call for different degrees of eloquence or skill. In order to gain this power, lord of the 2nd must be well aspected and conjoined. Mercury must be free from affliction if one is not to become witty in the vulgar sense.

For being an eloquent speaker, the lord of the 2nd should join a trine or a quadrant with Jupiter or get exalted. Parvatamsa, Simhasanamsa, etc., have been defined *infra*. The nature of vocabulary and the dignified or low tone of the speech depends upon the good and malefic influences the planet of speech is subjected to.

156. Parihasaka Yoga

Definition.—The lord of the Navamsa occupied by the Sun should attain Vaiseshikamsa and join the 2nd house.

Results.—The person becomes a humorous and witty speaker.

Remarks.—People of jolly temperament take things easy and lightly while there are some who take even trifles as serious. Humour is the spice of life and all cannot claim it with equal facility.

The Sun occupies some Navamsa and its lord should be in the 2nd besides attaining Vaiseshikamsa.

It will be seen that a planet can occupy its own Rasi, its own Amsa, its own Drekkana, etc., in which case it is said to be in Swarasi or Swakshetra, Swahora, Swadrekkana, etc. In all these cases it is in Swavarga. There are *Shodasa Vargas* or sixteen types of divisions. A planet can therefore occupy its own varga sixteen times. Astrological writers have attached great significance to the special distinction of a planet being in its own varga more than once. The following are the important Amsas (distinctions) often alluded to in the astrological literature.

When a planet is in its own varga—

Twice it is said to have attained		Parijatamsa
Thrice	do.	Uttamamsa
Four times	do.	Gopuramsa
Five ,,	do.	Simhasanamsa
Six ,,	do.	Parvatamsa
Seven ,,	do.	Devalokamsa
Eight ,,	do.	Kunkumamsa
Nine ,,	do.	Iravathamsa
Ten ,,	do.	Vaishnavamsa
Eleven ,,	do.	Saivamsa
Twelve ,,	do.	Bhaswadamsa
Thirteen ,,	do.	Vaiseshikamsa

When a planet attains Vaiseshikamsa, it is *par excellence*.

157. Asatyavadi Yoga

Definition.—If the lord of the 2nd occupies the house of Saturn or Mars and if malefics join kendras and thrikonas, the above Yoga is caused.

Results.—The native will be a liar.

Remarks.—According to this combination, lord of the 2nd must occupy Aries, Scorpio, Capricorn or Aquarius and the kendras and thrikonas must have malefics. The same Yoga is also said to be caused if the lord of the Navamsa occupied by the lord of the 2nd happens to be either Mars or Saturn or happens to stay in the signs of these two planets.

158. Jada Yoga

Definition.—The lord of the 2nd should be posited in the 10th with malefics or the 2nd must be joined by the Sun and Mandi.

Results.—The person becomes nervous in public assemblies.

Remarks.—There are some people who though learned, well-informed and capable of eloquence lose their balance of mind and become extremely nervous when they are called upon to speak in large gatherings. Such people will generally have the 2nd lord afflicted. Even when the above combination is present, if the 2nd lord is in a benefic Navamsa, the Yoga is found to lose its significance.

159. Bhaskara Yoga

Definition.—Mercury in the 2nd from the Sun, the Moon in the 11th from Mercury and Jupiter in the 5th or 9th from the Moon give rise to Bhaskara Yoga.

Results.—The native will be wealthy, valorous, aristocratic, learned in Sastras, Astrology and Music, and will have a good personality.

Remarks.—Three planets figure in this Yoga but their location relative to the Lagna or their signs of dignity or fall is not taken into consideration. It is required that Mercury should be in the 2nd from the Sun and the Moon in the 11th from Mercury, *i.e.*, the 12th from the Sun. In other words the Moon, Sun and Mercury should occupy three successive signs and Jupiter should be in a thrikona from the Moon.

The above horoscope is typically illustrative of Bhaskara Yoga as Mercury is in the 2nd from the Sun, the Moon is in the 11th from Mercury, and Jupiter occupies a trine from the Moon.

Chart No. 75.—*Born on 3-3-1894 at 3-16 p.m. (L.M.T) Lat. 12° 52' N.; Long. 74° 54' E.*

Mercury Rahu		Jupiter	
Sun	RASI		Lagna
Moon Venus	101.7		
Mars		Saturn	Kethu

	Sun		
Moon Jupit.	NAVAMSA		Kethu
Rahu			
	Saturn	Lagna Mars	Mercury Venus

Balance of Sun's Dasa at birth : years 2-5-18.

160. Marud Yoga

Definition.—Jupiter in 5th or 9th from Venus, the Moon in the 5th from Jupiter and the Sun in a kendra from the Moon give rise to Marud Yoga.

Results.—Good conversationalist, large-hearted, rich, learned, successful businessman, king or equal to him and having protruding belly.

Remarks.—This presupposes the disposition of Jupiter, Moon and Venus in mutual thrikonas and the Sun in a quadrant from the Moon. Several variations of the yoga are possible and the reader will do well to study the scope and significance of such variations in the light of actual examples.

Chart No. 76.—*Born on 29-2-1932 at 5-30 a.m. (L.M.T.) Lat. 13° N.; Long. 77° 35° E.*

Rahu Venus			
• Sun Mercury Mars Lagna	RASI		Jupit.
Saturn	141.5		
	Moon		Kethu

Sat. Sun Merc. Venus			
Kethu Jupit.	NAVAMSA		
Moon Mars			Rahu
	Lagna		

Balance of Mercury's Dasa at birth: years 11-4-5.

Mark the dispositions of Jupiter, Moon and Venus in mutual thrikonas and the presence of the Sun in a kendra from the Moon causing Marud Yoga.

161. Saraswathi Yoga

Definition.—If Jupiter, Venus and Mercury occupy Lagna, 2nd, 4th, 5th, 7th, 9th or 10th either jointly or severally, Jupiter being in his own, exaltation or friendly sign, the combination goes under the name of Saraswathi Yoga.

Results.—Poet, famous, learned in all sciences, skilled, rich, praised by all, and good wife and children.

Remarks.—This above yoga is not a rare one. Benefics are to be disposed in any of the 7 houses, *viz.*, 1st, 2nd, 4th, 5th, 7th, 9th or 10th. If the planets are strong, the Yoga will be prominently visible. Otherwise it may merge with other more powerful yogas.

Chart No. 77—*Born on 7-5-1861 at 4-2 a. m. (L.M.T.) Lat. 22° 40′ N.; Long. 88° 30′ E.*

Lagna Moon	Sun Mercury Venus		Mars Kethu
	RASI		Jupit.
	83.4		Saturn
Rahu			

Lagna Jupit.		Kethu	Mercury
	NAVAMSA		Saturn
Moon			
	Venus Sun Rahu	Mars	

Balance of Mercury's Dasa at birth: years 9-5-22.

Chart No. 77 is illustrative of Saraswathi Yoga. Jupiter is in the 5th, Venus and Mercury are in the 2nd. Jupiter is exalted. The native enjoyed all the blessings of Saraswathi Yoga.

162. Budha Yoga

Definition.—Jupiter in Lagna, the Moon in a kendra, Rahu in the 2nd from the Moon and the Sun and Mars in the 3rd from Rahu.

Results.—Kingly comforts, powerful, famous, aristocratic, learned in sciences, intelligent, and devoid of enemies.

Remarks.—Budha Yoga comprehends the strength of Lagna and the Moon. When Jupiter is in Lagna, the Lagna gains considerable strength. The disposition of the Moon in a kendra from Jupiter gives rise to Gajakesari Yoga. Rahu's situation in the 2nd from the Moon and the presence of Sun and Mars in the 3rd from Rahu (4th from the Moon) is said to produce Budha Yoga.

163. Mooka Yoga

Definition.—The 2nd lord should join the 8th with Jupiter.

Results.—The person becomes dumb.

Remarks.—The yoga does not apply if the 8th house happens to be Jupiter's own or exaltation sign. Ganapathi, an ancient astrological writer, includes the 12th house also as harmful for the conjunction of Jupiter and the 2nd lord.

164. Netranasa Yoga

Definition.—If the lords of the 10th and 6th occupy Lagna with the 2nd lord, or if they are in Neechamsa, the above yoga is caused.

Results.—The native loses his eyesight owing to the displeasure of the rulers.

Remarks.—The lords of the 2nd, 6th and 10th should all join the Lagna. This implies that one becomes blind due to the wrath of the ruler of the Government. But in actual practice such a combination makes one blind some time in life. The Sun and Moon rule the eyes. When these two planets are strongly and favourably situated, one should not predict loss of sight.

Chart No. 78.—*Born on 22-8-1915 at 6-30 a.m. (I.S.T.) at 12° 58′ N.; 77° 34′ E.*

Jupiter			Mars Sat.
	RASI		Kethu
Rahu	6.49		Sun Lagna Merc. Venus
Moon			

	Saturn Venus	Sun	
Kethu	NAVAMSA		Lagna
Mars			Mercury Jupiter Rahu
Moon			

Balance of Moon's Dasa at birth: years 4-10-2.

In Chart No. 78 combination 164 is present with a slight variation. The 10th and 2nd lords are in Lagna but the 6th lord Saturn aspects the Lagna instead of occupying it. The native lost his sight in his 10th year during Chandra Dasa Sani Bhukthi.

165. Andha Yoga

Definition.—Mercury and the Moon should be in the 2nd or the lords of Lagna and the 2nd should join the 2nd with the Sun.

Results.—The person will have defective sight during night or he will be born blind.

Remarks.—Mercury is the planet of nerves and the Moon is the karaka of vision. A conjunction of these two planets in the 2nd is held to make one nightblind. To be born blind, the 2nd house must be occupied by the Sun, the 2nd lord and the lord of Lagna. One should use his discretion in the matter of assigning the exact strengths of these three planets as if the 2nd house happens to be the exaltation place of one of the three members of the combination, the results will have to be modified.

166 and 167. Sumukha Yogas

Definition.—The lord of the 2nd should be in a kendra aspected by benefics, or benefics should join the 2nd house—166.

The lord of the 2nd should be posited in a kendra which should be his exaltation, own or friendly sign and the lord of the kendra should attain Gopuramsa —167.

Results.—The subject will have an attractive and smiling face.

Remarks.—Speech, eyes and facial appearance are all signified by the 2nd house. It must follow therefore that when the 2nd house and the 2nd lord are afflicted, his speech must be harsh, eyesight defective, and facial appearance ugly. In reality this will not be the case because an ugly looking person may have a polished tongue and clear sight or a man of defective vision may have a gifted tongue. In all these cases, apart from how a yoga is defined, the disposition of the karaka should receive prime consideration.

168 and 169. Durmukha Yogas

Definition.—Malefics should occupy the 2nd and its lord should join an evil planet or be in debilitation—168.

The lord of the 2nd being evil, should join Gulika or occupy unfriendly and debilitated Navamsa with malefics.—169.

Results.—The person will have an ugly or repulsive face and he becomes angry and irritable.

Remarks.—The intensity of beauty or ugliness of the face depends upon the good or evil influences which have reference to the 2nd house. Some are ugly from birth and some become ugly on account of disfiguration by accidents and these accidents happen during the periods and sub-periods of the planets concerned.

170. Bhojana Soukhya Yoga

Definition.—The powerful lord of the 2nd should occupy Vaiseshikamsa and have the aspect of Jupiter or Venus.

Results.—The subject becomes rich and will always have good and delicious food.

Remarks.—Venus is the karaka or indicator of *bhukth* or food. Therefore he should be well placed and free from affliction. In all these yogas, the first consideration should go to the karaka.

171. Annadana Yoga

Definition.—The lord of the 2nd should join Vaiseshikamsa and be in conjunction with or aspected by Jupiter and Mercury.

Results.—The person will have a hospitable nature and will feed a large number of people.

Remarks.—Annadana or feeding the hungry is considered a charitable act amongst the Hindus. Human nature is such that man's thirst for wealth, comforts, material possessions, fame and name can never be quenched. But when one is hungry and is fed sumptuously, one gets really satisfied. Hence the sanctity attaching to Annadana.

The above chart is a typical illustration of combination 171. The 2nd lord is Mercury and he is in the 10th with Jupiter. The subject of the horoscope was famous for his generous instincts and for the huge charities by way of food he used to give to the Brahmins, the poor and the needy.

Chart No. 79.—*Born on 12-2-1856 at 12-21 p.m. (L.M.T.) Lat. 18° N.; Long. 84° E.*

	Moon Rahu	Lagna	Saturn
Sun Mercury Jupiter	RASI		
Venus		Mars Kethu	

Jupit.		Lagna	Rahu
	NAVAMSA		
Merc.			
Kethu		Moon Sun Saturn Venus Mars	

Balance of Venus' Dasa at birth : years 6-11-3.

172. Parannabhojana Yoga

Definition.—The lord of the 2nd should be in debilitation or in unfriendly navamsas and aspected by a debilitated planet.

Results.—The person will live upon food doled out by others or will be a dependent.

Remarks.—When one is unable to eke out one's existence, then naturally one must be a dependent upon others. If the 2nd lord is in a debilitated *navamsa*, or in an inimical navamsa, the above result holds good. If, in addition to occupying a neecha navamsa, the lord of the 2nd is also aspected by a neecha planet, then he will be a hater of food.

173. Sraddhannabhuktha Yoga

Definition.—If Saturn happens to own the 2nd, or join the 2nd lord or if the 2nd is aspected by debilitated Saturn, the above yoga is caused.

Results.—The subject gets food prepared at the times of obsequies.

Remarks.—Much stigma is attached to eating food prepared at times of death ceremonies of those who are not one's nearest relatives. Getting such food is a misfortune. Saturn should have nothing to do with the 2nd house if one is to be spared this misfortune.

174. Sarpaganda Yoga

Definition.—Rahu should join the 2nd house with Mandi.

Results.—The person will be bitten by a snake.

Remarks.—A belief is current amongst the Hindus that one should be 'fated' to be bitten by a snake. There seems to be some justification in this view. It is often found that serpents, particularly cobras, will turn their faces away when accosted by certain persons, while some people will find themselves suddenly bitten in spite of being careful. When the 2nd is free from Rahu-Mandi affliction, one need not be afraid of ever being bitten by a snake.

175. Vakchalana Yoga

Definition.—If a malefic happens to own the 2nd joins a cruel navamsa and if the 2nd is devoid of benefic aspect or association, the above yoga is formed.

Results.—The native becomes a stammerer.

Remarks.—Stammering is a great disadvantage for a man's progress and success in life. He cannot express himself clearly nor can he impress his point upon others. As usual, the 2nd lord is to be afflicted. We would like to lay stress on Jupiter rather than on the 2nd lord.

176. Vishaprayoga Yoga

Definition.—The 2nd house must be joined and aspected by malefics and the 2nd lord should be in a cruel navamsa aspected by a malefic.

Results.—The person will be poisoned by others.

Remarks.—Death by being poisoned is a common feature generally in court life where rivalries, jealousies and hatred play a great part in setting people against one another.

177. Bhratruvriddhi Yoga

Definition.—The 3rd lord, or Mars, or the 3rd house should be joined or aspected by benefics and otherwise strong.

Results.—The person will be happy on account of his brothers who will attain great prosperity.

Remarks.—Children of the same parents would be brothers and sisters when young. As they grow up, they become enemies. There may be noble exceptions but as a general rule one would hardly come across brothers and sisters amongst whom cordial relations exist. Quarrels arise on account of petty things and they assume serious proportions. To have brothers and sisters and to be happy with them is indeed a fortune. Generally speaking, the 3rd lord should not occupy malefic vargas and particularly those of Mars. If, however, Mars becomes the lord of the 3rd, the stigma loses its sting considerably. Having brothers is different from living cordially with them. When the Bhava has inherent strength the subject will have brothers, but when the Bhava has a number of evil vargas, the brothers will be a source of annoyance

Chart No. 80.—*Born on 16-10-1918 at 2-20 p.m. (L.M.,) Lat. 13° N.; Long. 77° 34′ E.*

		Kethu	Jupit.			Saturn Jupiter	
Moon Lagna	RASI			Rahu	NAVAMSA		Venus
			Saturn	Moon			Kethu
	Mars Rahu	Sun Mercury	Venus	Mars		Lagna Sun Mercury	

Balance of Rahu's Dasa at birth : years 12-10-21.

In Chart No. 80 the 3rd house falls in Aries. The 3rd from the Moon is free from malefic association or aspect. The 3rd lord is in the 10th bhava. He has gained six navamsas. The native has five brothers and sisters alive. Unfortunately, the 3rd house has acquried the lordship of Mars in all the six vargas. Consequently, the relationship is not very cordial for no fault of the native.

178. Sodaranasa Yoga

Definition.—Mars and the 3rd lord should occupy the 8th (3rd, 5th or 7th) house and be aspected by malefics.

Results.—The person will be devoid of almost all brothers and sisters.

Chart No. 81.—*Born on 22-7-1916 at 8-34 p.m. (I.S.T.) Lat. 9° 30' N.; Long. 76° 13' E.*

	Jupiter Moon		Venus
Lagna	RASI		Sun Merc. Saturn Kethu
Rahu	41.5		
			Mars

Rahu Mars			
	NAVAMSA		Mercury Jupiter Saturn
Venus			Moon
	Lagna		Sun Kethu

Balance of Venus' Dasa at birth : years 16-4-6.

Remarks.—Mars is the karaka for brothers. The 3rd house and the 3rd lord have governance over brothers. A happy disposition of these three factors is absolutely necessary if one's brothers are to live. According to the above yoga, the presence of Mars and the 3rd lord in the 8th denotes that all the brothers would be destroyed. There is also the suggestion that the 3rd, 4th and 7th are also not suitable places for Mars or the 3rd lord to occupy. Practical experience shows that the disposition of Mars in the 7th is not as harmful as in the 8th. A karaka in the appropriate bhava is held to give rise to harmful results. I am not able to appreciate as to why the 4th should be deemed unfit for either Mars or the 3rd lord to join.

Here (Chart No. 81) Mars, the Bhratrukaraka, happens to be 3rd lord. He is in the 8th from Lagna, further aspected by Saturn.

179. Ekabhagini Yoga

Definition.—Mercury, the lord of the 3rd and Mars should join the 3rd house, the Moon and Saturn respectively.

Results.—The person will have only one sister.

Remarks.—The yoga as given here is restricted in its application. A number of variations have to be thought of by assuming similar dispositions in the navamsa and other shadvargas. The yoga assumes fortification of the 3rd house and the 3rd lord and the corresponding weakness of Mars.

180. Dwadasa Sahodara Yoga

Definition.—If the 3rd lord is in a kĕndra and exalted Mars joins Jupiter in a thrikona from the 3rd lord, the above yoga is caused.

Results.—The native will be the third out of the twelve brothers (and sisters) he will have.

Remarks.—The yoga is typical inasmuch as it is rare. The original construction is confounding. But it can be reduced to the simple proposition that in respect of Gemini, Leo, Scorpio, Sagittarius and Pisces, the 3rd lord should be in a kendra and Mars and Jupiter in conjunction in Capricorn. The other signs are to be omitted because the 3rd lord cannot occupy a kendra which should be a place of trine from Capricorn. When Mars is expected to be in *Swa-occha* with Jupiter, then the only possible place would be Capricorn. This should be a trine from the position of the 3rd lord, who in his turn should have occupied a kendra from Lagna. Taking Aries, lord of the 3rd is Mercury. He cannot occupy a kendra consistent with such a kendra being a thrikona from Mars-Jupiter combination which as per the requirements of the yoga is a fixed point. Taurus has to be rejected for the same reason. Gemini is a possibility because the yoga can arise by the Sun occupying Virgo. Cancer has to be ignored while for Leo, Venus can occupy Taurus. Virgo, Libra, Capricorn and Aquarius cannot be thought of as the lord happens to be either Mars or Jupiter. For Scorpio, Saturn can occupy

Taurus and for Sagittarius, the suitable place is Virgo. Thus the yoga is as limited in its application as it is rare in its occurrence.

It is important to remember that in interpreting yogas bearing on the number of children, brothers, etc., one has to carefully take note of the correct social conditions, the facilities available to regulate the birth of children, etc.

Chart No. 82.—*Born on 5-11-1937 at 4-24 p.m. (I.S.T.) Lat. 13° N.; Long. 77° 35' E.*

Lagna Saturn		Kethu	
	RASI		
Mars Jupiter	i-h.		
	Rahu Moon	Sun Mercury	Venus

Lagna	Sun	Mercury Kethu	
Mars	NAVAMSA		
Jupit.			
	Moon Rahu		Venus Saturn

Balance of Saturn's Dasa at birth : years 1-0-25.

Chart No. 82 is clearly illustrative of the above combination. The 3rd lord Venus is in the 7th, a kendra and exalted Mars has joined (debilitated) Jupiter, in a thrikona from the 3rd lord. Jupiter has obtained neechabhanga.

181. Sapthasankhya Sahodara Yoga

Definition.—Lord of the 12th should join Mars and the Moon should be in the 3rd with Jupiter, devoid of association with or aspect of Venus.

Results.—The native will have seven brothers.

Remarks.—A large number of combinations is to be found in traditional astrology bearing on the determination of the number of brothers, their prosperity and adversity and other peculiarities connected with them. Since people possessing a definite number of brothers such as seven or twelve are not a common phenomenon, combinations bearing on this peculiarity are of typical interest. Hence the distinction attached to their inclusion in this book. Generally, the number of Navamsas gained by the lord of the 3rd or Mars determines the number of brothers—the surviving ones depending upon the number of benefics intervening from the first navamsa to the one occupied by the planet in question.

182. Parakrama Yoga

Definition.—The lord of the 3rd should join a benefic navamsa being aspected by (or conjoined with) benefic planets, and Mars should occupy benefic signs.

Results.—The subject will possess much courage.

Remarks.—By courage is implied preserving one's balance of mind in the face of grave danger to one's own life and interests. The 3rd house is called 'Parakrama' and hence its lord should occupy a benefic navamsa besides receiving the aspect of a good planet. Mars should also be similarly situated. If the lord or the karaka has a predominance of evil vargas then the person becomes very funky.

Chart No. 83—*Born on 14-7-1926 at 3-21 p.m. (I.S.T.) Lat. 13° N.; Long. 77° 35' E.*

Mars		Venus	Sun Rahu
Jupiter	RASI		Merc.
	6		Moon
Kethu	Lagna	Saturn	

Mars		Rahu	Sun Saturn
Merc.	NAVAMSA		
	Kethu Jupiter	Lagna	Venus Moon

Balance of Venus' Dasa at birth: years 11-9-0.

In Chart No. 83, the 3rd lord is exalted having occupied a benefic navamsa. Saturn is also aspected by Jupiter. The native even from a very young age was a dare-devil.

183. Yuddha Praveena Yoga

Definition.—If the lord of the navamsa joined by the planet who owns the navamsa in which the 3rd lord is placed, joins his own vargas, the above yoga is caused.

Results.—The person becomes a capable strategist and an expert in warfare.

Remarks.—The combination is a bit round about. First, the 3rd lord is placed in some navamsa; second, the owner of this navamsa has joined some other navamsa. The lord of this navamsa should occupy his own shadvargas. Suppose Lagna is Aquarius, and Mars and the Sun are in Leo and Sagittarius navamsa. Then, the lord of the 3rd being Mars occupies Leo; the lord of this navamsa, *viz.*, the Sun is in Sagittarius. The lord of this, *viz.*, Jupiter should be in his own Varga. When the planets are situated as above, then the person will be a clever strategist and he will have the knack to give battles in such a way as to overcome the resistance offered by the enemy without much bloodshed. In this connection, the horoscopes of great military commanders may be studied with advantage.

Chart No. 84.—*Born on 19-12-1630 at 6-26 p.m. (L.M.T) Lat. 18° 32′ N.; Long. 73° 53′ E.*

Mercury	Venus		Rahu Mars
Sun Jupiter	RASI		
	P. N. 35		Lagna
Kethu		Saturn	Moon

Sat.	Kethu	Sun	
Mars	NAVAMSA		Venus
Lagna Jupit.		Rahu	Mercury Moon

Balance of Mars Dasa at birth: years 4-1-17.

In Chart No. 84 the 3rd lord Venus is in the navamsa of Cancer. The lord of this is in Virgo navamsa. The lord of this, *viz.*, Mercury has obtained the majority of his own shadvargas. The native was an expert in strategy and with his limited resources defied the Mughal Emperor, and brought him down to his knees.

184. Yuddhatpoorvadridhachitta Yoga

Definition.—The exalted lord of the 3rd should join malefics in movable Rasis or Navamsas.

Results.—The person will be courageous before the commencement of the war.

Remarks.—Evidently, the combination makes it clear that until the native actively participates in the war, he shows courage but as soon as he gets into the actual theatre, he loses his balance of mind, becomes funky and beats an ignominous retreat. The name of Uttara, a character of Mahabharatha, has become proverbial for all those who show initial zeal but lose heart as soon as they come into actual grips with reality.

185. Yuddhatpaschaddrudha Yoga

Definition.—The lord of the 3rd should occupy a fixed Rasi, a fixed Navamsa and a cruel Shahtiamsa and the lord of the Rasi so occupied should be in debility.

Results.—The person gets courage after the commencement of the war.

Remarks.—Some people get afraid to join military service but become sufficiently courageous after reaching the battlefield. The lord should be in a fixed Rasi and a fixed Navamsa and cruel Shashtiamsa, besides the lord of the house occupied by the 3rd lord getting debilitated. All the above yogas pertaining to courage, valour, strategic proficiency, etc., cannot be applied in a literal manner. The underlying principles can be extended to apply to day-to-day activities inasmuch as one has to come across a large number of pitfalls and face critical periods. To come out successful from life's ordeals, one has to be strong-minded, courageous and intelligent. There are moments in one's life when one is likely to lose heart just because one cannot control the situation.

Yogas 184 and 185 can be made use of for judging one's capacity to brave odds in life and come out successful in trying and hopeless circumstances.

186. Satkathadisravana Yoga

Definition.—The 3rd house should be a benefic sign aspected by benefic planets and the 3rd lord should join a benefic amsa.

Results.—The native will always be interested in reading high-class literature and in listening to religious discourses.

Remarks.—Irrespective of the fact whether or not the 3rd house is a benefic sign, the 3rd lord should have the aspect of one of the natural benefics.

187. Uttama Griha Yoga

Definition.—The lord of the 4th house should join benefics in a kendra or thrikona.

Results.—The subject will possess good houses.

Remarks.—Possession of a good house is held to be a great fortune. Astrological writers attach much importance to the lucky or unlucky nature of a house a man lives in or owns. Some houses bring in success and happiness while some lead the owner to failure and misery. This particular yoga indicates the possession of a good house. The 4th lord must be strongly disposed in a quadrant or trine. The 4th lord must be associated with a benefic, or at least receive the aspect of a benefic. When the Lagna is not strong, the yoga must be applied with reference to Chandra Lagna. This is, of course, our opinion though the original writers have not said anything specifically about this.

In Chart No. 85 the 4th lord Mercury is exalted in the 7th, a kendra and is aspected by Jupiter. Mercury is also associated with a benefic Venus, who though debilitated has Neechabhagna. The subject owns a very good house.

Chart No. 85.—*Born on 24-9-1890 at Gh. 37-10 after Sunrise. Lat. 13° N.; Long 77° 35' E.*

Lagna		Rahu	
	RASI		
Jupiter	10		Sun Sat.
	Moon Mars Kethu		Merc. Venus

Kethu	Jupiter		
Moon Merc. Lagna	NAVAMSA		Sun
Mars			Venus Saturn
			Rahu

Balance of Mercury's Dasa at birth: years 7-3-24.

It must be noted that the yoga given above is not exclusively typical. It is one of the important combinations denoting acquisition of immovable property.

188. Vichitra Saudha Prakara Yoga

Definition.—If the lords of the 4th and 10th are conjoined together with Saturn and Mars, the above yoga is given rise to.

Results.—The person acquires innumerable mansions.

Remarks.—The combination comprehends two conditions. First, there must be a conjunction of the 4th and 10th lords; second, these two planets together must join Saturn and Mars. Evidently this is a four-planet combination, rather rare of occurrence. Yet in regard to Thula, Vrischika, Makara and Simha, these planets cause the yoga, because the 4th lord invariably happens to be either Saturn or Mars. Likewise in regard to Mesha, Vrishabha, Kataka and Kumbha, the yoga could exist due to the conjunction of only three planets. Usually Saturn-Mars combination is harmful, as it is capable of immense mischief, but here probably the general rule is excepted.

Chart No. 86.—*Born on 15-12-1899 at 5-42 a.m. (L.M.T.) Lat. 10° 45' N.; Long. 5h. 16m. 48s. E.*

		Moon Kethu	
	RASI		
	H.J.H. 30		
Sun Mars Saturn Venus	Mercury Jupiter Lagna Rahu		

Moon Rahu	Sun	Saturn	Mars
Lagna	NAVAMSA		
	Mars Venus		Jupiter Kethu

Balance of the Sun's Dasa at birth: years 1-2-12.

Chart No. 86 illustrates the above yoga. The lords of the 4th and 10th are Saturn and Sun respectively. They are associated with Mars. Here the entire combination is purely malefic but for the association of Venus. The native possesses quite a good number of palatial buildings though the place of his own residence is as unpretentious as could be imagined.

189 and 190. Ayatna Griha Prapta Yogas

Definition.—Lords of Lagna and the 7th should occupy Lagna or the 4th, aspected by benefics—189.

The lord of the 9th should be posited in a kendra and the lord of the 4th must be in exaltation, moolathrikona or own house—190.

Results.—The subject acquires substantial house property with hardly any effort.

Remarks.—It must be a matter of common experience that some people will never be able to own a house for themselves in spite of their best efforts, while others will acquire house property with hardly any effort. The causes for such disparity are purely astrological. According to cambination 189, the lords of Lagna and the 7th should occupy Lagna or the 4th. If there is no aspect by a benefic, some effort is necessary.

In this case (Chart No. 87) lords of Chandra Lagna (Venus) and the 7th (Mars) are posited in the 4th in association with a benefic. Some effort was necessary on the part of the native to own a decent residence. There are of course other notable combinations also, but they are not relevant to the present discussion. Combination 190 is simple and does not need any elucidation.

Chart No. 87.—*Born on 8-8-1912 at 7-23 p.m. (L.M.T.) Lat. 13° N.; Long. 77° 35′ E.*

Rahu		Moon Saturn	
Lagna	RASI		Sun
			Mars Merc. Venus
.	Jupiter		Kethu

	Saturn	Venus	
Rahu Sun	NAVAMSA		
Lagna			Kethu Moon Mercury
	Jupiter	Mars	

Balance of Mars' Dasa at birth: years 6-0-10.

191 and 192. Grihanasa Yogas

Definition.—The lord of the 4th should be in the 12th aspected by a malefic—191.

The lord of the navamsa occupied by the lord of the 4th should be disposed in the 12th—192.

Results.—The person will lose all the house property.

Remarks.—These two yogas are very important because they give a clue for ascertaining whether one would lose one's property, already acquired or ancestral. The yogas refer to the 4th lord being situated in the house of loss. This must evidently imply the 12th from the 4th and not from Lagna. In other words when either the lord of the 4th or the lord of the navamsa occupied by the 4th is situated in the 3rd, there will be loss of house property.

193 and 194. Bandhu Pujya Yogas

Definition.—If the benefic lord of the 4th is aspected by another benefic and Mercury is situated in Lagna, the above yoga is given rise to—193.

The 4th house or the 4th lord should have the association or aspect of Jupiter—194.

Results.—The person will be respected by his relatives and friends.

Remarks.—A slight distinction is to be noted in the results suggested between the combinations 193 and 194. The former makes one respected by his relatives while the latter makes one loved by his relatives.

In actual practice, it is difficult to differentiate between the two. Respect may be shown for one's character, integrity and great qualities of head and heart while in showing love, other considerations may set in. The first combination refers to the *benefic lord of the 4th.* This means that it is applicable to those born in Mesha, Mithuna, Kataka, Dhanus and Meena. The 2nd combination is more general and broad-based.

In this horoscope, (In chart No. 88) not only is the 4th house aspected by Jupiter but also the 4th lord is in conjunction with Jupiter. The subject of the horoscope was loved and respected by all his relatives and friends for his character and generous instincts. All these various yogas should never be applied *literally.* There are quite a number of other factors to be considered,

Chart No. 88.—*Born on 12-2-1856 at 12-21 p.m. (L.M.T.) Lat. 18° N.; Long. 84° E.*

	Moon Rahu	Lagna	Saturn
Sun Mercury Jupiter	RASI		
Veuns		Mars Kethu	

Jupit.		Lagna	Rahu
	NAVAMSA		
Merc.			
Kethu		Moon Sun Saturn Venus Mars	

Balance of Venus' Dasa at birth : years 6-11-3.

not the least important of which is the predominance of the malefic or benefic shadvargas in regard to the 4th house.

Take the horoscope of Mahatma Gandhi. He was universally beloved and respected. The 4th is a malefic sign and Kethu is situated there. But both the 4th house and the 4th lord are powerfully aspected by Jupiter. Here the terms 'benefic and malefic' refer to the inherent nature of a sign or planet and not to the acquired qualities.

195. Bandhubhisthyaktha Yoga

Definition.—The 4th lord must be associated with malefics or occupy evil shashtiamsas or join inimical or debilitation signs.

Results.—The person will be deserted by his relatives.

Remarks.—The yoga takes into account three circumstances, *viz.*, (*a*) the 4th lord must be in evil shashtiamsa ; (*b*) he must be associated with malefic planets ; and (*c*) he must occupy his place of debilitation or that of an enemy. According to our humble experience, much reliance cannot be placed on this particular yoga because of its very general nature. One possessing this combination could be misunderstood by his associates, friends and relatives, ostensibly for no fault of his.

196 and 197. Matrudeerghayur Yogas

Definition.—A benefic must occupy the 4th, the 4th lord must be exalted, and the Moon must be strong—196.

The lord of the navamsa occupied by the 4th lord should be strong and occupy a kendra from Lagna as well as Chandra Lagna—197.

Results.—The native's mother will live long.

Remarks.—These two combinations give a clue for ascertaining the longevity of one's mother. The 4th lord, the Moon and the 4th house must all be strong and free from evil aspects and association. Even assuming that the 4th house is afflicted, long life for the mother can be predicted if the Moon is waxing and occupies a friendly place which should be a kendra or a thrikona from the 4th lord.

198 and 199. Matrunasa Yogas

Definition.—The Moon should be hemmed in between, associated with or aspected by evil planets—198.

The planet owning the navamsa, in which the lord of the navamsa occupied by the 4th lord is situated should be disposed in the 6th, 8th or 12th house—199.

Results.—The person's mother will have a verv early death.

Remarks.—According to combination 198, the Moon should be afflicted in order to render a man lose his mother early. Here affliction means, being subjected to Papakarthari Yoga, or being aspected by or conjoined with malefics. One of the three conditions must prevail. If all the three are present, the mother will die immediately after the birth of the subject. If the Moon is in conjunction with Saturn but aspected by Jupiter, or the Moon is in the 4th subjected to the above influences, the Yoga for killing the mother is there, but the benefic aspect of Jupiter delays the event. Added to this disposition, if the 4th lord is also afflicted, then early death to the mother is inevitable.

In chart No. 89 the Moon is in the 4th in conjunction with Saturn. Jupiter aspects the combination but unfortunately the 4th lord Venus is associated with Mars in the 4th from the Moon. The mother died in the 2nd year of the native.

Chart No. 89.—*Born on 8-8-1912 at 7-35 p.m.* (*I.S.T.*) *Lat. 13° N.; Long. 77° 35′ E.*

Rahu		Moon Saturn	
Lagna	RASI		Sun
			Mars Merc. Venus
	Jupiter		Kethu

	Saturn	Venus	
Sun Rahu	NAVAMSA		
Lagna			Kethu Moon Mercury
	Jupiter	Mars	

Balance of Mars' Dasa at birth : years 6-0-10.

Combination 199 is somewhat round about. Say (*a*) the 4th lord occupies some navamsa ; (*b*) its lord is in some other navamsa ; (*c*) the owner of this navamsa must occupy (in the Rasi chart) a position which should be the 6th, 8th or 12th from Lagna.

Chart No. 90 typically illustrates the combination in question. (*a*) The 4th lord is Venus and he is in the navamsa of Thula. (*b*) The lord of this navamsa is of course Venus. (*c*) The third condition becomes merged with the 2nd because the navamsa lord occupies his own house. Venus is in the 12th from Lagna. The native lost his mother early.

In Chart No. 91 (*a*) the 4th lord Venus is in the navamsa of Mesha, (*b*) the lord of this navamsa, *viz.*, Mars is in Simha navamsa, and (*c*) the lord of this navamsa, *viz.*, the Sun is in the 12th from

Chart No. 90.—*Born on 19-6-1904 at 7-30 a.m. (L.M.T.) Lat. 13° N.; Long. 76° 9' E.*

Kethu	Jupiter	Mercury	Sun Mars Venus
	RASI		Lagna
Saturn			Moon
			Rahu

		Jupiter Mercury	
	NAVAMSA		Lagna Kethu
Rahu			Moon
	Sun	Venus Mars	Saturn

Balance of Venus' Dasa at birth: years 15-11-3.

Chart No. 91.—*Born on 19-1-1913 at 8-30 a.m. (I.S.T.) Lat. 13° N.; Long. 77° 35' E.*

Rahu		Moon Saturn	
Lagna Venus	RASI		
Sun	i. h.		
Mercury Jupiter Mars			Kethu

Sun	Venus	Kethu	Moon
Sat.	NAVAMSA		Jupiter
			Mars
	Rahu Lagna	Mercury	

Balance of the Moon's Dasa at birth: years 3-2-3.

Lagna. The native lost his mother when he was about 9 years during the Bhukthi of Venus (4th lord) and the Dasa of Mars.

200. Matrugami Yoga

Definition.—The Moon or Venus should join a kendra in conjunction with or aspected by a malefic, and an evil planet should occupy the 4th house.

Results.—The person will be guilty of committing adultery with his own mother.

Remarks.—No greater sin can be conceived of than association with one's own mother. Unless a man is utterly shameless and completely depraved of all feelings of conscience, he cannot be guilty of such a heinous crime as the one mentioned in this combination. Here, by the term mother is implied not only the lady who has given birth to the person (step-mother also included) but to ladies who are held in equal esteem, *viz.*, *the ruler's wife, preceptor's wife, brother's wife, wife's mother and his own mother.

The Moon is the karaka of the mind and also mother. Venus is the karaka of sexual passions. According to this combination, *the Moon and Venus* should be afflicted in the manner suggested.

Adultery in any form is a consequence of mental filth and therefore both the planets and particularly the Moon must be devoid of association or aspect, if one is to entertain healthy thoughts.

---

* Raja patnee gurah patnee tathaiva cha patnce mata swamata cha panchaite matarustatha.

201. Sahodareesangama Yoga

Definition.—If the lord of the 7th and Venus are in conjunction in the 4th house and are aspected by or associated with malefics or are in cruel shashtiamsas, the above yoga is given rise to.

Results.—The person will be guilty of intercourse with his own sisters.

Remarks.—The combination is simple and does not require further elucidation. Intimacy with a sister is as heinous a crime as with a mother or a lady equal to a mother but men sometimes behave worse than beasts for the gratification of their bestial instincts. The best safeguard against any form of sexual immorality is an *unafflicted* disposition of Venus.

202 to 204. Kapata Yogas

Definition.—The 4th house must be joined by a malefic and the 4th lord must be associated with or aspected by malefics or be hemmed in between malefics—202.

The 4th must be occupied by Sani, Kuja, Rahu and the malefic 10th lord, who in his turn should be aspected by malefics—203.

The 4th lord must join Saturn, Mandi and Rahu and aspected by malefics—204.

Results.—The person becomes a hypocrite.

Remarks.—In my leading articles in THE ASTROLOGICAL MAGAZINE, I have clearly shown that the first-rate malefics, *viz.*, Saturn, Mars and Rahu, should occupy such positions in the horoscopes of political leaders and statesmen, as would render them absolutely harmless. Whenever there is a conjunction between Saturn-Rahu, Saturn-Mars and Mars-Rahu, the person will always be actuated by selfish and mean motives. Generally Kapata Yogas are to be found in the charts of diplomats, for diplomacy always implies dignified hypocrisy. The 4th rules the heart and the presence there of these incendiary planets makes the person conceal his real feelings and gives an impure heart. These three combinations are of common occurrence in the horoscopes of ordinary people. Some are very hypocritical by nature and they seldom give out their minds. Much more than a malefic afflicting the 4th house, the association of Saturn or Rahu with the 4th lord is not desirable.

Chart No. 92 is the horoscope of an important International Pact and not that of an individual.

The 4th is occupied by Kethu and the 4th lord Venus has joined two first-rate malefics the Sun and Mars, not relieved by any other benefic influences. The chart is clearly indicative of the free expression of hypocrisy under the guise of diplomacy, on the part of all the celebrated statesmen who joined together to sign the pact.

Chart No. 92.—*Born on 4-4-1949 at 12 noon (L.M.T.) Lat. 38° 53' N.; Long. 77° 3' E.*

Mars Sun Venus Mercury	Rahu		Moon
	RASI		Lagna
Jupiter	P.N. 101		Sat.
		Kethu	

Jupit.		Rahu	Saturn
	NAVAMSA		
Sun			Lagna
Venus Mars	Kethu Mercury	Moon	

Balance of Mars' Dasa at birth: years 3-0-26.

205 and 206. Nishkapata Yogas

Definition.—The 4th house must be occupied by a benefic, or a planet in exaltation, friendly or own house, or the 4th house must be a benefic sign—205.

Lord of Lagna should join the 4th in conjunction with or aspected by a benefic or occupy Parvata or Uttamamsa.—206.

Results.—The person will be pure-hearted and hates secrecy and hypocrisy.

Remarks.—According to the above two combinations, the 4th house must be occupied by a benefic or it must have an exalted planet or the sign in the 4th house must be a friendly one to the planet situated there. The combination is very flexible and is capable of loose interpretation. Just because the 4th house happens to be a benefic sign, it cannot make one an angel. On the contrary, it is the 4th lord that we have to look to. So long as the 4th lord does not conjoin Rahu or Saturn or if he conjoins, so long as there is the aspect of Jupiter or Venus, preferably Jupiter, there is no fear of the person being a hypocrite. The above two combinations are given for what they are worth. But in our opinion, great care must be exercised in applying them to actual horoscopes.

207. Matru Satrutwa Yoga

Definition.—Mercury, being lord of Lagna and the 4th, must join with or be aspected by a malefic.

Results.—The person will hate his mother.

Remarks.—Evidently this combination is applicable only to Mithuna Lagna horoscopes. For in regard to no other sign can Mercury become the lord of Lagna and the 4th. It occurs to us that when the lords of the Navamsas in which the Moon in the horoscopes of the mother and son are placed, are mutual enemies, cordial feelings do not exist between them. This is only an observation and must be further tested before it could be raised to the distinction of an astrological principle.

208. Matru Sneha Yoga

Definition.—The 1st and 4th houses must have a common lord, or the lords of the 1st and 4th must be temporal or natural friends or aspected by benefics.

Results.—Cordial relations will prevail between mother and son.

Remarks.—The 1st and 4th houses can have common lords only in respect of Mithuna and Dhanus. When the lords of Lagna and the 4th are mutual friends or *Tatkalika* friends, the yoga is said to prevail. Here also, the relationship between the Navamsa lords, adverted to in regard to combination 207, may be applied with advantage.

209 and 210. Vahana Yogas

Definition.—The lord of Lagna must join the 4th, 11th or the 9th—209.

The 4th lord must be exalted and the lord of the exaltation sign must occupy a kendra or trikona—210.

Results.—The native will acquire material comforts and conveyances.

Chart No. 93.—*Born on 8-8-1912 at 7-23 p.m. (L.M.T.) Lat. 13° N., Long. 77° 35′ E.*

Rahu		Moon Saturn	
Lagna	RASI		Sun
			Mars Merc. Venus
	Jupiter		Kethu

	Saturn	Venus	
Sun Rahu	NAVAMSA		
Lagna			Kethu Moon Mercury
	Jupiter	Mars	

Balance of Mars' Dasa at birth : years 6-0-10.

Remarks.—In the modern world, vahana must refer to bicycles and automobiles and not to the time-honoured carriages drawn by horses or palanquins carried by bearers. Any person of average means can possess a bicycle, but very few can afford to own an automobile. Therefore, there must be some distinct combinations present in a horoscope to enable the subject to acquire a vahana. The lord of Lagna must not only join the 4th, 9th or 11th but must be equally strong. Otherwise, the yoga cannot function properly.

The following observations may also be noted :—

Vahanakaraka is Venus and Vahanasthana is the 4th. Therefore, if Venus joins the 4th with the 4th lord, the person could possess ordinary vehicles. If Venus or lord of the 4th is in the 11th or 9th, the native will possess a number of conveyances. If the 4th lord is connected with the Moon, then the person will have carriages drawn by horses or motor cars in modern parlance.

In Chart No. 93 lord of Lagna Saturn has joined the 4th house, while the 4th lord Venus is in the 7th in association with Mercury, lord of the 5th (and 8th) and Mars, lord of the 10th (and 3rd). The 4th is also aspected by Jupiter. The native acquired an automobile as soon as Sukra Bhukthi in Guru Dasa commenced.

211. Anapathya Yoga

Definition.—If Jupiter and the lords of Lagna, the 7th and the 5th are weak, the above yoga is given rise to.

Results.—The person will have no issues.

Remarks.—Birth of children is considered to be a great blessing and the feelings of parents, not fortunate to get any issues, could better be imagined than adequately described. The Hindu considers childlessness as a great sin or misfortune and resorts to all kinds of vows to get a child.

Jupiter and the lord of Lagna, the 7th and the 5th should all be weak, to make one childless. If Jupiter and the 5th lord are strong, then the yoga gets somewhat modified.

212 to 215. Sarpasapa Yogas

Definition.—The 5th should be occupied by Rahu and aspected by Kuja or the 5th house being a sign of Mars, should be occupied by Rahu—212.

If the 5th lord is in conjunction with Rahu, and Saturn is in the 5th house aspected by or asssociated with the Moon, the above yoga is given rise to—213.

The karaka of children in association with Mars, Rahu in Lagna, and the 5th lord in a dusthana gives rise to this yoga—214.

The 5th house, being a sign of Mars, must be conjoined by Rahu and aspected by or associated with Mercury—215.

Results.—There will be death of children due to the curse of serpents.

Remarks.—Whether or not we believe in blessings and curses, afflictions to the 5th house as per the above combinations, are sure to cause premature death of children. It must be noted that the common factor in all the four yogas mentioned above is the affliction of the 5th bhava, karaka or the lord of children by Rahu. According to combination 212, either the 5th house should be occupied by Rahu and aspected by Mars; or the 5th house happening to be Aries or Scorpio should have the association of Rahu. The latter part of the combination is applicable only in respect of Kataka and Dhanur Lagnas. Combination 213 which is of a more general character is suggestive of severe affliction to the 5th house. The 5th lord must join Rahu and Saturn must be in the 5th having the aspect or conjunction of the Moon. The combination of the Moon and Saturn is always indicative of sorrow and suffering. When it has reference to the 5th house, it clearly implies that one must suffer great sorrow owing to the loss of children.

The karaka for children, *viz.*, Jupiter is brought into the picture in combination 214. He should be associated with Mars. Rahu must be in Lagna and the 5th lord should occupy either the 6th, the 8th or the 12th. Here it must be noted that the yoga could manifest fully only when Jupiter is weak. If he has sufficient Shadbala strength. The yoga becomes null and void. In a horoscope belonging to a certain young man, Jupiter is in the 5th (Cancer) exalted and in association with Mars, Rahu is in Lagna and the Moon is in Libra. But as Jupiter has obtained nearly 8 units of Shadbala strength, the yoga has become defunct for all practical purposes. The native has 2 children living but the evil due to the position of the 5th lord, etc., appears to have found expression in the shape of the native's wife having had a few abortions.

Combination 215 is merely a repetition of the earlier yoga but the difference that here Mercury is brought in and his aspect or association made a condition for the presence of the yoga.

Chart No. 94.—*Born on 11-3-1858 at 9 p.m. (L.M.T.) Lat. 13° N.; Long. 77° 36′ E.*

Venus	Jupiter		
Sun Mercury Rahu	RASI		Saturn
Moon			Kethu
	Mars	Lagna	

Lagna	Mercury	Moon	Sun Rahu
	NAVAMSA		Venus Saturn
Kethu		Jupiter	Mars

Balance of the Moon's Dasa at birth: years 7-2-8.

In Chart No. 94 mark the position of Rahu in the 5th, and his being aspected by Mars thus fulfilling combination 212. There are, of course, certain relieving features also but they are not of consequence from the point of view of illustrating this particular yoga.

In Chart No. 95 there is a powerful Sarpasapa Yoga (214). Putrakaraka Jupiter is associated with Mars, Rahu occupies Lagna and the 5th lord Sun is in a dusthana. In spite of the presence of Sarpasapa

Chart No. 95.—*Born on 2-12-1948 at 2-28 p.m. (I.S.T.) Lat. 18° 4' N.; Long. 83° 26' E.*

	Lagna Rahu		
	RASI		
Mandi	U. 839		Sat.
Moon Jupiter Mars	Mercury Sun	Venus Kethu	

	Lagna Mandi		Moon
Venus	NAVAMSA		Mars Rahu Jupiter
Kethu			Saturn
Sun		Mercury	

Balance of Kethu Dasa at birth : years 2-8-20.

Yoga, the inherent strength of Putrakaraka, derived by virtue of his situation in his own house and association with the Moon forming Gajakesari Yoga, acts as an antidote. But we are here concerned only with the Sarpasapa Yoga and not its neutralisation.

A stronger Anapathya Yoga than that present in Chart No. 96 cannot be met with. The 5th lord Mars is associated with Rahu and Saturn occupies the 5th aspected powerfully by the Moon. The yoga is present *in toto*. And the native will lose quite a number of children but the Putrakaraka Jupiter being disposed in the 10th, unafflicted, can take away much of the sting.

Chart No. 96.—*Born on 9/10-8-1928 at 4-46 a.m. (I.S.T.) Lat. 25° 22′ N.; Long. 68° 20′ E.*

	Jupiter	Mars Moon Rahu	Mandi
	RASI		Merc. Lagna Sun
	P. H. 34		Venus
	Kethu Saturn		

Mars Mandi	Moon	Venus Rahu	
Sun	NAVAMSA		Lagna
Sat.			
Merc.	Kethu		Jupiter

Balance of Moon's Dasa at birth: years 8-5-8.

216. Pitrusapa Sutakshaya Yoga

Definition.—The Sun must occupy the 5th house which should be his place of debilitation, or the amsas of Makara and Kumbha, or in between malefics.

Results.—The subject will lose issues on account of his father's wrath.

Remarks.—The wording of the combination is a bit confusing. One of the following three conditions can give rise to this yoga:

(*a*) The 5th must be occupied by debilitated Sun. This is possible only in regard to Mithuna in which case the Sun happens to own the 3rd house and hence becomes blemished.

(*b*) The Sun must join the 5th house, but the Navamsa should be Makara or Kumbha. This combination cannot be applied for persons born in Mesha, Simha and Dhanus, because, in respect of these three, Makara and Kumbha navamsas cannot rise in the 5th house, as the last navamsa ends with Dhanus. With regard to Vrishabha, Kanya and Makara the Sun's situation in the 5th house coincident with Makara or Kumbha navamsa can happen provided the Sun is within 6° 40′ from the beginning of the sign concerned. In regard to Mithuna, Thula and Kumbha, the Sun's 5th house position must fall within the arc of 10° to 16° 40′ of the sign concerned. Similarly, in reference to Kataka, Vrischika and Meena the Sun's 5th bhava position must correspond to the area between 20° and 26° 40′ of the sign concerned. Suppose Vrishabha is Lagna and the Sun occupies the 5th degree of Kanya, which is the same as the 2nd navamsa, *viz.*, Kumbha. Conditions necessary for the fulfilment of the yoga may be said to exist in this case. Here again due consideration must be given to the fact whether the Sun is actually in the 5th house or 5th sign. If latter, the yoga cannot exist. Let us assume that the 3rd degree of Cancer is Lagna, and the 5th degree of Scorpio rises in the 5th house, the 5th bhava ending at the 19th degree of Scorplo. If the Sun is in Scorpio 19th degree, the combination does not exist because the navamsa cannot be Makara or Kumbha. If the Sun is in the 21st degree of Vrischika, even then the combination cannot hold good because he will be actually in the 6th house. These subtle differences due to bhava positions should be carefully balanced before making sure that the Yoga really exists. I may add *en passant* that the mere fact of the 5th house falling in the navamsa of Saturn is enough to indicate death of children, unless there are other counteracting influences.

In the various combinations dealt with above and in the following pages, causes for the death of children due to various kinds of curses *sapas* given by parents, brothers, elders and others are enumerated. Loss of progeny is an irreparable and heart-rending misfortune. Blessings and curses work on a subtle plane. But the results they produce are often demonstrable and remarkable. The mysterious force or energy manifests itself in various ways and curious forms. When a man is angry or out of temper, reason and logic are generally thrown to the winds and the ill-temper discharges itself in various ways. Curses are the resultants of various causes proceeding from different sorts of temperaments or provocations whether they are real or imaginary. There are some people born with intense passions developed as a result of their previous karma which always find expression in inflicting injuries on others. Take the case of what is called the 'evil eye'. Here what happens is this: The man has strong passions developed in him like the poison of cobra or the sting of a scorpion which is able to discharge electric or ethereal energy with a tremendous force directed for the destruction or the injury of an object.

Examples illustrating the Sun's debilitation in the 5th house can be had in plenty and therefore

I do not propose to give an example for this combination.

In Chart No. 97 the Lagna is Libra and the 5th house is occupied by the Sun who joins Makaramsa. Therefore, Pitrusapa Sutakshaya Yoga is present.

(*c*) The 3rd variation of the yoga is simple. The Sun must occupy the 5th house, hemmed in on either side by malefics.

Chart No. 97.—*Born on 22-2-1863 at Gh. 39-40. Lat. 13° N.; Long. 77 34′ E.*

	Moon	Mars Kethu	
Venus Sun	RASI		
Mercury	3-60		
	Rahu	Jupiter Lagna	Saturn

Lagna		Saturn	Moon Venus
	NAVAMSA		Kethu Mercury
Sun Mars Rahu			
Jupit.			

Balance of Kethu Dasa at birth: years 1-9-13.

The following dispositions of planets also constitute Yoga No. 216:

(*a*) The Sun, being lord of the 5th, should occupy a trine, and be hemmed in between or aspected by malefics. Evidently this combination can hold good only for Mesha Lagna.

(*b*) Jupiter's disposition in Leo, the association of the 5th lord with the Sun and the 5th and Lagna being occupied by malefics—children die on account of the father's wrath.

(*c*) If Mars as lord of the 9th joins the 5th lord and malefics occupy Lagna and the trikonas, death of children due to father's curse should be predicted.

In the practical application of these yogas, one should use one's power of discretion, taking into consideration the fact whether or not the 5th house as such is strongly disposed.

217. Matrusapa Sutakshaya Yoga

Definition.—If the 8th lord is in the 5th, the 5th lord is in the 8th and the Moon and the 4th lord join the 6th, the above yoga is given rise to.

Results.—There will be loss of children due to the curse of the mother.

Remarks.—The depth of Indian astrological lore is clearly revealed by the innumerable number of combinations given by the sages for the happening of event like the death of children. Such a variety of yogas appears to be absolutely necessary, in view of the fact that children die on account of various causes.

In the yoga under consideration, there must be Parivarthana between the 5th and 8th lords, and the Matrukaraka Moon and the Matrusthanadhipathi (lord of the 4th house) should join a dusthana like the 6th. For Simha and Kumbha Lagnas, the yoga cannot operate as the same planet happens to own both the 5th and 8th houses.

Chart No. 98.—*Born on 18-11-1900 at 4-17 p.m. (L.M.T.) Lat. 13° N. ; Long. 77° 35° E.*

	Lagna	Kethu	
	RASI		
			Mars
Saturn	Sun Jupiter Mercury Rahu		Venus Moon

	Kethu		Mars
Jupit.	NAVAMSA		Saturn Moon
			Sun Venus Lagna
		Rahu	Mercury

Balance of Moon's Dasa at birth : years 0-9-13.

Here is a typical horoscope illustrating combination 217. Lords of the 5th and 8th have interchanged places. The 2nd part of the yoga can also be said to exist as the Moon happening to be lord of the 4th is posited in the 6th.

218. Bhratrusapa Sutakshaya Yoga

Definition.—The lords of Lagna and the 5th must join the 8th and the lord of the 3rd should combine with Mars and Rahu in the 5th.

Results.—There will be death of children due to curses from brothers.

Remarks.—In this yoga, some sort of connection has been brought about between lord of Lagna, 5th, 3rd, 8th, Rahu and Bhratrukaraka Mars. The principle enumerated in this yoga may be extended to include a few variations in the dispositions suggested. The 5th lord in association with Mars, or Mars and Rahu in the 5th, may also give rise to the same yoga. Here, what is of importance is the connection between 5th and 3rd houses and Mars in such a way as to cause affliction to the 5th house.

219. Pretasapa Yoga

Definition.—The Sun and Saturn in the 5th, weak Moon in the 7th, Rahu in Lagna and Jupiter in the 12th give rise to Pretasapa Yoga.

Results.—Children will die through the curses of Pretas or manes of the dead.

Remarks.—The individual soul just after its release from the mortal coil is supposed to be in a state of transition for the period of the death ceremonies which generally lasts for two weeks. The disembodied soul in this state of transition is termed Preta. It is held that the Preta reaching a higher or lower plane of existence, consistent with its karma during its sojourn on the earth, depends entirely upon the satisfactory performance of the obsequies by the sons or dependents of the deceased concerned. When these ceremonies are not properly performed, the *Preta* is denied safe-conduct in the ethereal regions with the result curses are sent to the persons responsible for such omission. The yoga in question reveals death of children from the curses of such

Pretas. Whether or not we believe in such things death means disappearance of some mysterious force from the physical body and this subtle force cannot go to nothingness nor could it have come from nothingness. It is far more reasonable to suppose that the soul or the subtle aspect of existence moves on to a different plane, invested with karma done during its sojourn on the earth plane. The sages must have seen the further evolution of the soul, after *death* here, through intuition, and because known laws of science cannot explain the mysteries of life and death it does not mean that existence ends with physical death.

When the weak Moon is in the 7th, Rahu is in Lagna, and the Sun and Saturn are in the 5th, the Moon becomes subject to a series of afflictions—Kethu's association, Rahu's aspect and Saturn's aspect. The Moon-Rahu-Saturn connection, in any form, is always indicative of the influences of what are generally known as devils, spirits, ghosts and other destructive denizens.

In Chart No. 99, the Sun and Saturn are in the 5th. The Moon, in this case weak, is in the 7th with Mars and Kethu. Jupiter is in the 12th and Rahu occupies Lagna. The yoga is powerful, and there are absolutely no relieving features. We can anticipate death of almost all issues that may be born to the subject.

Chart No. 99.—*Born on 28-6-1914 at 9-57 p.m. (I.S.T.) Lat. 13° N. ; Long. 77° 35′ E.*

			Sun Saturn
Lagna Rahu	RASI		Venus Merc.
Jupiter			Mars Moon Kethu

			Mars
Sun Rahu	NAVAMSA		
			Mercury Kethu Moon
Venus		Lagna Saturn	Jupiter

Balance of Venus Dasa at birth: years 16-2-3.

220 and 221. Bahuputra Yogas

Definition.—Rahu in the 5th house, in a Navamsa other than that of Saturn, gives rise to this yoga —220.

The same yoga arises if the lord of the Navamsa occupied by a planet who is in association with the 7th lord is in the 1st, 2nd or 5th house—221.

Results.—The person will have a large number of children.

Remarks.—Nature is full of anomalies. Side by side with persons who are longing for issues, there are people who have any number of children and who are unable to rear them due to financial and other misfortunes. A perfectly normal couple, perfect in the sense of sexual compatibility, is denied the birth of even a single issue thus demonstrating fully the law of karma and its mysterious manifestations.

Combination 220 is highly important because of the fact that it is an exception of the general rule that the 5th house should not be occupied by Rahu. It is only in the Navamsa of Saturn that Rahu's disposition is held to be harmful. Combination 220 is almost the same as combination 216 but with the difference that instead of the Sun, Rahu is brought in.

Combination 221 is a bit confusing. It may be explaind thus : Some planet is in association with the 7th lord. This associate occupies a certain Navamsa and the lord of this Navamsa should be posited in the 1st, 2nd or 5th house. Say, for example, Aquarius is Lagna, and the 7th lord, *viz.*, Sun is with Mars, who in his turn occupies the Navamsa of Dhanus and the lord of this Navamsa should, in order to give rise to this yoga, occupy either Kumbha, Mithuna or Meena.

Chart No. 100.—*Born on 30-8-1927 at 12-30 p. m. (L.M.T.) Lat. 21° N ; Long. 72° 50′ E.*

Jupiter			Rahu
	RASI		
	P.I. 84		Sun Merc.
Kethu	Lagna Saturn		Mars Venus Moon

	Kethu		Moon
	NAVAMSA		Mercury
Venus Mars			Sun
	Lagna	Saturn Rahu	Jupiter

Balance of Moon's Dasa at birth : years 3-8-21.

Chart No. 100 illustrates combination 221. Mars is in association with the lord of the 7th. The lord of the Navamsa occupied by Mars, *viz.*, Saturn is in Lagna. Hence, the yoga is present.

222 and 223. Dattaputra Yogas

Definition.—Mars and Saturn should occupy the 5th house and the lord of Lagna should be in a sign of Mercury, aspected by or in association with the same planet—222.

The lord of the 7th must be posited in the 11th, the 5th lord must join a benefic and the 5th house must be occupied by Mars or Saturn—223.

Results.—The person will have adopted children.

Remarks.—According to Hindu beliefs, if a man does not have issues born to him, he should adopt a son with a view not only to continuing the line but also to be helpful to the person during his old age. Several species of combinations to be found are given in ancient astrological books but here we have given only two typical ones. Combination 222 requires that Mars and Saturn should be in the 5th house. This means the affliction of the house of children. The disposition of the lord of the asscendant in the sign of Mercury or his association with, or his being subjected to the aspect of Mercury, may deprive the native of the *power to procreate* as Mercury is a neutral planet.

The last part of combination 223 and the 1st part of combination 222 are more or less the same. In addition to this, lord of the 7th must be in the 11th and the 5th lord must conjoin a benefic. The retionale of these combinations is not clear. But horoscopes, in which these yogas are present, generally show the results attributed.

Chart No. 101.—*Born on 22-1-1914 at 6-40 a.m. (I.S.T.) Lat 13° N.; Long. 80° 14' E.*

		Saturn	Mars
Rahu	RASI		
Lagna Sun Mercury Jupiter Venus			Kethu
	Moon		

Jupit. Merc. Sun Mars	Lagna	Rahu	
Venus	NAVAMSA		Saturn
Moon	Kethu		

Balance of Mercury's Dasa at birth : years 14-4-19.

Here is an illustration of combination 223. Lord of the 7th Moon is in the 11th; the 5th lord Venus joins a benefic and Saturn occupies the 5th.

224. Aputra Yoga

Definition.—The lord of the 5th house should occupy a dusthana.

Results.—The person will have no issues.

Remarks.—This is a general combination denoting birth of no children at all. In some of the yogas dealt with earlier, combinations are suggested for the loss of children due to various causes. But Aputra Yoga reveals that there will be no birth of issues at all. Dusthanas are the 6th, 8th and 12th. The lord of the 5th should not join any of these houses. Chart No. 102 is typically illustrative of Aputra Yoga.

Chart No. 102.—*Born on 31-7-1910 at Gh. 32-15 after sunrise. Lat 8° 44' N ; Long. 77° 44' E.*

	Saturn	Moon Rahu	Venus
	RASI		Merc. Sun
Lagna	U. 187		Mars
	Kethu		Jupit.

Merc.		Moon Mars	Jupiter
Venus	NAVAMSA		Kethu Lagna
Rahu			Saturn
	Sun		

Balance of Moon's Dasa at birth : years 7-3-18.

It must be noted that the combination sketched above is of a very general character and it should not be literally applied without making a thorough examination of the 5th house and its relative strength and weakness.

225. Ekaputra Yoga

Definition.—Lord of the 5th house should join a kendra or trikona.

Results.—The person will have only one son.

Remarks.—The combination is simple and calls for no explanation. Most of these yogas bearing on the 5th house cannot be applied verbatim. The 5th house must be carefully studied and if there are any serious afflictions, then alone the loss of children should be anticipated.

These yogas help us to form a rough estimate of the disposition of the 5th house, but it is the intrinsic strength or weakness of the house that really gives us all the details about the 5th house, whether one will have issues and if so, how many will survive and what will be their future, etc.

226. Suputra Yoga

Definition.—If Jupiter is lord of the 5th house and the Sun occupies a favourable position, this yoga is caused.

Results.—The native will have a worthy son.

Remarks.—An object which, in the beginning, is a source of pleasure, may eventually become a source of pain. A son generally sought after by the majority of human beings, a source of extreme joy as a child, may cause, when grown up, lot of misery and suffering to the parents provided the combination referred to above or a variation of it is not present in one's horoscope. The yoga in question is applicable only in respect of Simha and Vrischika Lagnas, as it is only with regard to these that Jupiter can own the 5th and not for persons born in other lagnas. It occurs to us that when the lord of the 5th house or the 5th house itself has a number of benefic vargas, the son will be a beacon light to the family.

227 and 228. Kalanirdesat Putra Yogas

Definition.—Jupiter should be in the 5th house and the lord of the 5th should join Venus—227.

Jupiter must also occupy the 9th from Lagna and Venus should be in the 9th from Jupiter, in conjunction with the lord of Lagna—228.

Results.—The native begets a son either in his 32nd, 33rd or 40th year.

Remarks.—These two yogas enable us to predict the probable period when one will have a son. If Jupiter is in the 5th and Venus is in conjunction with the 5th lord, birth of a son in one's 32nd or 33rd year can be predicted, *provided* the appropriate directional influences operate at the time the native reaches the above age; otherwise the yoga will not be valid.

Combination 228 says that Jupiter must be in the 9th from Lagna and Venus must be in the 9th from Jupiter. This is as good as saying that Venus must be in the 5th from Lagna. One born in this yoga will have a son in his 40th year, provided the appropriate Dasa and Bhukthi are current.

229 and 230. Kalanirdesat Putranasa Yogas

Definition.—Rahu must occupy the 5th house, the lord of the 5th must be in conjunction with a malefic and Jupiter should be debilitated—229.

Malefics should be disposed in the 5th from Jupiter and Lagna—230.

Results.—The person will suffer loss of issues in his 32nd and 40th years respectively.

Remarks.—These two combinations enable us to predict loss of sons at certain years of one's life. For one to lose a son in his 32nd year, Rahu should occupy the 5th, whose lord should have association with evil planets and Jupiter must get debilitated. In other words, all the three factors bearing on the house of children, *viz.*, the house, the lord and the karaka must have some sort of affliction. In actual practice, such a yoga has been found to give rise to more serious effects than those ascribed in classical works. For instance, we have a number of horoscopes in our collections, containing this combination, and the results in almost all cases have been either still-births or death of all the children within the first year of their birth. This is a peculiar phenomenon we have noticed.

Combination 230 is more general. If a malefic is present in the 5th from Lagna and also from Jupiter, there will be loss of an issue in the 32nd or 40th year. In actual practice, this combination appears to manifest in the shape of a few children dying and a few issues surviving.

Whenever an affliction by way of a malefic occupying a certain house or joining with a certain planet is suggested, by implication an aspect is also meant, though an affliction caused by aspect is comparatively less malevolent.

Chart No. 103.—*Born on 23-10-1883 at 10 a.m. (L.M.T.) Lat. 12° N.; Long. 76° 38′ E.*

	Kethu	Saturn	
	RASI		Moon Mars Jupit.
Lagna		Venus Sun Rahu	Merc.

Venus		Lagna	Saturn
	NAVAMSA		Mercury Kethu
Rahu			
Sun	Mars	Moon Jupiter	

Balance of Saturn's Dasa at birth : years 7-5-6.

In Chart No. 103 the 5th from Lagna is occupied by Kethu and aspected by Rahu while the 5th from Jupiter is equally afflicted by the aspect of Saturn. The horoscope clearly illustrates the above combination.

231. Buddhimaturya Yoga

Definition.—If the 5th lord, being a benefic, is either aspected by another benefic or occupies a benefic sign, the above yoga is given rise to.

Results.—The person will be a man of great intelligence and character.

Remarks.—The 5th lord can be a benefic only in regard to Vrishabha, Mithuna, Simha, Vrischika, Makara, Kumbha and Meena. If the definition is literally interpreted, then the yoga cannot operate in respect of the remaining five signs. Conversely it means that persons born in Mesha, Kataka, Kanya, Thula and Dhanus cannot become intelligent or men of character. Such a suggestion would be preposterous especially in view of the fact that several geniuses and men of great integrity have been born in signs for which the 5th house can never be a benefic sign. Therefore, the yoga may be deemed to be present in case the 5th house, irrespective of its being a benefic or a malefic sign, is occupied by benefics and 5th lord is in association with Jupiter, Mercury and Venus.

Chart No. 104 is the horoscope of a retired Judge. Mark the unique disposition of the 5th house, it being occupied by Venus its own lord and Mercury lord of (the 6th and) 9th. The native is a man of great intelligence and integrity. Even at this advanced age, his powers of memory and comprehension are extraordinarily good.

Chart No. 104.—*Born on 5-5-1871 at 11-14 p.m. (L.M.T.) Lat. 13° N., Long 76° 9 E.*

	Sun	Mercury Venus	Jupit. Rahu
Mandi	RASI		
Lagna	5.47		Mars
Saturn Kethu	Moon		

Merc.			
Lagna	NAVAMSA		Kethu
Rahu			Moon
Mars	Mandi Jupiter Sun		Veuns Saturn

Balance of Saturn's Dasa at birth : years 17-10-10.

Chart No. 105.—*Born on 12-2-1856 at 12-21 p.m. (L.M.T.) Lat. 18° N., Long. 84° E.*

	Rahu Moon	Lagna	Saturn
Sun Mercury Jupiter	RASI		
Venus		Mars Kethu	

	Lagna Jupiter		Rahu
	NAVAMSA		
Merc. Kethu		Moon Mars Saturn Venus Sun	

Balance of Venus' Dasa at birth : years 6-8-12.

Chart No. 105 is that of late Prof. B. Suryanarain Rao. The 5th house is Virgo, the sign of a benefic planet, while the 5th lord Mercury is in the 10th in association with benefic Jupiter. It is a matter of common knowledge that the Professor was an extraordinarily intelligent man and had retained his great intellectual faculties until the day of his death. Noble-hearted and incorruptible, he was a great philanthropist and delighted himself in helping the poor and the needy. His moral stature won for him great respect both from relatives and friends. All these qualities are not a little due to the strength the 5th lord has derived by virtue of his association with the philosophical and intellectual planet Jupiter.

232. Theevrabuddhi Yoga

Definition.—The lord of the navamsa, in which the lord of the 5th is placed, should be aspected by benefics, and the 5th lord himself should be a benefic.

Results.—The person will be precociously intelligent.

Remarks.—This combination is to be usually found in the horoscope of geniuses. It occurs to me that the suggestion in the 2nd part of the yoga, that the 5th lord should be a benefic, is not warranted. Because, in actual practice, we find that the 5th lord should have good associations or aspects, irrespective of his being a natural malefic or natural benefic. According to the yoga in question the lord of the Navamsa occupied by the 5th lord should receive the *aspect* of a benefic. The yoga can be assumed to be present even if the said Navamsa lord is in conjunction with a natural benefic.

In the following horoscope, the 5th lord, *viz.*, Venus is in a benefic Navamsa. The lord of this Navamsa, *viz.*, Mercury is in the 2nd house in association with two first-rate benefics.

Consequently Theevrabuddhi Yoga may be said to be present. The native is a man of very great intelligence, an astute politician, an able lawyer and a brilliant writer.

Chart No. 106.—*Born on 20/21-2-1879 at 4-50 a.m. (L.M.T.) Lat. 10° 43' N. ; Long. 76° 48' E.*

Saturn			
Sun Venus Moon Merc. Jupiter	RASI		Kethu
Lagna Rahu	A.5		
Mars			

	Rahu Sun		Venus Lagna
	NAVAMSA		
Moon		Saturn Merc. Jupiter Kethu Mars	

Balance of Rahu's Dasa at birth : years 14-6-29.

233. Buddhi Jada Yoga

Definition.—If the lord of the Ascendant is conjoined with or aspected by evil planets, Saturn occupies the 5th and the lord of Lagna is aspected by Saturn, the above yoga is caused.

Results.—The person will be a dunce.

Remarks.—All the various yogas enumerated in these pages comprehend two basic conditions, *viz.*, (1) the benefic disposition of the karaka, lord or bhava of the signification concerned and, (2) affliction to either or all of the three factors concerned. Since each bhava comprehends more than one event, one should very carefully analyse the bhava concerned in order to locate the particular event involved in an affliction or benefic disposition. In the yoga under consideration which is supposed to indicate dullness of intellect, a connection is envisaged between Saturn, Lagnadhipathi and the 5th house. The same combination is also capable of a different interpretation, *viz.*, the death of children. But if Jupiter, the karaka for children, is well placed, the person may have children who may remain dunces. Intellectual bankruptcy is not the sole monopoly of people having no issues. What I wish to impress upon my readers is that a snap-shot judgement because a certain yoga if present, is always a dangerous thing. A beginner should never attempt predictions where he will be required to deal with the house of children, house of death or house of wife, until he has gained sufficient practical experience.

Chart No. 107.—*Born on 26-6-1920 at 2-6 p.m. (L.M.T.) Lat. 24° 54′ N.; Long. 4th. 28m. E.*

Lagna	Kethu		Sun Venue	Lagna	Moon Rahu		
	RASI		Merc. Jupit.	Jupit. Sun	NAVAMSA		
	3.46		Saturn	Venus			
		Moon Mars Rahu			Mars	Kethu	Mercury Saturn

Balance of Jupiter's Dasa at birth: years 11-10-17.

Chart No. 107 belongs to a man whose mental dullness almost borders on insanity. With Jupiter exalted and in conjunction with Mercury, the native should have become a man of very great intelligence. But contrary is the case. The 5th lord Moon is in conjunction with Mars and Rahu, aspected by Saturn from an inimical sign. A more malefic combination cannot be conceived. The subject whiles away his time like a child. He cannot think, he cannot use intelligence and sometimes he behaves like a mad man.

234. Thrikalagnana Yoga

Definition.—Jupiter should occupy Mrudwamsa in his own navamsa, or Gopuramsa and be aspected by a benefic planet.

Results.—The native becomes capable of reading the past, present and future.

Remarks.—An astrologer with the aid of his art can read the past, present and future. But here the reference is to *Thrikalagnana* or the faculty of seership which enables a man *intuitively* to prophesy things. This particular yoga can be assumed to be present if (*a*) Jupiter being in his own Navamsa has obtained Mrudwamsa or (*b*) being in Gopuramsa is aspected by a benefic.

Readers must be aware of the Shashtiamsa or 1/60th division of a Rasi. Mrudwamsa will be the 19th part (9 to 9½°) of this division in an odd sign or the 42nd (20½ to 21°) part in an even sign. Jupiter can have Mrudwamsa in his own Navamsa, provided his longitude is between 9 and 9½° in Mithuna,

Thula or Kumbha. When he is in any other sign other than the above, he cannot have Mrudwamsa consistently with his situation in a Swa-navamsa because of the fact that 20½ to 21°, which means the 7th navamsa, can never fall under Jupiter.

The other combination denoting the same yoga requires the situation of Jupiter in Gopuramsa. A planet is said to attaian Gopuramsa if he occupies his own varga four times. Suppose Jupiter is in the first degree of Dhanus, then he occupies his own Rasi, his own Drekkana, his own Chaturthamsa and his own Sapthamsa, having attained his *Swavarga* four times.

The following horoscope is illustrative of the presence of Thrikalagnana Yoga.

In the following chart Jupiter's longitude being 9° 16′ in Thula, an odd sign, he occupies his own Navamsa consistent with the longitude falling in a Mrudwamsa :

Chart No. 108.—*Born on 30-9-1946 at 5-30 a.m. (I.S.T.) Lat. 25° N. ; Long. 82° 30′ E.*

		Rahu	
	RASI		Saturn
	9.16		
	Moon Kethu	Mars Jupiter Venus	Sun Merc. Lagna

Lagna		Sun	Venus
Kethu	NAVAMSA		
Mars			Rahu Mercury
Jupit.	Saturn		Moon

Balance of Saturn's Dasa at birth : years 12-11-18.

235. Putra Sukha Yoga

Definition.—When the 5th is occupied by Jupiter and Venus, or when Mercury joins the 5th, or the 5th happening to be the sign of a benefic, is occupied by benefics, Putra Sukha Yoga exists.

Results.—There will be happiness on account of children.

Remarks.—The yoga is very flexibly defined. The 5th house must be the sign of a benefic (Mercury, Jupiter, Venus) and occupied by a benefic, or even without the 5th being a benefic sign, mere Jupiter and Venus there could also give rise to the same yoga. In other words, the yoga assumes the general strength of the 5th house. To become happy on account of children is indeed a great fortune. Many hearts have ached because of dislike, disobedience or disrespect on the part of grown-up children towards their parents.

236. Jara Yoga

Definition.—The 10th house must be occupied by the lords of the 10th, 2nd and 7th.

Results.—The person will have extra-marital relations with a number of women.

Remarks.—There are several combinations for making one a *Jara* or a debauchee and the yoga herein described is one such. In interpreting such yogas, one should exercise great care and skill. I am not able to follow as to how lords of the 2nd, 7th and 10th in the 10th could make one loose in sex life. Suppose the Lagna is Kanya, then the lords of the 2nd, 7th and 10th would be Venus, Jupiter and Mercury. When all these three join in the 10th, the subject must be very strict and principled in regard to his sex-relations though Mercury-Venus conjunction will also render him sensual. With due deference to the Sages who have formulated this yoga, we have to observe that unless the 7th lord happens to be Mars or Venus and unless the conjunction happens in the 10th, it is not advisable to conclude that the person concerned would be of questionable character. Mars and Venus in the 7th make one highly passionate. When there is a benefic aspect on this combination, the over-sexuality is tempered considerably and the person confines his appetites within reasonable bounds.

Chart No. 109.—*Born on 10-6-1910 at 3-20 p.m. (I.S.T.) Lat. 13° N.; Long. 77° 35 E.*

	Saturn Venus	Sun Rahu Mercury	
	RASI		Moon Mars
	Kethu	Lagna	Jupit.

Merc.		Jupiter	
Rahu	NAVAMSA		Saturn
Lagna			Venus Moon Mars Kethu
			Sun

Balance of Saturn's Dasa at birth : years 15-3-16.

This horoscope typically illustrates Jara Yoga.

237. Jarajaputra Yoga

Definition.—Powerful lords of the 5th and the 7th must join with the lord of the 6th and be aspected by benefics.

Results.—The person lacks the power of procreation but his wife will have a son from another man.

Remarks.—This is very important yoga inasmuch as it enables one to ascertain whether an issue is really the product of one's own seed or the result of illegitimate intimacy of one's wife with another person. According to this yoga, both the husband and the wife will be guilty of extramarital adventures, because the husband will be attached to other women, while the wife will have her own way of seeking illegitimate gratification of her baser instincts. When both the husband and wife prove ungrateful to each other, children born to such parents cannot be expected to be morally strong.

238. Bahu Stree Yoga

Definition.—If the lords of the Lagna and the 7th are in conjunction or aspect with each other, the above yoga is given rise to.

Results.—The person will have any number of wives.

Remarks.—Man's sexual appetites are various and curious and express themselves in strange and unbelievable manners. There are people who are scrupulously clean mentally and physically that women other than their own wives are always considered equal to their own mothers and sisters. There are others apparently respectable but thoroughly immoral, who hunt after all sorts of dirty women to have their bestial instincts gratified. Even though the yoga is said to indicate a 'number of wives', in actual practice it should be interpreted to mean that the person would be in intimacy with a number of women. The following is a typical horoscope illustrative of man's depravity of character.

In Chart No. 110 the 7th lord Mars and the Lagna lord Venus are in mutual aspect besides being

Chart No. 110.—*Born on 6-4-1886 at about 6-30 p.m. (L.M.T.) Lat. 17° 30′ N., Long. 78° 30′ E.*

Sun	Moon Mercury		Saturn
Kethu Venus	RASI		
	3.100		Rahu Mars
		Lagna Mandi	Jupit.

Jupit.	Mercury	Kethu	
Sun	NAVAMSA		
Sat. Venus			Mars
Mandi	Rahu	Lagna	Moon

Balance of Venus' Dasa at birth : years 11-9-9.

associated with the shadowy planets Rahu and Kethu. The 7th lord Mars is aspected by Saturn also. The native who has a flexible conscience was reputed to have a number of wives.

The yoga is also said to arise when the lord of the 9th is in the 7th, the lord of the 7th is in the 4th and the lord of Lagna or the lord of the 11th is in a kendra. Some of these yogas seem very simple but their practical application is always a matter of great risk and difficulty.

239. Satkalatra Yoga

Definition.—The lord of the 7th or Venus should join or be aspected by Jupiter or Mercury.

Results.—The native's wife will be noble and virtuous.

Remarks.—Nobility of character is a precious commodity not easily to be found in the majority of people—men or women. The wife of one having the above combination will be a woman of strict moral discipline, god-fearing and attached to her husband. Modern eves would not perhaps like to have such combinations present in their husbands' horoscopes! Under a false sense of equality, there are some respectable (?) women, within our knowledge, who are worse than public prostitutes, and who are ever prepared to sell their honour just to get the appellation of society cocks.

In Chart No. 111, note 7th lord Mars occupying the Ascendant with two benefics Venus and Mercury. The native's wife was an ideal, chaste and devoted lady who regarded her husband as her god.

Chart No. 111.—*Born on 2-10-1869 at 7-45 a.m. (L.M.T.) Lat. 21° 37′ W., Long. 69° 49′ E.*

		Jupiter			Moon Kethu	Venus	Sun Mars
	RASI		Rahu		NAVAMSA		
Kethu			Moon	Jupit. Lagna Merc.			
	Saturn	Lagna Venus Mars Mercury	Sun	Sat.		Rahu	

Balance of Kethu Dasa at birth : years 6-10-28.

Chart No. 112.—*Born on 18-11-1943 at 1-43 a.m. (L.M.T.) at 17° 20′ N., 78° 30′ E.*

		Mars	Saturn			Venus Jupiter	Kethu
	RASI		Moon Rahu		NAVAMSA		Sun
Kethu			Jupit.	Lagna			
	Sun Mercury		Lagna Venus	Rahu	Saturn	Moon	Mercury Mars

Balance of Saturn Dasa at birth : years 8-9-83.

Neither the 7th lord Jupiter nor Venus come under any benefic influences. There is very little understanding between the native and his wife which has resulted in separation.

240. Bhaga Chumbana Yoga

Definition.—If the lord of the 7th is in the 4th in conjunction with Venus, the above yoga is caused.

Results.—The person will indulge in *Bhaga Chumbana* (caressing the *pudendum muliebre*).

Remarks.—The same result may also be anticipated in case Lagna lord is debilitated in the Rasi or in the Navamsa.

241. Bhagya Yoga

Definition.—A strong benefic should be in Lagna, the 3rd or 5th, simultaneously aspecting the 9th.

Results.—The subject will be extremely fortunate, pleasure-loving and rich.

Remarks.—Two conditions are specified for the occurrence of this yoga, *viz.*, a strong benefic must occupy Lagna, the 3rd or 5th. It must at the same time aspect the 9th. Obviously, Jupiter alone can cause yoga when in Lagna, or in the 5th house for no other benefic can be in Lagna and aspect the 9th. Any benefic planet can cause the yoga from the 3rd house Here also due consideration must be given to the nature of the ownership of the benefic concerned before actually evaluating the yoga. Cancer Lagna with Jupiter there constitutes a powerful *Bhagya Yoga* as Jupiter, as lord of the 9th, aspects the 9th and occupies Lagna in exaltation. The same yoga forming from Mithuna becomes almost ineffective because of Kendradhipatya dosha for Jupiter. Consideration of the temporal nature of a benefic is not suggested in the original but it is clearly implied that the potency of the yoga should be based upon the sum-total of the strength of the benefic concerned, for the yoga *rests* on the presence of a strong benefic in Lagna, the 3rd or 5th.

242. Jananatpurvam Pitru Marana Yoga

Difinition.—The Sun must be in the 6th, 8th or 12th; lord of the 8th must be in the 9th; lord of the 12th in Lagna and the lord of the 6th in the 5th.

Results.—The subject will be a posthumous child.

Remarks.—Birth of posthumous children is a somewhat rare phenomenon but not an infrequent one. The yoga here defined is a round-about one involving the Sun, and lords of the 6th, 8th and 12th, and their disposition in certain mutual positions. It occurs to me that in order to produce the full effects, the entire yoga, and not a part of it, should be present in the horoscope.

Chart No. 113—*Born on 22-3-1929 at 5-10 p.m. (L.M.T.) Lat. 20° N.; Long. 77° 30' E.*

Sun	Venus Jupiter	Rahu	Mars
Mercury	RASI		
			Lagna Moon
Saturn	Kethu		

Merc.		Moon	Saturn
	NAVAMSA		Kethu
Rahu Mars			Venus
	Lagna		Jupiter Sun

Balance of Kethu's Dasa at birth: years 4-7-19.

In Chart No. 113, Yoga No. 242 is present *in toto*. The Sun is in the 8th; lord of 8th Jupiter is in the 9th; lord of the 12th Moon is in Lagna; and finally lord of the 6th, *viz.*, Saturn is in the 5th.

243. Dhatrutwa Yoga

Definition.—The lord of the 9th should be exalted, and aspected by a benefic, and the 9th should be occupied by a benefic.

Results.—The person will be an embodiment of generosity.

Remarks.—The yoga assumes the strength of the 9th lord and the 9th house to make one charitable in one's outlook. the 9th is termed Dharma as well as Bhagya and Dana or charity being an indispensable part of one's Dharma, one should be fortunate enough to possess the instinct of generosity. Here again, there are various grades of charity ranging from giving away gifts without entertaining any profit-motives, to giving huge sums seemingly for charitable purposes but ostensibly to serve selfiish ends. Karna of the Mahabharatha fame and Emperor Bali had been known for their absolutely motiveless acts of charity. But such men belong to the age of legend. Even today there are people who take immense pleasure in helping others without expecting anything in return for their acts of sacrifice. Such noble instincts should always be attributed to the strength of the 9th house. Malefics in the 9th house, otherwise strong and capable of conferring Rajayoga, deaden the finer instincts of the person. He would no doubt make large endowments for so-called charitable purposes, etc., but he does all this with an ulterior motive, to get some title or to get into the good graces of influential people. A man engaged in the perfidious task of filling his coffers by creating conditions for starving the poor man, and later on passing an insignificant part of this ill-gotten fortune towards a charitable purpose is worse than a thief wedded to rob the rich and help the poor. Here, the yoga is applicable to really sincere and humanitarian persons whose generous instincts find a spontaneous expression for the good of the suffering humanity.

Chart No. 114 belongs to a late Maharaja. Lord of the 9th Jupiter is *exalted* in Lagna with another benefic Venus and 9th is aspected by the lord himself. The 9th is of course aspected by Mars, but Jupiter is exceptionally beneficial and powerful. The native was noted for his great humanitarian instincts and never lost an opportunity to help the needy and the deserving.

Chart No. 114.—*Born on 4-6-1884 at 10-18 a.m. (L.M.T.) Lat. 12° N.; Long. 76° 38′ E.*

Kethu		Saturn Sun Mercury	
	RASI		Lagna Jupit. Venus
	P. N. 46		Mars
		Moon	Rahu

Lagaa Kethu			Mars
	NAVAMSA		Sun Venus Saturn
Merc.			
		Moon Jupiter	Rahu

Balance of Mars' Dasa at birth : years 1-11-12.

Dhatrutwa Yoga can also be said to exist, (*a*) when the Lagna or the lord of Lagna is aspected by the 9th lord who in his turn occupies a kendra, and (*b*) when the 9th lord is in the 4th, the 10th lord is in a kendra and the 12th lord is aspected by Jupiter. Several variations of these yogas can also be attempted.

244. Apakeerti Yoga

Definition.—The 10th house must be occupied by the Sun and Saturn who should join malefic amsas or be aspected by malefics.

Results.—The person will have a bad reputation.

Remarks.—Reputation is a bubble and it can burst at any moment. Some are fortunate in commanding an unsullied name throughout their lives, while others suddenly shoot into lime-light and disappear ignominously like a meteor. For one to possess a good name, there should be no mutual conjunction or aspect between the Sun and Saturn especially in the 10th house. According to Yoga No. 244, the 10th house should be occupied by the Sun and Saturn and aspected by malefics, or the Sun and Saturn should occupy malefic navamsas. Conversely it means, the mere presence of these two planets in the 10th unaspected by other malefics cannot constitute Apakeerti Yoga, if benefic navamsas are held. In our humble opinion, Jupiter's aspects on the Sun-Saturn combination in the 10th can no doubt act as a powerful antidote, but nevertheless, the person will have a setback in his reputation at least temporarily.

245 to 263. Raja Yogas

245

Definition.—Three or more planets should be in exaltation or own house occupying kendras.

Results.—The person becomes a famous king.

246

Definition.—When a planet is in debilitation but with bright rays, or retrograde, and occupies favourable positions, Raja Yoga will be caused.

Results.—The person will attain a position equal to that of a ruler and will command all the insignia of royalty.

247

Definition.—Two, there or four planets should possess Digbala.

Results.—A person, even though born in an ordinary family, will become a ruler.

Remarks.—The above there Raja Yogas are capable of elevating a man, though born in humble surroundings, to the position of a ruler. Hundreds and thousands of Raja Yogas are enumerated in classical astrological works, but I am confining my attention to just a few important ones which could really produce results attributed to them. According to Yoga No. 245, three or more planets should be exalted or in swakshetra and *at the same time* occupy kendras. Evidently the definition resembles a Panchamahapurusha Yoga. In actual practice, it has been found that these *three or more* planets in swakshetra or uchcha need not necessarily be in kendras. Even trikonas will do.

Combination 246 is more general and widely applicable. The only condition is the debilitated planet must be of *bright rays, i.e.,* free from combustion; or retrograde and occupy houses which are not dusthanas (6th, 8th or 12th). I am afraid a planet like Saturn debilitated in the 10th and vakra, unless there are other relieving features, can cause quite a good deal of harm and completely shatter the career of the person. It is held by the framers of this yoga, that the Raja Yoga gets fructified by the debilitated planet occupying auspicious navamsas also.

According to combination 247, the mere possession of Digbala by two to four planets is said to give rise to Raja Yoga. Mercury and Jupiter in Lagna, Mars and the Sun in the 10th, Saturn in the 7th and the Moon and Venus in the 4th respectively get Digbala. Here again consideration should be given to the general strength or otherwise of the planets causing Raja Yoga by the possession of Digbala. A Raja Yoga caused by Mesha being Lagna with Sani and Kuja in the 7th and 10th respectively cannot be equated with a Raja Yoga caused by Thula being Lagna and Sani and Kuja being placed in Mesha and Kataka respectively. In the first instance, the yoga is *par excellence* because of the exaltation of Saturn in the 7th and Mars in the 10th in addition to their possessing Digbala. Mars gets added strength by virtue of this uchcha in the 10th from Lagna, as lord of Lagna. In the second instance, Saturn being neecha, has no doubt Digbala besides being a yogakaraka. But his power to confer yoga is considerably restricted on account of his debilitation, while Mars though possessing Digbala is powerless, as he would be debilitated in the 10th.

In Chart No. 115 three planets, *viz.*, Saturn, Mars and the Sun are exalted and occupy kendras form Chandra Lagna and hence illustrative of combination 245. There are, of course, certain breaks which have impeded the smooth flow of fortunate currents such as mutual aspects between the Sun

Chart No. 115.—*Born on 14/13-4-1924 at 2-34 a.m. (L.M.T.) Lat. 13° N.; Long. 77° 34′ E.*

	Sun Mercury	Venus		Jupit.	Sun		Venus Rahu
Kethu Lagna	RASI		Moon		NAVAMSA		
Mars	S. 234		Rahu	Mars			
	Jupiter	Saturn		Kethu Moon Sat.	Lagna	Mercury	

Balance of Mercury's Dasa at birth: years 14-4-27.

and Saturn and Mars aspecting Rahu, etc. But, nevertheless, from Raja Yoga point of view, the Sun's Dasa should prove excellent. And it did prove so.

Chart No. 116.—*Born on 10-10-1871 at 2-0 p.m. (L.M.T.) Lat. 51° 26′ N., Long. 2° 35′ W.*

			Rahu		Mercury	Kethu	Moon
	RASI		Jupit.	Venus	NAVAMSA		
	P. N. 36		Moon				Saturn Sun
Lagna Kethu Saturn	Mars		Sun Merc. Venus (R)	Mars	Lagna Rahu		Jupiter

Balance of Kethu's Dasa at birth: years 1-9-25.

In Chart No 116 though Venus is debilitated in the 10th, he is not only bright but retrograde. The native served as Dewan in Kashmir, Mysore and Cochin, enjoyed all the royal paraphernalia and lived upto a good old age. This chart is no doubt clearly illustrative of combination 246, but there are others equally powerful Raja Yogas which have contributed to the general strength of the horoscope.

Chart No. 117.—*Born on 4-6-1884 at 10-18 a.m. (L.M.T.) Lat. 12° N.; Long. 76° 38' E.*

Kethu		Sun Saturn Mercury	
	RASI		Lagna Venus Jupit.
	P.N. 46		Mars
		Moon	Rahu

Lagna Kethu			Mars
	NAVAMSA		Sun Venus Saturn
Merc.			
		Moon Jupiter	Rahu

Balance of Mars' Dasa at birth: years 1-11-12.

Chart No. 117 illustrative of combination 247 is that of an Indian Maharaja. Jupiter and the Moon have obtained Digbala by virtue of situation in Lagna and the 4th respectively. This has acted as a powerful Raja Yoga. The native was an ideal ruler and had earned the respect and affection of his subject by his great qualities of head and heart.

248 to 250

Definition.—The Lagna must be Kumbha with Sukra in it and four planets should be exalted without occupying evil navamsas or shastiamsas—248.

The Moon must be in Lagna, Jupiter in the 4th, Venus in the 10th and Saturn exalted or in his own house—249.

The lord of the sign, a planet is debilitated in, or the planet, who would be exalted there, should be in a kendra from the Moon or Lagna—250.

Results.—The subject becomes a ruler or an equal to him.

Remarks.—In the treatment of Raja Yogas, I have included what are all called Neechabhanga Raja Yogas also. Generally the latter type of Raja Yogas are said to denote elevation from ordinary or low births. But, in actual practice, it has been found that Raja Yogas as well as Neechabhanga Raja Yogas function more or less similarly subject to such difference as may be due to the inherent nature and functions of the planets involved.

Combination 248 is of rare occurrence and not of universal application as it is confined to only one Lagna and as it requires the exaltation of four planets and their non-occupation of malefic navamsas or shashtiamsas. If the exalted planets are in evil navamsas or shashtiamsas, the yoga does not function and the native may become a tyrant or malevolent dictator.

Yoga No. 249 requires that the Moon, Jupiter and Venus should occupy Lagna, the 4th and 10th, Saturn being disposed in exalation or own house. Here again, the vitality and potentiality of the yoga depend upon the Lagna concerned. The most important point involved in this yoga is the fortification of the 4th and 10th houses by presence of two first-rate benefics.

Chart No. 118.—*Born on 21-7-1895 at 12 noon. Lat, 40° N.; Long. 0°.*

Lagna Moon Rahu	Mars		Jupit.
	RASI		
Sun Mercury Venus		Saturn	Kethu

Lagna			Mars
Saturn Kethu	NAVAMSA		Moon
			Rahu Mercury
Jupit. Venus		Sun	

Balance of Jupiter's Dasa at birth: years 3-3-11.

Chart No. 118 is an example for Yoga No. 249. The Moon, Jupiter and Venus are situated respectively in Lagna, the 4th and 10th, while Saturn is in exaltation. The yoga obtains *in toto*.

As regards combination 250, there has been quite a lot of discussion about the planet "who would be exalted in the sign of the debilitated planet" in the pages of THE ASTROLOGICAL MAGAZINE. The term used in the original is *thaduchchanatha* and this has been interpreted by some scholars as 'the lord of the exaltation sign of the debilitated planet'. Arguments offered by such critics have not been convincing. According to savants like Prof. B. Suryanarain Rao, *thaduchchanatha* means the planet who gets exalted there, and not the lord of the exaltation sign of the debilitated planet. This is still a controversial matter and I do not therefore propose to discuss it in this book which is mainly intended for students of astrology. Since astrology is a practical science any interpretation that we put upon a certain combination must be capable of verification when applied to practical horoscopes. As most of the astrological terms are expressed in very suggestive, symbolic or euphemistic language, no amount of scholarship in Sanskrit or Grammar or Literature would enable one to appreciate the subject in its proper perspective. On the contrary, the more one tries to grammatically interpret such terms the more absurd becomes one's conclusion. A literal and matter-of-fact interpretation leaves no scope for imagination with the result original ideas would be narrowed down to mere confusion. Most of these yogas are to be reckoned both from Lagna and the Moon.

Here is an illustration for Neechabhanga Raja Yoga. The Sun is neecha, and Saturn, the planet who is to get exalted in the Rasi occupied by the Sun is in a kendra from Lagna. The horoscope is that of a great scientist who has won international laurels. Apart from Neechabhanga Raja Yoga, the conjunction of Saturn and Rahu in the 10th aspected by Mars is higly significant.

Chart No. 119.—*Born on 8-11-1888 at 5-47 a.m. (L.M.T.) Lat. 10° 47' N.; Long. 79° 10' E.*

				Saturn	Lagna	Sun	
	RASI		Saturn Rahu	Kethu Venus	NAVAMSA		
Kethu	P.N. 57			Merc.			Rahu
Mars Moon	Jupiter Venus	Lagna Sun Mercury		Jupit.		Moon Mars	

Balance of Venus' Dasa at birth : years 8-2-21.

251 to 253

Definition.—The Moon must be in a kendra other than Lagna and aspected by Jupiter, and otherwise powerful—251.

Planets in debilitated Rasis should occupy exalted Navamsas—252.

Jupiter in Lagna and Mercury in a kendra must be aspected respectively by the lords of the 9th and 11th—253.

Results.—The native becomes a ruler or an equal to him, in wealth, power and influence.

Remarks.—Raja Yogas like any other yogas have to be adopted to suit modern conditions. Most of the Raja Yogas mentioned in classical works must have been framed, when monarchial forms of rule were the order of the day. But now in this age of 'democracy', when Kingship as an institution has been practically wiped out, the presence of Raja Yogas need not suggest that one would become a ruler. A powerful Raja Yoga may confer a position equal to that of a king. There are different grades of Raja Yoga capable of conferring different degrees of political power. If the Raja Yoga planets are intimately connected with the Sun and the Moon, political power may result. If the Raja Yoga planets are connected with Mars, one may become a dictator or a Commander-in-Chief. It would require quite a good deal of study and investigation before one could definitely say in what manner a particular Raja Yoga is likely to manifest.

Combination 251 requires the disposition of the powerful Moon in a kendra other than the Lagna and subject to the aspect of Jupiter.

Chart No. 120.—*Born on 8-8-1912 at 7-23 p.m. (L.M.T.) Lat. 13° N.; Long. 77° 35' E.*

Rahu		Saturn Moon	
Lagna	RASI		Sun
			Mars Merc. Venus
	Jupiter		Kethu

	Venus Saturn		
	NAVAMSA		Kethu
Lagna Rahu Sun			Moon Mercury
	Jupiter	Mars	

Balance of Mars' Dasa at birth: years 6-0-10.

In Chart No. 120 the Moon is in a kendra other than Lagna, and is aspected by Jupiter. The Moon being exalted may be said to be fairly powerful. A Raja Yoga is therefore clearly present, and it is further fortified by the Moon and Jupiter being in mutual kendras thus causing Gajakesari Yoga. The Raja Yoga has however nothing to do with political power, as neither the 10th nor the 10th lord has any contact with the political planet, Sun. Mars no doubt aspects the 10th as 10th lord, but the dominating planet is Jupiter. Short of political power, the Raja Yoga could confer all the other results consistent with the strength of the planets causing the yoga.

Chart No. 121.—*Born on 8-11-1903 at 2-38 p.m. (L.M.T.) Lat. 17° 30′ N.; Long. 73° 30′ E.*

Lagna Kethu			Moon
Jupiter	RASI		
Saturn	5.128		
Mars		Sun Mercury	Venue Rahu

Venus	Jupiter Saturn	Sun Rahu	
Merc.	NAVAMSA		Mars
			Lagna
	Moon Kethu		

Balance of Mars' Dasa at birth: year 0-11-7.

In Chart No. 121, the Moon is in the 4th aspected by Jupiter from the 12th. Combination 251 is present. The Moon is aspected by Mars from the 10th. Therefore the Raja Yoga should have expressed itself in the shape of the native getting political power. But actually, he is a buisnessman and has nothing to do with politics. The reason appears to be due to his not getting the Moon and Mars Dasas. Jupiter Dasa merely built his business career. We may therefore infer that a Raja Yoga could confer political power, provided, one of the Yogakarakas is connected with Mars or the Sun who in his turn should own or occupy the 10th house. Mark also another Neechabhanga Raja Yoga caused by the disposition of Venus (lord of the sign the Sun is debilitated in) in a kendra from Lagna. The native is a very rich man having inherited lakhs of rupees from his father.

In Chart No. 122, Yoga No. 252 is illustrated. All the neecha planets in Rasi are exalted in Amsa.

Chart No. 122.—*Born on 5-11-1915 at 11-30 a.m. (I.S.T.) Lat. 15° N.; Long. 77° E.*

			Saturn
Jupiter	RASI		Mars Kethu
Lagna Rahu			
	Venus	Sun Mercury	Moon

	Sun	Saturn	Jupiter
	NAVAMSA		Rahu Moon
Kethu Lagna Mars			Venus
		Mercury	

Balance of Moon's Dasa at birth: year 0-11-21.

Chart No. 123.—*Born on 22-5-1921 at 2-5 p.m. (I.S.T.) Lat. 18° 52' N.; Long. 72° 35' E.*

	Kethu Venus	Sun Mars Mercury	
	RASI		
	5.217		Jupit. Lagna Sat.
	Moon	Rahu Mandi	

Sun		Venus Kethu	
Mandi	NAVAMSA		Mars Mercury
Lagna	Rahu Moon Saturn		Jupiter

Balance of Saturn's Dasa at birth : years 1-9-28.

Chart No. 123 fulfils all the requirements of combination 253, excepting one, *viz.*, Mercury receiving the aspect of the lord of the 11th. Since Mercury himself happens to be lord of the 11th, the yoga can be assumed to be present. Jupiter is in Lagna and Mercury is in the 10th, another kendra and Jupiter is aspected by Mars lord of the 9th. Mark also the conjunction of lord of Lagna with Yogakaraka Mars and the lord of the 11th Mercury —all in the 10th from Lagna.

254 to 258

Definition.—Saturn in exaltation or Moola-thrikona should occupy a kendra or thrikona aspected by the lord of the 10th—254.

The Moon should join Mars in the 2nd or 3rd and Rahu must occupy the 5th—255.

The lord of the 10th should occupy an exalted or friendly navamsa in the 9th having attained Uttamamsa—256.

Jupiter must be in the 5th from Lagna and in a kendra from the Moon and the Lagna being a fixed sign the lord should occupy the 10th—257.

The lord of the navamsa occupied by the Moon should be disposed in a quadrant or trine either from Lagna or Mercury—258.

Results.—The native becomes a ruler or an equal to him.

Remarks.—Saturn's exaltation sign is Thula and Moolathrikona is Kumbha. For combination 254 to obtain, Saturn must occupy either Thula or Kumbha which should happen to be a kendra or thrikona from Lagna. In other words, this yoga can operate in respect of all signs except Kanya, Dhanus and Makara because they cannot be kendra or thrikona either from Thula or Kumbha. Therefore Saturn in Kumbha or Thula, aspected by the lord of the 10th, can give rise to the Raja Yoga defined in combination 254, provided the Lagna is not Kanya, Dhanus or Meena.

The theoretical presence of Raja Yogas is of no consequence unless the Raja Yogas have inherent vitality to produce the results ascribed to them. The student must first learn to pick up Raja Yogas and then weigh their relative strengths and weaknesses. Chart No. 124 illustrates the presence of Raja Yoga as per combination 254. Saturn is not only in exaltation occupying a thrikona but is aspected by Jupiter lord of the 10th from Lagna. The subject was a big zamindar.

Chart No. 124—*Born on 15-5-1895 at 9-17 p.m. (L.M.T.) Lat. 22° 25' N.; Long. 87° 21' E.*

		Sun Mercury	Venus Jupit. Mars Lagna
Rahu	RASI		
Moon	5.107		Kethu
		Saturn	

	Mars	Moon Mercury	Rahu Lagna
Jupit.	NAVAMSA		
Sat. Sun Venus			
Kethu			

Balance of Moon's Dasa at birth : years 5-9-0.

A Chandra Mangala Yoga in the 2nd or 3rd with Rahu in the 5th is also said to give rise to a Raja Yoga (255). Rahu's situation in the 5th is not good for children. When Kuja is in the 2nd and Rahu is in the 5th, Kuja aspects Rahu thus increasing the affliction on the 5th house. The Raja Yoga in question is perhaps an exception to the general dictum that Rahu-Mars influences on the 5th would adversely affect the house of children. In about a dozen horoscopes (containing this combination) I have examined, the Raja Yoga appears to be nominal inasmuch as the subjects concerned belong to mediocre status and have not been noted either for wealth, or power or intellect. I should feel thankful to readers who could pass on to me charts illustrative of Raja Yoga mentioned in combination 255.

Yoga No. 256 seems to require a little explanation. First, the 10th lord should occupy the 9th; second, in the 9th house, the Navamsa occupied should be an exalted or friendly one; and third, the 10th lord should have attained Uttamamsa. If a planet is in its own varga three times, it is said to be in Uttamamsa.

Chart No. 125.—*Born on 27-3-1902 at 10-15 a.m. (L.M T.) Lat. 31° 43' N.; Long. 77° 35' E.*

Sun Mars	Kethu	Lagna	
Mercury Venus	RASI		
Jupiter Saturn	5.44		
		Moon Rahu	

Moon Merc.			Jupiter
Saturn Rahu	NAVAMSA		Lagna
			Kethu
	Sun Mars	Venus	

Balance of Rahu's Dasa at birth: year 0-9-22.

Chart No. 125 is an example for combination 256. The 10th lord, Saturn, is in the 9th occupying his own (instead of exalted or friendly) Navamsa and Saturn has attained Uttamamsa as he occupies his own vargas thrice.

Two out of three factors, involved in causing Yoga No. 257, are constant, for, the positions of Jupiter and Lagnadhipathi are fixed. It is only the position of the Moon that is variable. The Lagna must be a fixed sign, Jupiter should occupy the 5th from Lagna and the Moon must be in a kendra from Jupiter. Lagnadhipathi should, of course, be in the 10th. When the Moon is to be in a kendra from Jupiter, the existence of Gajakesari Yoga is clearly implied. The Moon could occupy the 2nd, 11th or 8th from Lagna, the first two positions being good, as they would have reference to the houses of wealth and gains (provided the Moon is not blemished by lordship), while the third position is not recommended. As the yoga takes into account the presence of Gajakesari *plus* Jupiter's aspect on Lagna, its potentiality could be considerable, provided, Lagnadhipathi and Jupiter are both strongly disposed. The yoga is capable of a number of variations, as it can arise with regard to four signs and as the Moon's position is variable.

Yoga No. 257 is present in Chart No. 126. Jupiter is in the 5th from Lagna and the Moon is in a kendra from Jupiter. The Lagna is a fixed sign and the lord of Lagna occupies the 10th.

Combination 258 requires the fulfilment of the following conditions. The Moon occupies some Navamsa. The lord of this Navamsa should be in a kendra or thrikona either from Lagna or from Mercury. This does not appear to be a powerful Raja Yoga. It is quite a common combination.

In Chart No. 127, the Moon is in Mesha Navamsa. The lord of the Navamsa, *viz.*, Mars is in a kendra from Mercury and in a thrikona from Lagna. Thus the yoga is present *in toto*. Yet the subject is neither a king nor a big personality. There are quite

Chart No. 126.—*Born on 6-6-1913 at 11-59 a.m. (G.M.T.) Lat. 51° N.; Long. 1° W.*

Rahu	Venus Mars	Saturn Sun Mercury	Moon
	RASI		
			Lagna
Jupiter			Kethu

Kethu	Mars		Saturn
Moon	NAVAMSA		Venus
			Sun
Lagna	Jupiter		Mercury Rahu

Balance of Rahu's Dasa at birth : years 6-2-24.

Chart No. 127—*Born on 10-5-1916 at Gh. 39-15 after sunrise. Lat. 13° N.; Long. 77° 35′ E.*

Jupiter		Sun Mercury	Venus Saturn
	RASI		Kethu
Rahu			Mars
Lagna Moon			

Saturn Rahu Jupit.	Venus Moon Mars		Mercury
Sun	NAVAMSA		
		Lagna	Kethu

Balance of Kethu's Dasa at birth : years 5-4-0.

a number of afflictions present which must have countered the Raja Yoga.

259

Definition.—The Lagna being Taurus with the Moon in it, Saturn, the Sun and Jupiter must occupy the 10th, 4th and 7th houses respectively.

Results.—The person becomes a commander or an equal to a ruler.

Remarks.—The yoga is applicable only to those born in Vrishabha Lagna. The yoga comprehends the strength of four important planets, *viz.*, the Moon exalted in Lagna, Saturn, the Yogakaraka for Vrishabha in the 10th in its own house, the Sun lord of the 4th in his own house, and Jupiter, the greatest benefic in the 7th in the house of a friend, constituting a powerful Gajakesari Yoga. Mars being excluded and yet the yoga being capable of making the person a commander appears somewhat inconsistent. This yoga is taken from the famous work *Sambhuhora Prakasha.* It would be plausible to suppose that under a combination such as this, a democratic tyrant may be born.

260 and 261

Definition.—The lord of the Navamsa occupied by a debilitated planet should join a quadrant or trine from Lagna which should be a movable sign and the lord of the Lagna should also be in a movable sign—260.

The lord of Lagna should join a debilitated planet and Rahu and Saturn should occupy the 10th, aspected by the lord of the 9th—261.

Results.—The native becomes a ruler or an equal to him.

Remarks.—When the Lagna is a movable sign and the Lagnadhipathi occupies a movable sign, the lord of the Navamsa held by a debilitated planet is said to become capable of conferring Raja Yoga, provided the said planet is in a kendra or thrikona from Lagna. This is a round-about combination and I have not tested its practical applicability.

Chart No. 128.—*Born on 21-9-1866 at 3-33 p.m. Lat. 51° 24′ N.; Long. 0° 15′ E.*

Kethu			Mars	Sun Sat.	Rahu	Venus	
	RASI			Mars	NAVAMSA		
Lagna Jupiter Moon	P.N. 10		Merc.	Lagna Jupit.			
		Venus Saturn Mandi	Sun Rahu	Merc.		Kethu Mandi	Moon

Balance of Mars' Dasa at birth: years 5-1-3.

The native of Chart No. 128 was a prince of literature and commanded considerable respect and riches. The Lagna is Makara, a movable sign and the lord Saturn occupies Thula, another movable sign. Jupiter is debilitated and the lord of the Navamsa Jupiter is in, *viz.*, Saturn conferred all the blessings of a Raja Yoga. The above horoscope is clearly illustrative of combination 260.

As regards combination 261, I am unable to appreciate the rationale of a Raja Yoga being caused by the situation of two of the worst malefics, like Rahu and Saturn in the 10th and the conjunction of Lagnadhipathi with a debilitated planet. Probably, the double evil of Rahu-Saturn association aspected by the 9th lord and Lagnadhipathi-neecha planet combination gets mutually cancelled. I should be glad to have the views of scholars who have tested this Raja Yoga. In a couple of horoscopes containing this yoga, which I have seen, it looks as though the debilitated planet gets all the Raja Yoga power while Lagnadhipathi and the two planets in the 10th become enfeebled or weakened to such an extent they can confer no Raja Yoga results.

Chart No. 129.—*Born an 17-11-1944 at 3-17 a.m. (Z.S.T.) Lat. 33° N.; Long. 49° 15' E.*

			Saturn Rahu
	RASI		
Venus Kethu	Mars Moon Mercury Sun		Lagna Jupit.

Sat.			Venus Rahu
	NAVAMSA		Sun Mars Lagna
Jupit.			
Kethu Merc.	Moon		

Balance of Saturn's Dasa at birth · years 1-10-15.

Chart No. 129 has Rahu and Saturn in the 10th and Lagnadhipathi Mercury is with a debilitated planet. Yoga No. 261 is therefore completely present.

262 and 263

Definition.—Out of the lords of the 11th, the 9th and the 2nd houses, at least one planet should be in a kendra from the Moon and Jupiter must be lord of the 2nd, 5th or the 11th house—262.

Jupiter, Mercury, Venus or the Moon should join the 9th, free from combustion and be aspected by or associated with friendly planets—263.

Results.—The native becomes a great man or a respected ruler.

Remarks.—With the above two combinations, the chapter on Raja Yoga is completed. For causing Yoga No. 262, either the 11th lord or the 9th lord or the 2nd lord should be disposed in a kendra from the Moon and Jupiter should own the 2nd, 5th or or 11th and this would be possible, provided the Lagna is Kumbha, Simha, Vrishabha or Vrischika. By implication, it means that the yoga cannot apply to the remaining eight Lagnas.

In Chart No. 130 the 11th lord Mercury is in a kendra from the Moon and Jupiter owns the 2nd as well as the 5th, thus illustrating Yoga No. 262.

Combination 263 is very simple to understand and needs no explanation. Jupiter, Venus, Mercury, or the Moon must be in the 9th house aspected or associated with *friendlly* planets and free from combustion. Here again, due care is necessary to assess the exact nature and strength of the yoga.

Chart No. 130.—*Born on 30-7-1863 at 2-9 p.m. Lat. 42° 5' N.; Long. 83° 5' W.*

		Kethu	
	RASI		Sun Merc.
Moon	P.N. 17		Mars
	Lagna Rahu		Venus Jupit. Sat.

	Saturn Kethu		Mars
	NAVAMSA		Moon
Venus			Lagna
	Sun	Mercury Rahu	Jupiter

Balance of Moon's Dasa at birth : years 2-1-6.

Arishta Yogas

Misfortunes or miseries are more important than fortunes or sources of happiness. The best general is he who first makes and takes suitable precautions to beat a sound retreat and then begins to fight the battle. If success attends his attempts, he will have no difficulty and everything goes off well. But if misfortune overtakes him, he must see and make provision for the safety of his army and give no room for its utter annihilation. Similarly when bright fortunes overtake a man, he will have no difficulty in adjusting his surroundings and enjoying their results but when sudden misfortunes overtake him, he will be not only unnerved but will be at a loss to know how he should meet them. Misfortunes or arishtas are of a wonderful variety and though there is a general resemblance, the feelings of pain and miseries do not appear to be the same among all the individuals. Misfortunes affect persons on three planes two of which, *viz.*, bodily and mental, are demonstrable and the third, *viz.*, pertaining to the soul, is universally recognised though not demonstrable to the naked eye. In a horoscope, ordinarily most of the arishtas have reference to the 6th house, but the Arishta Yogas detailed in this book affect almost all houses. In interpreting Arishta Yogas due consideration should be given to combinations which may act as antidotes or minimising factors.

264. Galakarna Yoga

Definition.—The 3rd house must be occupied by Mandi and Rahu or by Mars in the shashtiamsa of Preta Puriha.

Results.—The native suffers from ear troubles.

Remarks.—According to some astrological treatises, the yoga is also caused by the mere presence of malefics in the 3rd house. But in actual practice, this theory is not borne out. Rahu's disposition in the 3rd house in a cruel shashtiamsa is a sure indication of some sort of trouble in the ear.

For details about shashtiamsas, see my book A MANUAL OF HINDU ASTROLOGY.

265. Vrana Yoga

Definition.—The 6th lord, being a malefic, should occupy the Lagna, 8th or 10th.

Results.—The person suffers from dreadful disease of cancer.

Remarks.—A literal application of the yoga is not at all recommended. *Firstly*, the 6th lord must be a malefic. This would be possible provided the ascendant is Gemini, Leo, Virgo, Scorpio or Pisces. It occurs to me that Scorpio must be excepted as the 6th lord happens to be Lagnadhipathi himself. And *secondly*, he should occupy either the Lagna, the 8th or the 10th. The presence of 6th lord, whether a benefic or malefic, in Lagna is always held to deplete the vitality of the horoscope. Probably, the malefic 6th lord, in addition to weakening the general structure of the horoscope, would also cause physical troubles.

The seat of disease should be located by taking into consideration the planet involved. If the planet in question be the Sun, then the person suffers from cancer of the head; if the planet is the Moon—cancer of the face; Mars—throat or neck (or rectum); Mercury—lower stomach; Jupiter nose; Venus—eyes; Saturn—legs; and Rahu and Kethu—abdomen. If the malefic planet in question is aspected by benefics there will not be much trouble. The allocation of the seat of disease to different planets appears to be incomplete inasmuch as several organs have been omitted.

Cancer is a general name applied to all malignant tumours. Cancer is liable to damage important or vital organs or tissues in the human body. Modern medicine has yet to find a remedy for this diabolical disease. It must be said to the discredit of modern civilisation that the more highly organised and artificial the state of society in a country, the more frequent is the occurrence of cancer.

In Chart No. 131 the 6th lord Mars is a malefic and he is in the 10th, the sign of another malefic and aspected powerfully by Saturn another equally strong malefic. Against these malefic influences, Jupiter's association with Mars is not of much significance. The subject suffered from the cancer of rectum. She suffered for a long time from dreadful pains at the lower end of the spinal column and across the bowels. Mars has governance over rectum. From

Chart No. 131.—*Born on 14-7-1897 at 4 p. m. (L.M.T.) Lat. 41° 15′ N.; Long. 0°.*

		Venus	Merc.
	RASI		Sun Kethu
Moon Rahu			Jupit Mars
	Lagna Saturn		

Moon		Venus Rahu	Mercury
	NAVAMSA		Sun Saturn Mars
	Kethu Lagna		Jupiter

Balance of Sun's Dasa at birth: years 1-1-4.

standard books on the subject, I have been able to gather the following details regarding the rulership of the different organs by the different planets:

Sun—Spleen, heart.

Moon—Oesophagus, alimentary canal.

Mars—Genitals, left cerebral hemisphere, red-colouring matter in blood, rectum.

Mercury—Nerves, right cerebral hemisphere, cerebrospinal system, bronchial tubes, ears, tongue.

Jupiter—Liver, suprarenals.

Venus—Throat, kidneys, uterus, ovaries.

Saturn—Teeth, skin, vagus nerve.

Rahu—Pituitary body.

Kethu—Pineal glands.

This allocation is based upon our own findings. Therefore they could only be provisional and not final. There is, however, considerable scope for research in medical astrology and it is hoped that students of astrology will be able to collect important material by a study of a large number of horoscopes.

266. Sisnavyadhi Yoga

Definition.—Mercury should join Lagna in association with the lords of the 6th and 8th.

Results.—The native will suffer from incurable sexual diseases.

Remarks.—Sisna means sexual organ. Combination 266 merely says that under the planetary dispositions defined by it, one would suffer from sex complaints. Sexual diseases are of various kinds. Hydrocele, epididymitis, orchitis, phimonis, genital fistula, gonorrhoea, tumours of the ovary, dysmennorrhea are all diseases pertaining to the sex, while there are any number of social diseases largely due to sexual perversions and excesses. Classical texts on astrology furnish no clue for predicting such social diseases, probably due to the fact of such diseases not obtaining in ancient times.

In Chart No. 132 Mercury has joined Venus, lord of the 6th, who also happens to be Lagnadhipathi, and there is Bhava conjunction between Mercury and the lord of the 8th Jupiter. Consequently Sisna Yoga is present. The subject suffered from sexual troubles during Jupiter's Dasa.

Combination 266 can be extended by suitable variation, to include different types of sexual diseases.

Saturn's presence in the above combination and the absence of benefic aspects would involve surgical treatment of the sex-organ.

Chart No. 132.—*Born on 13-5-1917 at 6-36 a.m. (I.S.T.) Lat. 20° 53' N.; Long. 75° 39' E.*

	Mars Jupiter	Venus Lagna Sun Mercury	Kethu
	RASI		Saturn
Moon	R. 17		
Rahu			

Balance of Moon's Dasa at birth: years 4-10-2.

267. Kalatrashanda Yoga

Definition.—The lord of the 7th should join the 6th with Venus.

Results.—The person's wife will be frigid.

Remarks.—Impotency is the inability to perform the act of sexual intercourse due to undeveloped sex-organs or excessive indulgence over a long period of time or due to certain psychological inhibitions. In the case of a woman, impotence means inability to give satisfaction to her partner. When the wife is unfit for fulfilling her sexual obligations, the husband should consider himself really unfortunate. In order to make the wife frigid, the 7th lord must be in the 6th with Venus. Since I have not tested this yoga in regard to a large number of horoscopes, I am unable to endorse its practical applicability. Readers will do well to test the combination and convince themselves how far it holds good in actual practice.

268 and 269. Kushtaroga Yogas

Definition.—The lord of Lagna must join the 4th or 12th in conjunction with Mars and Mercury—268.

Jupiter should occupy the 6th in association with Saturn and the Moon—269.

Results.—The person suffers from leprosy.

Remarks.—The dreadful disease of leprosy, though said to be caused by insanitary and unclean habits of living, is generally traced to moral turpitude in one's previous life. In spite of all medical pretensions, leprosy could never really be checked. But during certain periods, it seems to subside slightly. According to combination 268, Lagnadhipathi, Mars and Mercury should be found in the 4th or 12th. Here again the nature of the ascendant and the general strength of the horoscope should be carefully considered. Combination 269 requires the presence of Jupiter, Saturn and the Moon in the 6th. In applying these yogas, due consideration should be given to the disposition of the 6th Bhava. When Saturn, Mercury and Lagnadhipathi are together and Rahu and the Sun are in the 6th, the person suffers from a severe form of leprosy. Lomasa goes to the extent of suggesting that the mere presence of Jupiter and the Moon in the 6th house gives rise to leprosy between the ages of 19 and 22. The truth of this has to be tested by applying the principles to a large number of horoscopes. My Research Department has been collecting a large number of horoscopes of persons suffering from various types of diseases and I hope to place before my esteemed readers, the results of my investigations in due course. I must caution amateur astrologers against coming to premature conclusions regarding the nature of diseases one is likely to suffer from unless they have gained sufficient practical experience.

270. Kshayaroga Yoga

Definition.—Rahu in the 6th, Mandi in a kendra from Lagna, and the lord of Lagna in the 8th gives rise to this yoga.

Results.—The person suffers from tuberculosis.

Remarks.—Combination 270 is very simple to understand and it calls for no explanation. However, I propose to make a few observations on the relation of astrology to disease in general and consumption in particular.

Consumption is a disease of very ancient origin perhaps almost co-eval with man's existence. The Hindus seemed to have known a lot about this disease and even now it is held to be one of the visitations that are to come upon man for the sins committed by him in previous births. This opinion may be held by some to be a mooted question, notwithstanding what was believed but that this together with other diseases was the result of violated law, there could be little doubt. In the recent times deaths by consumption are on the increase in spite of the measures adopted by the medical fraternity to check the infection in its initial stages. There must be something fundamentally wrong with medical theories as regards how one would succumb to this dreadful disease. Medical men seem to be quite ignorant, in spite of the high sounding medical terms they use, of the true cause of this disease. The treatment applied and the measures adopted are curative rather than preventive. Modern medicine has miserably failed to tackle this dreadful disease successfully and therefore it will do well, in the interests of humanity, to seek for the planetary causes of consumption. There are many combinations given in astrological books but such combinations are often made at random and in obscure places and are not indexed or codified. No systematic book has so far been published on medical astrology and the various combinations for diseases lie scattered in the different books. In order to get these combinations into classified form we have conceived the idea of dealing with medical astrology in an elaborate manner. This book when published will enable one to have bird's eye-view of the entire range of astrological science in its application to disease diagnosis. It will give the planetary influences which cause the various diseases, afflictions, events and injuries in life.

According to Karma theory 'all disease is the result of sin or broken law'. The law was not necessarily broken by the individual suffering, but may be by some progenitor dating far back, possibly some generations before the birth of the sufferer. In this way, we have tuberculosis, transmitted hereditarily—may not as disease—but as a tendency to the disease like a weak contracted lung or a general constitutional weakness that could develop into tuberculosis. This tendency is so very well indicated in the horoscope that an adept in astrology can tell whether one is likely to suffer from consumption and if so the probable period.

We have now to digress a bit and state the medical view on the matter. According to medical theories, the disease is transmitted by the tubercular bacilli. Popularly understood, consumption has been regarded as a disease of the lungs. The medical profession is responsible for that popular belief overlooking possibly the fact that consumption may be a disease of any organ.

The tripod of life is famed by the Sun (ego), the Moon (mind) and the Lagna (body) and too much affliction to any or all these three factors will result in some kind of mental or physical disease or disturbance.

The doctrine of infection by bacilli tuberculosis is accepted as the true cause of consumption by all the 'up-to-date' thinkers. Whether this theory has any scientific basis, we shall discuss subsequently.

Suffice it to say that the germ theory of disease has many pitfalls and cannot stand the test of human experience, scientific investigation and common-sense reasoning. If the theory is correct, then all the persons living near consumptive patients should get the disease. In reality, the contrary has been the case. Astrologically, if no combination for consumption is present, then the body of the individual will be immune to the disease even though he may have to live amidst a number of consumptive patients.

Saturn is associated with consumption as its ruler. Tendency to suffer from it is shown in charts in which Saturn and Mars are in the 6th house with powerful aspects by the Sun and Rahu. Lagna being hemmed in between Rahu or Kethu and another malefic indicates death by consumption. The presence of Rahu or Kethu in the 6th is also indicative of tubercular tendencies. If the Moon is severely afflicted, then the root cause of consumption would be mental. If Venus is highly afflicted with Rahu and Mars, then the native may contact consumption after marriage. In such cases, selection of the bride or bridegroom must be carefully made. If the 6th or the 8th lord is with Rahu or Kethu, then also the native is likely to suffer from consumption.

An examination of a large number of horoscopes of persons who have died of consumption reveals that all the malefics have their share of evil to contribute, including of course afflicted Mercury. Consumption of the bowels is caused by Saturn's or Rahu's affliction in Kanya, perticularly when it happens to be Lagna. Inflammatory tubercular trouble in the bowels will be caused if Mars is in a common Navamsa, especially Kanya. Mars in Cancer and aspecting Sun in Libra—the Sun further receiving the aspect or conjunction of Saturn indicates acute phthisis. If the Sun and Saturn are in mutual kendras afflicting the Lagna, death by phthisis is denoted. If Gemini is Lagna or one of the kendras and the Sun occupies the sign being afflicted, pulmonary tuberculosis will be caused. Consumption of the lungs will also occur if the Sun is afflicted in a common sign. The Moon in debilitation, associated with the Sun and aspected by Mars or Saturn gives rise to pulmonary consumption. Various forms of consumption are caused by different malefic combinations and it is not possible to catalogue al! of them here. The above combinations are due to our own studies and observations and we shall herewith inculcate some combinations from ancient texts.

(1) Rahu in the 8th, Mandi in a kendra and lord of Lagna in the 8th cause consumption in the 28th year. (2) Mercury in the 6th with Mars aspected by Venus and the Moon. (3) Mars and Saturn in the 6th aspected by the Sun and Rahu. (4) The Moon hemmed in between Saturn and Mars and the Sun in Capricorn. (5) The Moon in conjunction with Saturn and aspected by Mars. (6) Waxing Moon in a watery sign in conjunction with or aspected by malefics.

We shall now consider two typical horoscopes :

The native of Chart No. 133 had a very strong constitution being an athletic instructor. The Moon powerfully aspected by Saturn without any beneficial associate to relieve, is suggestive that consumption was due to mental worry. Lagna is hemmed in between Rahu and Saturn and Lagnadhipathi is

Chart No. 133.—*Born on 28-6-1897 at 6-50 p.m. (L.M.T.) Lat. 13° N.; Long. 77° 35′ E.*

		Mercury Moon Venus	Sun
	RASI		Kethu
Rahu	M.R.S.		Mars Jupit.
Lagna	Saturn		

	Mars		Rahu
Sun	NAVAMSA		Saturn
Venus			Jupiter
Kethu		Lagna	Moon Mercury

Balance of Mars' Dasa at birth : years 4-2-12.

considerably afflicted. The disease made its appearance in Rahu's sub-period in Jupiter's Dasa and the native died in Saturn's Dasa in his own Bhukti. Mark how Saturn is a maraka and how Jupiter caused the disease.

In Chart No. 134, the Moon in the 5th is aspected by Mars. From the Moon, the 6th is a watery sign occupied by Mars. The 8th lord from the Moon, Mercury, is in the 11th with Rahu and the Sun. The disease made its appearance at the end of Saturn Dasa and the person died in Mercury's sub-period in the Dasa of Mercury.

Chart No. 134.—*Born on 18-12-1898 at about 2-20 a.m. (L.M.T.) Lat. 13° N. ; Long 77° 35′ E.*

			Kethu
Moon			Mars
	RASI		
Sun Mercury Rahu	Saturn Venus	Jupiter Lagna	

Balance of Rahu's Dasa at birth : year 0-0-8.

In order to successfully combat this destructive disease, it is essential that a careful study of the horoscopes of all individuals is made by expert astrologers. This is possible only when the state encourages astrology and gives it at least the status that is enjoyed by medicine. Collect the horoscopes of different individuals and subject them to a thorough astrological analysis. When any tendencies are astrologically present, suitable remedies, astrological as well as medical, should be resorted to. The medical remedies would be stimulating the nutritive or metabolic processes to build and restore the wasted structures of the body and development of the chest by expansion of the lungs in order that deep, full and free breathing may be practical. Saturn, as we have seen, is the prime causer of consumption. Blue rays in sunlight seem to possess Saturnine energy in a considerable measure. By passing sunlight through blue glass, the heat rays are rejected, and blue light which is not sufficiently hot can be obtained. The patient must be subjected to the influence of these blue rays and he will thereby be highly benefited. The influence may be to supply the difficiency of Saturn's rays or it may be the direct action of light on bacilli, or upon the blood which passes underneath the large area bathed in the actinic light. Immediate effects will be seen if the experiment is properly done.

Astrology tells in advance whether a particular horoscope has any consumptive tendencies and if so the period of their manifestation and the remedies to be adopted for the prevention of the disease.

Medicine is 'empirical practice' and therefore not a science. To classify, it is necessary to observe, compare, reflect and record. This the ancient astrologers have done as best as they could from the days of Parasara down to the present time with 'something' of agreement on the part of the leading lights, as embodied in the treatises of experienced authors. Nevertheless, it is proverbial that astrologers like doctors rarely agree and they are honest in their disagreement. The horoscope therefore is the revealer of exact science and when the medical profession begins to consult its aid, then true progress in the diagnosis and classification of disease could be made.

271. Bandhana Yoga

Definition.—If the lord of the Lagna and the 6th join a kendra or thrikona with Saturn, Rahu or Kethu, the above yoga is given rise to.

Results.—The native will be incarcerated.

Remarks.—The cause of the imprisonment is not made clear in this yoga. Imprisonment may be due to political or criminal offences. The lords of Lagna and the 6th should occupy a kendra or thrikona in association with Saturn or Rahu or Kethu. If the lord of Lagna happens to be Saturn, by implication the evil is either lessened or completely neutralised. Benefic aspects lessen the evil.

272. Karascheda Yoga

Definition.—Saturn and Jupiter should be in the 9th and the 3rd.

Results.—The native's hands will be cut off.

Remarks.—The mere presence of Saturn in the 9th and that of Jupiter in the 3rd cannot make one lose one's limbs by way of punishment. It looks far more reasonable to assume that the result ascribed to the yoga can happen only when Saturn and Jupiter are highly afflicted and occupy cruel shashtiamsas. I have not so far come across horoscopes of persons who had their hands cut off. In this age of advancement and civilisation, deprivation of limbs as a means of punishment by the state is inconceivable. This combination, extracted from ancient works, is given for what it is worth. It is for intelligent readers to test its practical applicability.

Karascheda Yoga is also said to arise (*a*) by the disposition of Saturn and Jupiter in the 8th and 12th, (*b*) by the presence of the Moon in the 7th or 8th in association with Mars, and (*c*) by the conjunction of Rahu, Saturn and Mercury in the 10th.

273. Sirachcheda Yoga

Definition.—The lord of the 6th must be in conjunction with Venus while the Sun or Saturn should join Rahu in a cruel shashtiamsa.

Results.—The person's death will be due to his head being cut off.

Remarks.—Combinations denoting cutting off of the head or cutting off of the limbs should be applied consistent with the nature of the punishment now in force in different countries for different offences. Combination 273 indicates death by hanging. The nature of the offence for which one would be condemned to death should be ascertained by a careful study of the 8th house and the nature of the ownership held by the planets causing the yoga. Two conditions must be fulfilled for the operation of the yoga. First, Venus must be with the 6th lord and second, either the Sun or Saturn should be with Rahu in cruel shashtiamsa. This means, Sun-Rahu or Saturn-Rahu should be in the same shashtiamsa. By implication it means that if they are in conjunction but not in the same shashtiamsa, the yoga ceases to function. Some scholars are of the opinion that such rigid interpretation is not justified. They contend that the conjoining planet, *viz.*, Saturn or the Sun, should be in a cruel shashtiamsa and not Saturn or the Sun and Rahu. The *original simply means "the Sun or Saturn being in conjunction with Rahu should occupy a cruel shashtiamsa".

Chart No. 135.—*Born on 30-4-1894 at 11-5 p.m. (L.M.T.) Lat. 51° 31' N., Long. 6° 37' E.*

Rahu Mercury Venus	Sun	Jupiter	
Moon Mars	RASI		
	P. N. 24		
Lagna			Kethu Saturn Mandi

Merc. Mandi	Moon Lagna	Jupiter	Kethu
	NAVAMSA		
			Venus
Rahu		Mars	Sun Saturn

Balance of Jupiter's Dasa at birth: years 13-11-23.

* Ravow Sanou va phaninathayukte krooradi shashtyamsamanviteva.

In Chart No. 135 the lord of the 6th being Venus, the first condition of the yoga is fulfiilled. Saturn has joined Kethu in a cruel shashtiamsa (Rakshasa). The man was hanged by the international tribunal for alleged war crimes.

274. Durmarana Yoga

Definition.—The Moon being aspected by lord of Lagna should occupy the 6th, 8th or 12th in association with Saturn, Mandi or Rahu.

Results.—The person will meet with unnatural death.

Remarks.—The Lagnadhipathi and the Moon are two out of the three most important factors of a horoscope. When they are subjected to such serious afflictions as suggested in the yoga, they are bound to give rise to quite unfavourable results. Unnatural deaths may happen through quite a number of ways and for causing each kind of death there must be a distinct combination.

Death by suicide, death by poisoning, death by weapons, death by being killed by beasts or venomous reptiles, death by drowning, or death by accidents are all unnatural. The following combinations may also be noted :

(*a*) The conjunction of the Sun, Saturn and Rahu in the 7th—death by poisonous reptiles.

(*b*) Mars in Capricorn or Aquarius and Mercury in a house of Jupiter—will be killed by a tiger.

(*c*) Mars in the 9th and Saturn, Rahu and the Sun in association—death by weapons.

(*d*) 4th house being occupied by a debilitated or vanquished planet and the 6th falling in watery sign —death by drowning.

275. Yuddhe Marana Yoga

Definition.—Mars, being lord of the 6th or 8th, should conjoin the 3rd lord and Rahu, Saturn or Mandi in cruel amsas.

Results.—The person will be killed in battle.

Remarks.—Death in a battle fighting for one's own country is always glorified by sages as the gateway to Heaven. The yoga is applicable only to Mesha, Mithuna, Kanya and Vrischika Lagnas as Mars cannot own the 6th or 8th house for other Lagnas. In actual practice, persons born in almost all Lagnas have been killed in battle so that it looks far more reasonable not to restrict the definition of the yoga to the ownership of the 6th or 8th by Mars alone. If the 6th or 8th lord in conjunction with the 3rd lord, and Saturn, Rahu or Mandi occupies cruel amsas, combination 275 may be said to exist. When the 6th or 8th lord happens to be Saturn, then also the yoga could be caused by his association with the 3rd lord and Rahu, Mandi or Mars.

The same yoga is also said to be caused if the lord of the drekkana occupied by Saturn is in a Rasi or Navamsa of Mars or is aspected by Mars.

In Chart No. 136 the lord of the drekkana occupied by Saturn, *viz.*, Mercury is in a Navamsa of Mars.

Chart No. 136.—*Born on 29-7-1883 at 2-5 p.m. (L.M.T.) Lat. 45° 26′ N.; Long. 11° E.*

	Kethu	Moon Mars Saturn	Jupit. Venus
	RASI		Sun Merc.
	1.86		
	Lagna	Rahu	

			Moon Venus Saturn Jupiter
Rahu	NAVAMSA		Lagna Mars
			Kethu
	Sun Mercury		

Balance of the Moon's Dasa at birth : years 3-7-11.

In Chart No. 136 though death did not happen actually in the course of battle yet the end was undoubtedly due to the part played by him in the war. Mars as lord of the 6th and 1st has joined the 3rd lord who also happens to be Saturn. Mark the Mars-Saturn conjunction in the 7th. The subject met with death under tragic conditions.

276 and 277. Sanghataka Marana Yogas

Definition.—If there are many evil planets in the 8th occupying martian Rasi or Navamsa and joining evil sub-divisions the above yoga is given rise to—276.

The Sun, Rahu and Saturn being aspected by the 8th lord should join evil amsas—277.

Results.—The person will die with many others.

Remarks.—Sanghataka Maranas mean collective deaths such as in earthquakes, explosions in mines and factories, sinking of ships, aeroplane crashes, heat and cold waves, railway accidents and the like. If hundreds and thousands of people are to meet with the same kind of death at the same instant, then it is reasonable to assume the presence of some common combinations in all their horoscopes. Whether same or similar combinations are present in regard to all those who die at the same instant and by the same cause, nobody has tested. Here is a fruitful field for research and investigation. In all these misfortunes, malefics, particularly Mars, the 8th house and evil sub-divisions are involved.

278. Peenasaroga Yoga

Definition.—The Moon, Saturn and a malefic should be in the 6th, 8th and 12th respectively and Lagnadhipathi should join malefic Navamsa.

Results.—The person suffers from inflammation of Schneiderian Membrane.

Remarks.—Peenasaroga is a disease of the nose. The nasal canal rots and becomes full of foetid matter and sometimes discharges of blood mixed with pus from the nose. Heaviness of the head, disgust for food, watery discharges from the nose, weakness of the voice and repeated discharges of mucous secretion are symptoms that appear first.

Mercury is the planet associated with the nose and therefore any afflictions to him may find expression in the shape of the person suffering from nasal complaints. In the majority of the horoscopes studied by me, the Moon in the 6th and Lagnadhipathi in a malefic Navamsa has caused Peenasaroga.

Chart No. 137.—*Born on 15-10-1916 at 12-26 p.m. (I.S.T.) Lat. 13° N. ; Long. 77° 35′ E.*

Mandi	Jupiter	Moon	
	RASI		Kethu Sat.
Rahu	6.58		Venus
Lagna	Mars	Sun	Merc.

		Mercury	Moon
	NAVAMSA		Kethu Jupiter Mandi
Rahu			Mars
Lagna		Sun	Venus Saturn

Balance of the Moon's Dasa at birth : years 3-0-9.

The above horoscope is clearly illustrative of Peenasaroga Yoga. The Moon is in the 6th, Saturn is in the 8th and Mars another malefic is in the 12th. Of course, Jupiter Lagnadhipathi, has not joined a malefic Navamsa.

279. Pittaroga Yoga

Definition.—The 6th house must be occupied by the Sun in conjunction with a malefic and further aspected by another malefic.

Results.—The subject suffers from bilious complaints.

Remarks.—According to Ayurveda, the entire psychological activities of the body are controlled and brought about by three important forces or basic factors called *thridoshas*. They are Vatha (wind), Pitta (bile) and Sleshma (phlegm). Pitta is said to be responsible for metabolic activities. The thridoshas when excited or disturbed are said to cause diseases. Each dosha has got its own attributes. For instance, the attributes of pitta are heat, keenness, lightness and slight oiliness. When there is excitement of pitta, the effects are burning, warmth, suppuration, gangrenous ulcerations, secretions and redness of complexion. When there is Pitttavriddhi (increase of bile), there will be disposition to jaundice, sleeplessness and increase of hunger. Pittakshayam (decrease of bile) gives rise to colic troubles. I would refer the reader to standard works on Ayurveda for greater details. The Sun's position in the 6th by itself is good. When the Sun is in the house of diseases, joined and aspected by malefics, the native's health will not be good and he will always suffer from one complaint or the other due to excitement of pitta or bile.

280. Vikalangapatni Yoga

Definition.—Venus and Sun should occupy the 7th, 9th or 5th house.

Results.—The person's wife will have deformed limbs.

Remarks.—The mere presence of the Sun and Venus in the 5th, 7th or 9th cannot cause the yoga in question. There must be further afflictions for these two planets.

281. Putrakalatraheena Yoga

Definition.—When the waning Moon is in the 5th and malefics occupy the 12th, 7th and Lagna, the above yoga is formed.

Results.—The person will be deprived of his family and children.

Remarks.—In applying most of these yogas, it is experience and commonsense that should guide the reader. So far as this yoga is concerned, three variations for each Lagna or 36 variations in all are possible. The results in respect of all these variations cannot be same and they are bound to differ with regard to each variety of the yoga. The position of the Moon is constant or fixed. The malefics can change their positions. Thus the Moon is in the 5th and (*a*) the Sun in the 12th, Mars in the 7th and Saturn in Lagna; (*b*) Mars in the 12th, Saturn in the 7th and the Sun in Lagna; and (*c*) Saturn in the 12th, Mars in Lagna and the Sun in the 7th are the three varieties of the same yoga for a Lagna.

282. Bharyasahavyabhichara Yoga

Definition.—Venus, Saturn and Mars must join the Moon in the 7th house.

Results.—The husband and wife will both be guilty of adultery.

Remarks.—Mark the number and nature of the planets involved in the 7th house combination. The Moon-Saturn association denotes mental depression, due to want of satisfaction of the sexual urge denoted by Mars-Venus association. It will be seen that the chronic adulterers and adulteresses, the deliberate hunters for opportunities are either over-sexed (again Mars-Venus conjunction) or their cultural inhibitions (Mars-Saturn association) are underdeveloped.

Owing to the limited scope of this book, I have referred to one or two yogas in respect of each human event but I may make a casual reference to some of the horoscopes in my possession, which do not actually have combination 282 but which nevertheless are fully illustrative of sexual perversion and adultery of both the husband and the wife. Satyriasis (sexual insatiability in men) and nymphomania (sexual insatiability in women) are supposed by sexologists to be the two main causes for adultery. Nymphomania is frequently associated with mental disorder with the result higher inhibitions are eliminated.

In Chart No. 138, the 7th lord Mercury is in the 10th in conjunction with Venus and aspected by Saturn. The 7th house is aspected by Kethu, Saturn and Mars. Mark also the affliction of both Venus and the Moon by Saturn and Mars respectively. Though the native belonged to a respectable family, he was a glutton for the sexual experience. He could never

Chart No. 138.—*Born on 10-10-1871 at 2 p.m. (L.M.T.) Lat. 51° 26′ N.; Long. 2° 35′ W.*

			Rahu
	RASI		Jupit.
	P.N. 36		Moon
Lagna Kethu Saturn	Mars		Sun Merc. Venus

	Mercury	Kethu	Moon
Venus	NAVAMSA		
			Saturn Sun
Mars	Lagna Rahu		Jupiter

Balance of Kethu's Dasa at birth: years 1-9-25.

adapt himself to the requirements of the marriage with the result he went after every woman, respectable or disrespectable whom he could trap through the usual 'social contacts'. As he himself confessed to me just before his death, his wife was equally oversexed and experienced an irresistible compulsion to surrender to any man if an opportunity arose. The couple had agreed between themselves in regard to one thing, *viz.*, that each should have his or her own way so far as their sex life was concerned. Debauchery, drunkenness and mental instability were common to both. Unfortunately, the wife's horoscope is not available.

283. Vamsacheda Yoga

Definition.—The 10th, 7th and 4th must be occupied by the Moon, Venus and malefics respectively.

Results.—The person will be the extinguisher of his family.

Remarks.—Family extinction is considered to be one of the greatest misfortunes that could befall a man. The yoga as defined above is somewhat rare. In actual experience, we find the Moon and Venus in the 7th and malefics in the 4th and 10th would lead to family extinction.

284. Guhyaroga Yoga

Definition.—The Moon should join malefics in the Navamsa of Cancer or Scorpio.

Results.—The person suffers from diseases in the private parts.

Remarks.—Diseases in the private parts include piles, hernia and complicated forms of sexual troubles. According to this, the Moon may occupy any sign. But he must be in the Navamsa of Cancer or Scorpio. I am afraid that so general a definition of the yoga is not warranted by experience. The Moon in Cancer Rasi and Scorpio Navamsa, or *vice versa*, is also capable of giving rise to diseases in private parts.

The Moon in Chart No. 139 has joined a malefic in the Navamsa of Cancer. The person was suffering from bleeding piles since 1914. He also has dyspepsia and palpitation of the heart. It is amazing how most of these combinations can be so clearly illustrated in actual horoscopes.

Chart No. 139.—*Born on 26-8-1892 at 2-30 a.m. (L.M.T.) Lat. 12° 52′ N.; Long. 74° 54′ E.*

	Jupiter Rahu		Venus Lagna
	RASI		
Mars	R. 71		Sun Merc.
		Kethu	Moon Saturn

Saturu	Kethu	Jupiter Lagna	Mars Venus
	NAVAMSA		Moon Sun Mercury
		Rahu	

Balance of the Moon's Dasa at birth : years 1-5-21.

285. Angaheena Yoga

Definition.—When the Moon is in the 10th, Mars in the 7th and Saturn in the 2nd from the Sun, the above yoga is formed.

Results.—The person suffers from loss of limbs.

Remarks.—The original word used for defining the results of the yoga is Vikalaha or loss of limbs. This may mean deprivation of the use of, certain parts of the body by attacks of rheumatism or paralysis or by injuries inflicted by weapons or wild beasts. My book on *Medical Astrology* gives quite a number of combinations for paralysis, rheumatism and other forms of diseases with suitable illustrations.

286. Swetakushta Yoga

Definition.—If Mars and Saturn are in the 2nd and 12th, the Moon in Lagna and the Sun in the 7th, the above yoga is given rise to.

Results.—The person suffers from white leprosy.

Remarks.—Ayurveda comprehends varieties of Kushta Rogas falling under two main categories, *viz., Mahakushta* and *Kshudra kushta.* The horoscope does not say that the subject must get the disease. It merely shows the predisposition. Kshudra kushta or simple leprosy is said to be curable. When Jupiter aspects either Mars or Saturn in the above yoga, the disease could be checked by medicines and other astrological remedies.

Yoga No. 286 in Chart No. 140 is clearly present. Lagna has Saturn in the 12th and Mars in the 2nd and the Moon occupies Lagna and the Sun the 7th.

Chart No. 140.—*Born on 3-4-1920 at 5-13 p.m. (I.S.T.) Lat. 17° N. ; Long. 78° 15' E.*

Sun Mercury	Kethu		
Venus	RASI		Jupit.
			Sat.
		Rahu Mars	Lagna Moon

		Rahu	Venus
Lagna Mars	NAVAMSA		Moon Mercury
Sun			Saturn
Jupit.	Kethu		

Balance of Moon's Dasa at birth : year 0-7-11.

287. Pisacha Grastha Yoga

Definition.—When Rahu is in Lagna in conjunction with the Moon and the malefics join trines, the above yoga is given rise to.

Results.—The person suffers from the attacks of 'spirits'.

Remarks.—This yoga is similar to 288 given on page 290 except that the Moon here takes the place of the Sun in the next yoga. The Moon's conjunction with Rahu and Saturn is always undesirable as it makes the person mentally unsound. Whilst it may be conceded that some super-normal phenomena such as "possession by devils", etc., may be proved to be due to abnormal conditions of the brain, yet there will be found to remain well-attested facts which will compel science to admit the existence of pisachas, devils, spirits, hobgoblins and the like. Pisachas are supposed to be discarnate intelligent beings, some of whom occasionally get into communication with us through "mediums" or persons who are weak-minded. Various experiences recorded by trustworthy men do afford strong *prima facie* evidence of survival after *death* and pisachas are said to be souls of less evolved persons whose spiritual development is deficient and who die an early death without tasting any earthly pleasures. The subject of pisachas is a vast one and I would refer my readers to standard books on the subject particularly to

Dr. Ghose's *Adventures with Evil Spirits.* When the Moon is with Rahu and Saturn, or Saturn aspects Moon-Rahu combination, especially in Lagna, the person doubtless suffers from evil spirits or devils.

288 and 289. Andha Yogas

Definition.—The Sun must rise in Lagna in conjunction with Rahu and malefics should be disposed in thrikonas—288.

Mars, the Moon, Saturn and the Sun should respectively occupy the 2nd, 6th, 12th and 8th—289.

Results.—The person will be born stone-blind.

Remarks.—The Sun and the Moon are said to rule the right eye and the left eye respectively. The 12th house governs the left eye and the 2nd, the right eye. According to combination 288, the Sun is subject to severe affliction by association with Rahu and the 12th house by being aspected by Mars. Out of the four malefics, as the Lagna is to be occupied by the Sun and Rahu, the two others left, *viz.*, Saturn and Mars will have to be in thrikonas, *i.e.*, the 5th and 9th. Irrespective of whether Mars is in the 5th or 9th, he would be aspecting the 12th. If Saturn is in the 5th, he could aspect the 2nd ; if he is in the 9th, neither the 12th nor the 2nd would receive his aspect. The Moon is completely excluded.

Combination 289 can be considered more malignant because all the factors ruling the eyes, *viz.*, the Sun and the Moon and the 2nd and 12th houses become subject to the aspects or associations of Mars and Saturn. When Mars is in the 2nd and the Sun in the 8th, both the 2nd and the Sun are afflicted. When the Moon is in the 6th and Saturn is in the 12th, both the 12th and the Moon get involved. Since the 2nd house becomes more afflicted than the 12th, by virtue of martian position and Saturn's aspect, one born in this yoga would either be stone-blind or completely lose his right eye.

In actual practice, we find that when the 12th and 2nd houses, and the Sun and the Moon are in conjunction with or aspected by malefic planets or when they are in evil shadvargas, the subject will have either defective vision, loss of an eye, or complete loss of sight depending upon the intensity of the affliction.

Mark in Chart No. 141 the following evil combinations. The 2nd is aspected by Saturn. Both the Moon and the 12th have the conjunction of Saturn and the aspect of Mars. The native, a lady, is completely blind. Besides blindness, there is trouble with the elimination of the urine and bleeding piles.

290. Vatharoga Yoga

Definition.—When Jupiter is in Lagna and Saturn in the 7th house, the above yoga is caused.

Results.—The person suffers from windy complaints.

Remarks.—Jupiter in Lagna and Saturn in the 7th get Digbala. Depending upon their strengths, these planets may cause Raja Yoga also. But that does not deprive them of their capacity to cause diseases appropriate to their nature. When Jupiter is in Lagna, the person will have a tendency towards corpulence and a stout body is a breeding place for windy complaints. We have already observed elsewhere that according to Ayurveda, disease is due to the vitiation or excitement of one or more of the three doshas or basic factors. The attributes ascribed to Vayu are dryness, lightness and clearness. The indications of its abnormal functions are cheerlessness, pain in the body, swelling, contractions, numbness or paralysis of limbs. When there is Vathavriddhi (increase in wind) one is likely to suffer from constipation, flatulence, sleeplessness, loss of enthusiasm and fainting. When there is Vathakshayam (decrease in wind), one will suffer from emaciation, fainting and increase of hunger. Apart from the Raja Yoga aspect, Jupiter in Lagna aspected by Saturn in the 7th is not good for sound health. This is a powerful combination for rheumatism.

Chart No. 141—*Born on 13-6-1873 at 11-55 p.m. (L.M.T.) Lat. 42° N.; Long. 75° E.*

	Venus	Rahu	Sun Merc.
Lagna	RASI		
Moon Saturn			Jupit.
	Kethu	Mars	

Moon	Lagna Saturn	Jupiter	
	NAVAMSA		Kethu
Rahu			
Merc. Mars		Venus Sun	

Balance of the Sun's Dasa at birth: year 0-0-3.

In Chart No. 142 mark the disposition of Jupiter in Lagna and Saturn in the 7th. The martian aspect on Rahu is also not desirable. The native suffered from rheumatism and fallen arches.

Chart No. 142.—*Born on 14-8-1912 at 1-7 p.m. (I.S.T.) Lat. 13° N.; Long. 5h. 10m. 20s. E.*

Rahu		Saturn	
	RASI		Sun
			Moon Mars Merc. Venus
	Lagna Jupiter		Kethu

Sun	Saturn		
Rahu	NAVAMSA		Venus
			Mercury Kethu
	Mars Jupiter	Lagna Moon	

Balance of Venus' Dasa at birth: years 8-6-27.

291 to 294. Matibhramana Yogas

Definition.—Jupiter and Mars should occupy the Lagna and the 7th respectively—291.

Saturn must be in Lagna and Mars should join the 9th, 5th or 7th—292.

Saturn must occupy the 12th with the waning Moon—293.

The Moon and Mercury should be in a kendra, aspected by or conjoined with any other planet—294.

Results.—The person becomes insane.

Remarks.—The rationale of the various combinations for various diseases is not easily discernible. But when these combinations are present in the horoscopes of a large number of persons suffering from lunacy and insanity, we are justified in concluding that these various yogas are not merely the product of imagination, but that they must have been the result of keen observation and study on the part of the sages.

Four yogas for insanity are given above. They result by a certain juxtaposition of Saturn, Jupiter, Mars, the Moon and Mercury. In my humble opinion, combination 291 does not seem as harmful as it is said to be. I am convinced that unless the Moon and Mercury are involved in heavy afflictions, insanity or lunacy cannot be present. To assume that insanity always results by nervous debility which in its turn is due to mental disturbances is to ignore the fundamentals of commonsense, reasoning and ordinary logic. The mind is no doubt the root cause but the root cause itself is conditioned by certain acts done in the previous life so that a human being, however normal he may appear to be for all practical purposes, would lose the mental equilibrium when the moment for the fructification of the karmaic results expressed as sidereal influences arrives.

Astrologically, it is certainly possible to say in advance whether one is likely to suffer from insanity so that if indications are present, an environment from very early life may be so created as to lessen the chances of the individual's violent reactions to nervous and mental shocks.

According to Ayurveda, various causes bring about insanity, chief among them being inhormoniously combined food, certain poisons, insults to Gods, the pious, elders and preceptors; sudden fear or joy or grief, and acts which put a severe strain upon the nervous system, excite the doshas (three humours) and vitiate the seat of the understanding, the heart and all those ducts by which the mind communicates with the organs of sense. This leads to the disturbance of the mind causing insanity. Insanity is therefore a mental disease. The mind becomes restless and vacant, the vision becomes stale, and actions become purposeless and speech incoherent. Insanity born of the 'faults' is curable by administering medicine. Gluttony in the absence of proper physical exercise is said to provoke kapha (phlegm); the excited phlegm mixes with pitta (bile) and produces what is called kapha-born insanity. Each planet is said to rule a certain humour and when the said planet is highly afflicted and adversely situated with reference to the Moon or Mercury some form of insanity cannot be ruled out. One should be very careful in analysing horoscopes for this purpose. It is always advisable that such diagnosis be left to specialists in medical astrology as otherwise grave repercussions will follow. The following are the assignments of planetary rulerships for the three humours—the Sun—bile (pitta); the Moon—wind and phlegm (vayu and kapha); Mars—bile; Mercury—all the three; Jupiter—phlegm;

Venus—too much wind and phlegm; Saturn—wind. Mercury in the 6th afflicted by conjunction with Saturn is indicative of some form of insanity appearing especially in Sani Dasa, Budha Bhukthi or *vice versa.* The cause of madness in this case is physical and therefore the disease is curable. Sanskrit works describe that insanity in a large number of cases is caused by certain spirits of departed individuals, the asuras, yakshas and even pisachas and a sort of insanity is generated Whilst we may not accept this statement as 'sensible', let us not condemn it as superstitious or dismiss it lightly. It is full of significance and comprehends several of the psychological and psychoanalytical causes. Some insane people behave very violently while others are harmless. Medicine can give no explanations for these 'vagaries'. On the other hand, astrology can offer a reasonable explanation. Insanity caused by 'obsession' or 'possession' is hardly curable. It can be checked if treated within thirteen years; otherwise it becomes incurable.

From an astrological standpoint, this disease is to be viewed primarily from the afflictions to Lagna, the 6th house, the Moon and Mercury. Whether mental derangement is the resultant of 'obsession' or due to physiological causes can be easily ascertained from the horoscope. Rahu determines the issue. If the powerful affliction of Mercury or Lagna or the Moon has the contact of Rahu, one may be certain that no medical treatment would be of any avail. One has to seek remedies other than medical.

In a disease of this magnitude, the configuration and aspects in the horoscope must necessarily be very severe. In studying this disease, the Moon and Mercury should be primarily considered. Mental weakness is more apt to result where there is no aspect at birth between the Moon and Mercury and also when neither is disposed favourably from the Lagna; and at the same time greatly afflicted. If Saturn be the afflictor in a day birth, epilepsy is more apt to occur but in a night chart, if Rahu be the afflictor, insanity may follow. Virgo and Pisces are sensitive signs and afflictions occurring in them are always undesirable. If, on the other hand, Mars be the afflictor, insanity may prevail during the day and epilepsy during the night. In insanity, the Lagna is not necessarily afflicted but in epilepsy, the ascendant is usually badly aspected or conjoined. Before proceeding further, I shall take a typical case for illustration. I am purposely omitting the birth details as readers can easily follow my arguments without these particulars :

Lagna		Moon	
Jupiter Kethu	RASI		
Venus	P.N. 17		Rahu
Sun Mars Mercury	Saturn		

Lagna			
Jupit. Kethu	NAVAMSA		Saturn Moon Venus
			Mercury Rahu
	Sun Mars		

Although we may be unable to predict the dates of crisis with the present state of development in medical astrology, we can very easily say that the native is bound to suffer from insanity. Lagna is Pisces, a sensitive sign and the lord is in the 12th with Kethu. Let alone this combination as it made him highly stoical, religious and philosophical. The most important combinations relevant to the present discussion are :—

(1) The 6th is occupied by Rahu and aspected by Kethu.

(2) The 6th lord is further afflicted by conjunction with Mars.

(3) The planet of nerves Mercury is in a common sign in conjunction with two malefics, *viz.*, Mars and the Sun.

(4) In the Navamsa again Mercury occupies the 6th with Rahu and the 6th lord is in conjunction with Mars.

The benevolent aspect of Jupiter on the 6th is sterilised as he is with Kethu. The Moon being aspected by Saturn, the planet of gloom and melancholy, made the mind morbid. On account of all these adverse and perverse influences, the poor man was erratic, reckless and gloomy. Mark particularly the association of Mercury and Rahu in Amsa, Rahu's situation in the 6th in Rasi and the planet of nerves and brain in Sagittarius with Mars and the Sun (lord of the 6th) and the latter two planets in exact conjunction. A more typical case could not have been thought of. Mercury's Dasa commenced and the man was taken violently insane and had to be confined in an asylum. At this time Saturn was transiting the exact degree occupied by Mercury. This cannot be a coincidence. Our grand-father (late Prof. B. Suryanarain Rao) had warned 15 years before that when Mercury Dasa commenced, the native would become mad and might even be put into an asylum. The person was too proud to listen to his astrological advice. In 1938, the son of this subject consulted us about the longevity. Saturn causing *elarata* for the third time and a Maraka Dasa operating, we predicted that his death would happen when Saturn entered Aswini. Unfortunately the prediction was realised. So long as the person remained in the asylum, there was little or no improvement in regard to the mental condition. It is no doubt a hopeless case. But still Jupiter's aspect could have been made to operate by properly conditioning the environment when the first warning was given. In dealing with the question of insanity, we must always bear in mind that it is a rupture between the physical body and the vital body. Before naming the next yoga we may just mention a few more combinations, most of which are the result of our own observations :—

(1) The conjunction of Mercury and Gulika especially in the 6th house.

(2) The Moon in conjunction with Kethu and Saturn.

(3) Saturn and Mars in an angle but causing Papadhi Yoga from the Moon or from Mercury.

(4) Saturn and Rahu conjunction especially in the first degree of Virgo, Lagna being either Pisces or Virgo.

(5) Mars powerfully aspecting or in conjunction with Mercury in the 6th or 8th house.

(6) Mutable signs on the angles and greatly afflicted.

The astrologer, professional or amateur, would be rendering a distinct disservice to society if he attempts to predict insanity on superficial grounds. The general strength or weakness of the horoscope should not be ignored. Let readers use astrology to help and to heal and not to wound. Even if there are any indications to the effect, they must not be revealed direct to the person concerned. The nearest relatives and friends who have the good of the person should be told, so that they might take the necessary preventive measures. A weak-willed person may become despondent and will be surrounded by imaginary troubles. The *Meteria Medica* is easy to read, but it is only a specialist who can diagnose a disease properly and prescribe the remedy.

295. Khalwata Yoga

Definition.—The ascendant must be a malefic sign or Sagittarius or Taurus aspected by malefic planets.

Results.—The person will be bald-headed.

Remarks.—Astrological writers consider baldness as an arishta or misfortune. According to the definition given above, birth in a malefic sign., *viz.*, Aries, Leo, Scorpio, Capricorn or Aquarius, or in Taurus or Sagittarius gives rise to this yoga provided the Lagna is aspected by malefic planets. The type and time of onset of ordinary baldness cannot be easily found out with the aid of astrological knowledge as at present known. Examples of horoscopes for baldness could be had in plenty and therefore I do not propose to add an illustration for this yoga.

296. Nishturabhashi Yoga

Definition.—The Moon must be in conjunction with Saturn.

Results.—The person will be harsh in speech.

Remarks.—If Jupiter aspects the Moon-Saturn conjunction, the yoga gets neutralized. If the aspecting planet is Mars, then the person will not only be harsh and blunt in his speech but sarcastic also.

297. Rajabhrashta Yoga

Definition.—The lords of Aroodha Lagna and Aroodha Dwadasa should be in conjunction.

Results.—The subject will suffer a fall from high position.

Remarks.—Most astrologers pay attention to Raja Yogas and Dhana Yogas and hardly take into account combinations which either act as breaks to the functioning of Raja Yogas or completely neutralise the Raja Yogas with the result horoscope judgments invariably go wrong. When Raja Yogas are really more powerful than Rajabhanga Yogas, then alone the former could function. Aroodha Lagna is the sign arrived at by counting as many signs from Lagnadhipathi as the Lagnadhipathi is removed from Lagna. Similarly, Aroodha Dwadasa Rasi is as many signs away from the 12th lord as the 12th lord is from the 12th house. Supposing Lagna is Aries and the lord Mars is in Leo. Then the 5th from Leo, *viz.*, Sagittarius would be Aroodha Lagna. Likewise if the 12th is Pisces; and the 12th lord, *viz.*, Jupiter is in Taurus (the 3rd from 12th), then the Dwadasarudha would be Cancer, the 3rd from the 12th lord. In a horoscope, where Lagna is Aries and Lagnadhipathi is in Leo and the 12th lord Jupiter is in Gemini, Lagnarudha would be Sagittarius and Dwadasarudha would be Virgo. Conjunction between these two lords, *viz.*, Mercury and Jupiter would result in a Rajabhrashta Yoga.

298 and 299. Raja Yoga Bhangas

Definition.—The ascendant being Leo, Saturn must be in exaltation occupying a debilitated Navamsa or aspected by benefics—298.

The Sun must occupy the 10th degree of Libra —299.

Results.—The person though born in a royal family will be bereft of fortune and social position.

Remarks—Both the above yogas are quite simple to understand and they need no explanation. Yoga No. 298 requires that Saturn should occupy a debilitated Navamsa in his exaltation sign, and the Lagna must be Leo. This means Saturn must occupy the first pada of the constellation of Visakha or Libra 20° to 23° 20′. As for Yoga No. 299, the Sun must be in deep debilitation. I am afraid, in the absence of other powerful arishtas, the mere debilitation of the Sun cannot destroy all the Raja Yogas and render the person unfortunate and miserable.

Chart No. 143.—*Born on 14-5-1896 at Gh. 17 after sunrise. Lat. 13° N.; Long. 77° 35′ E.*

Mars	Venus	Sun Moon Mercury			Saturn		Kethu Lagna
Rahu	RASI		Jupit.		NAVAMSA		Moon
	1.138		Kethu Lagna	Sun			Mars Mercury
		Saturn		Rahu		Jupiter	Venus

Balance of Moon's Dasa at birth : years 2-5-21.

In Chart No. 143 the Lagna is Leo, Saturn is exalted in Rasi, debilitated in Navamsa and aspected by Mars. The Raja Yoga formed in the 10th house has been rendered infructuous.

300. Gohanta Yoga

Definition.—A malefic devoid of benefic aspect in a kendra and Jupiter in the 8th house gives rise to this yoga.

Results.—The person becomes a butcher.

Remarks.—Butchery was held by the framers of these yogas to be a disrespectable and degrading avocation. But in the modern world, especially in the West, no stigma could attach to the profession or butchery. The yoga is said to arise by the mere presence of Jupiter in the 8th and a malefic in kendra unaspected by benefics. I have not been able to test this yoga adequately. Any further observations would be unwarranted. I would refer the readers to Stanza 2 of Chapter XIX of *Brihat Jathaka*. When the Moon in Libra is aspected by Mars or Saturn, the native is supposed to become cruel. Some commentators suggest, by implication, that the person could take to occupations involving cruelty to animals. Unless one is hard-hearted and lacks the respect and sanctity for life, one cannot think of taking to an occupation involving the slaughtering of thousands of innocent lives. When the Moon is in the 1st quarter of Visakha and powerfully aspected by Saturn and the Sun, he would not only be lacking humanitarian feelings but would be completely impervious to human suffering.

Summary

We have been able to cover in the course of this book, *three hundred yogas.* In classical works on astrology are mentioned thousands of yogas bearing on every aspect of human activity. Yoga in astrology may be defined as a special combination indicating some definite or distinct feature pertaining to a particular signification of the horoscope. Yogas may be formed in several ways, but we can recognise three broad varieties, *viz.*, yogas formed between planets themselves ; yogas formed between planets and Rasis ; and yogas formed between planets and Bhavas.

The measurement of the strength of a yoga is a difficult process. No hard and fast rules have been laid down by ancient astrologers. Planets have been classified into benefics and malefics consistent with their inherent good or bad natures. In the formation of the several of the Raja Yogas, even these natural malefics have their own part to play. Just because a natural malefic causes a Raja Yoga, it does not mean that the yoga lacks vitality to give the results attributed to it. On the contrary, if the malefic happens to be a *benefic lord* also, then the potentiality of the yoga is considerably augmented. Similarly there is no warrant that a Raja Yoga could give rise to all the results ascribed to it simply because it is caused by a benefic. If the benefic happens to be a malefic lord, there will be adverse repercussions on the yoga. Readers must therefore note the difference between a benefic and a benefic lord and a malefic and a malefic lord. Jupiter, for instance, is a benefic but for Kumbha Lagna, he is a malefic lord. Therefore a benefic can become a benefic lord or a malefic lord depending upon the kind of ownership he obtains for a given Lagna. Likewise a malefic can become a malefic lord or a benefic lord depending on the kind of ownership he obtains for a given Lagna. The Sun could be a benefic lord as owning 1, 4, 7, 10, 5 and 9 which is possible in regard to Leo, Taurus, Aquarius, Scorpio, Aries and Sagittarius. He is neutral as lord of 2, 12 and 8, which is possible for Cancer, Virgo and Capricorn. He becomes a malefic lord as owner of 3, 6 and 11, which is possible for Gemini, Pisces and Libra. Other planets can become benefic and malefic lords as already elaborated from pages 3 to 5 to which the reader may refer.

As regards the interpretation of yogas, we do not have infallible clues in any of the classical works. The inherent and residential strengths of planets calculated as per methods outlined in my *Graha and Bhava Balas* will be of great use in assessing the potentiality of the Yogarkarakas. If the reader finds it difficult to ascertain the shadbalas owing to the cumbersomeness of the methods, at least the *saptavargabala* of the planets should be calculated. The residential strength of a planet is one when it is in the midpoint of a house and zero at the bhava sandhi or the beginning and termination points of the bhavas. The residential strength of a planet situated in the Poorvabhaga (between the first and the mid-point) can be obtained by the following formula :—

$$\frac{\text{Longitude of Bhavamadhya} - \text{Longitude of the planet}}{\text{Longitude of Bhavamadhya} - \text{Longitude of Arambha Sandhi}}$$

For a planet situated in the Uttarabhaga (between the mid and last points) the residential strength could be obtained thus :—

$$\frac{\text{Longitude of Bhavasandhi} - \text{Longitude of planet}}{\text{Longitude of Bhavasandhi} - \text{Longitude of Bhavamadhya}}$$

Residential strength reveals how much of the bhava effects a planet is capable of giving as a result of its position there. When we know (*a*) the benefic and malefic lords, (*b*) the inherent, and (*c*) the residential strengths of planets, the interpretation of yogas becomes simplified. A Yogakaraka could get strength (*a*) by being a benefic or good lord—1 unit, (*b*) by association with a benefic lord—1 unit, (*e*) by occupying own or exaltation house—1 unit, and (*d*) by receiving the aspect of a benefic lord $\frac{1}{4}$, $\frac{1}{2}$, $\frac{3}{4}$ or 1 unit depending upon the partial or full nature of the aspect.

All planets aspect the 7th house and the planet or planets therein fully. Saturn, in addition to the 7th house, aspects the 3rd and 10th also fully ; other planets aspect the 3rd and 10th with a quarter aspect. Jupiter, in addition to the 7th house, aspects the 5th and 9th also fully. Other planets aspect the 5th and 9th with half aspect. Mars, in addition to 7th house, aspects the 4th and 8th houses fully. Other planets aspect the 4th and 8th with a three-fourths aspect. We can enter the above aspects thus in a tabulated form :—

Planet	Full	$\frac{3}{4}$	$\frac{1}{2}$	$\frac{1}{4}$
Sun	7	4, 8	5, 9	3, 10
Moon	7	4, 8	5, 9	3, 10
Mars	7, 4, 8	...	5, 9	3, 10
Mercury	7	4, 8	5, 9	3, 10
Jupiter	7, 5, 9	4, 8	...	3, 10
Venus	7	4, 8	5, 9	3, 10
Saturn	7, 3, 10	4, 8	5, 9	...

The aspects of Rahu and Kethu need not be considered for this purpose.

A Yogakaraka could lose strength by being (*a*) a malefic or bad lord, (*b*) by associating with a malefic lord, (*c*) by joining neecha or inimical sign, and (*d*) by receiving the aspect of a malefic lord—$\frac{1}{4}$, $\frac{1}{2}$, $\frac{3}{4}$ or 1 unit depending upon the partial or full nature of the aspect.

For purpose of illustration let me take the horoscope of a person born on 8-8-1912 at 7-23 p.m. (L.M.T.) at Lat. 13° N., Long. 5h. 10m. 20s. E. The following are the Rasi and Navamsa positions and the residential and inherent strengths :—

Rahu		Moon Saturn	
Lagna	RASI		Sun
			Mars Merc. Venus
	Jupiter		Kethu

	Saturn Venus		
	NAVAMSA		Kethu
Lagna Rahu Sun			Mercury Moon
	Jupiter	Mars	

Balance of Mars' Dasa at birth : years 5-6-15.

	Inherent Strengths	Residential Strengths
Sun	6.2	24 per cent
Moon	8.9	40 "
Mars	6.4	31 "
Mercury	6.3	80 "
Jupiter	6.9	90 "
Venus	5.0	37 "
Saturn	6.8	95 "
Rahu (same as Jupiter)	6.9	24 "
Kethu (same as Mercury)	6.3	24 "

The benefic or malefic nature of aspect on a body or house is the sum-total of aspects of benefic and malefic lords. Take for instance, the Sun who is in the house in the *Standard Horoscope*. The aspects of Saturn, a benefic lord (positive) and of Jupiter a malefic lord (negative) are full (1 unit each). The Moon's aspect is 1/4th (negative or —). The sum-total of the three aspects is — 1/4 and hence the Sun (as well as the 6th house) is slightly afflicted by aspect.

The following is the table of aspects in the *Standard Horoscope* :—

Aspected Planets	*ASPECTING PLANETS							
	B.L. Sun +	M.L. Moon −	M.L. Mars −	N.L. Merc. ±	M.L. Jupit. −	B.L. Venus +	B.L. Sat. +	Total
Sun	....	$\frac{1}{4}$		....	1	....	1	$-\frac{1}{4}$
Moon	....	....	$\frac{1}{4}$	$\frac{1}{4}$	1	$\frac{1}{4}$	....	$-\frac{3}{4}$
Mars	....	$\frac{3}{4}$	....	....	$\frac{1}{4}$	....	$\frac{3}{4}$	$-\frac{1}{4}$
Mercury	....	$\frac{3}{4}$	....	....	$\frac{1}{4}$	....	$\frac{3}{4}$	$-\frac{1}{4}$
Jupiter	$\frac{1}{2}$	1	1	$\frac{3}{4}$	....	$\frac{3}{4}$	1	+1
Venus	....	$\frac{3}{4}$	....	....	$\frac{1}{4}$	....	$\frac{3}{4}$	$-\frac{1}{4}$
Saturn	....	....	$\frac{1}{4}$	$\frac{1}{4}$	1	$\frac{1}{4}$	....	$-\frac{3}{4}$

In the illustrated horoscope, let us take the planets Jupiter and the Moon, the two planets causing Gajakesari.

The Moon is a malefic lord		— 1 unit
The Moon is associated with Saturn, a benefic lord	....	+ 1 ,,
The Moon is exalted	....	+ 1 ,,
The Moon's aspect strength	....	— $\frac{1}{2}$,,
Total	....	+ $\frac{1}{2}$ unit

Jupiter is malefic lord	....	— 1 unit
Jupiter occupies a friendly sign	....	+ 1 ,,
Jupiter's aspect strength	....	+ $2\frac{1}{4}$,,
Total	....	+ $2\frac{1}{4}$ units

* B.L. = Benefic lord.
M.L. = Malefic lord.
N.L. = Neutral lord.

The Moon is slightly benefic and Jupiter is benefic. The Moon's shadbala strength (8.9) being higher than that of Jupiter (6.9) the Moon could fulfil the higher part of the yoga, but as the Moon's Dasa is not likely to be enjoyed, he can give rise to the yoga only as a sub-lord and that too to the extent of 40%, this being his residential strength. Jupiter, on the other hand, can give 90% of the results due by him in reference to the 10th house both in the capacity of a major lord and sub-lord.

There are different types of yogas, *viz*., Chandra Yogas, Surya Yogas, Panchamahapurusha Yogas, Nabhasa Yogas, Raja Yogas, Arishta Yogas and Parivraja Yogas. According to Varahamihira, the distingushing feature of the Nabhasa Yogas is that the effects are realised throughout life. But what is the channel through which the results can be felt, excepting the Dasas and the transits. The effects of any yoga, Nabhasa or otherwise, can only be realised during the periods and sub-periods of, or during the times of favourable transits of the planets causing the yoga.

Gajakesari (1) is caused by the disposition of Jupiter and the Moon in mutual kendras. The two lunar yogas Sunapha (2) and Anapha (3) arise by the situation of planets (excepting the Sun) in the 2nd and 12th from the Moon. Durdhura (4) and Kemadruma (5) result when the Moon has, and has not, respectively planets on either side. Kemadruma is an evil yoga but it gets cancelled if a kendra from Lagna or the Moon is occupied by a planet. Chandra Mangala Yoga (6) results by the conjunction of the

Moon and Mars. Its occurrence in unfavourable houses is not favoured. Adhi Yoga (7), another equally powerful yoga, results by the disposition of benefics in the 6th, 7th and 8th from the Moon. Even if one of the three places is occupied by a benefic, there will be a trace of Adhi Yoga. This contributes to character, wealth and longevity. When all the kendras have planets, Chatussagara Yoga (8) is formed. Benefics in Upachayas, and benefics in Lagna give rise to Vasumati (9) and Rajalakshana (10) Yogas respectively. The association of Lagnadhipathi or Lagna with Rahu, Saturn or Kethu or even Gulika results in Vanchanabheethi Yoga (11) indicating a fear-complex nature. This yoga has a few variations also (12). When dusthanas from Jupiter are occupied by the Moon, Sakata Yoga is formed, while a benefic in the 10th from the Moon produces Amala (13). Parvata Yoga (14) comprehends three sets of combinations and it cannot be considered as a Raja Yoga. Kahala (15) is formed when the lords of the 4th and 9th are in mutual kendras and Lagnadhipathi is strong. The three solar yogas Vesi, Vasi and Obhayachari (16, 17, 18) are the consequence of the disposition of planets (Moon excepted) in the 2nd, 12th and 2nd and 12th from the Sun. The yogas appear to have reference to the ego development of an individual. The Panchamahapurusha Yogas, *viz.*, Ruchaka, Bhadra, Hamsa, Malavya and Sasa (19 to 23) are formed when Mars, Mercury, Jupiter, Venus or Saturn respectively are in a kendra identical with their own or exaltation house. When powerful, they produce five distinct sorts of great personages. The

Sun-Mercury conjunction goes under the name of Budha-Aditya Yoga (24), provided, they are not within 10° from each other. The Sun, the Moon and Lagna in odd and even signs, in the cases of males and females respectively, give rise to Mahabhagya Yoga (25). Pushkala Yoga (26) is a fairly auspicious combination, while Lakshmi Yoga formed by the conjunction of the lords of Lagna and the 9th contributes to financial stability. The elevated position of the lord of the Navamsa held by the lord of the 10th produces Gauri Yoga (27), while the lords of the Navamsas occupied by the 2nd, 5th and 11th lords, in exaltation and with the 9th lord give rise to Bharathi Yoga (28). Both are subha yogas conducing to wealth and learning. Jupiter, the Moon and the Sun, in Lagna, 7th and 2nd respectively produce Kusuma Yoga (29), an important Raja Yoga. Chapa Yoga (30) is formed when lord of Lagna is exalted and the 4th and 10th lords have exchanged houses. Both these yogas are capable of conferring fame and power consistent with the strengths of the planets causing the yoga. Lord of the 10th with the 9th lord and the lord of the 7th exalted in the 10th produces Sreenatha Yoga (31). Malika Yogas (32 to 43) arise by the seven planets occupying the seven houses contiguously from any particular bhava. There are twelve types of this yoga. Sankha Yoga (44) is formed by the mutual disposition in kendras of the 5th and 6th lords. The Lagna must of course be strong General happiness is usually assured by Bheri Yoga (45) which is formed when Venus, Jupiter and lord of Lagna are in mutual kendras and the 9th lord is powerfully disposed. If the lord of the Navamsa occupied by an exalted planet, be posited in a trikona or kendra identical with friendly or exalted sign and the Lagna lord strongly disposed, Mridanga Yoga (46) is formed which assures royal honour and influence. Parijatha (47) is an important combination capable of conferring political or spiritual power. It is formed by the lord of the sign in which the lord of the house occupied by the ascendant lord in a quadrant, trine, or own or exaltation sign. Yogas 48 to 70 are all very important and some of them such as Gaja are of rare occurrence. Kalanidhi Yoga is a Raja Yoga and is capable of giving very auspicious results. Then we have Amsavatara, Harihara Brahma, Kusuma, Matsya, Kurma, Devendra, Makuta, Chandika, Jaya, Vidyut, Gandharva, Siva, Vishnu, Brahma, Indra, Ravi, Garuda, Go, Gola, Thrilochana and Kulavardhana, each of which is important in its own way. Nabhasa Yogas (71 to 102) consist of four groups, *viz.*, Akriti-20, Sankhya-7, Asraya-3 and Dala-2. The first four out of the 20 Akriti Yogas, *viz.*, Yupa, Ishu, Sakthi, and Danda (71 to 74) are produced when all the planets occupy four signs contiguously from Lagna and other kendras. The next four, *viz.*, Nav, Kuta, Chatra and Chapa (75 to 78) arise by virtue of the disposition of the seven planets in seven contiguous houses from Lagna and the other kendras respectively. When the seven planets occupy the seven houses from a Panapara or Apoklima, Ardha Chandra (79) is produced, while for the formation of Chakra, the seven planets should occupy odd bhavas. Gada, Sakata, Vihaga

(81 to 83) arise when the planets occupy two adjacent kendras, 1st and 7th houses, and 4th and 10th houses respectively. Benefics in Lagna and the 7th and malefics in 4 and 10 give rise to Vajra while the reverse holds good in regard to Yava. Sringhataka is the name given to a yoga formed when all the trines are occupied. If planets are confined to other triangles than Lagna, Hala Yoga results. Planets in all the kendras result in Kamala; in all the Apoklimas, or Panaparas give rise to Vapee. The last of the Akriti, *viz.*, Samudra Yoga is formed when all the even bhavas are occupied. The seven Sankhya Yogas, *viz.*, Vallaki, Dama, Pasa, Kendra, Sula, Yuga and Gola are formed by the seven planets occupying 7, 6, 5, 4, 3, 2 and 1 houses. The three Asraya Yogas, *viz.*, Rajju, Musala and Nala arise when the planets are exclusively in movable, fixed or common signs respectively. And the Dala Yogas, *viz.*, Srik and Sarpa arise by the kendras being occupied exclusively by benefics and malefics respectively. Sometimes Asraya Yogas merge with Akriti Yogas, Sankhya Yogas with Akriti Yogas and so on. When there is a merging or identification of two yogas belonging to two different groups of the Nabhasa Yogas, one of the two will cease to function. Rajju, Musala and Nala are more or less the same as Yava, Abja, Vajra, Andaja, Gola, Gada and Sakata (among Akriti Yogas) and Sula and Kendra (among the Sankhya Yogas). When Sankhya Yogas coincide with Akriti Yogas, the former become defunct. When Asraya coincides with Akriti, the latter alone functions. When Nala and Sankhya coincide, the former

alone functions. When Asraya and Sankhya coincide, the latter ceases to function and if Asraya coincides with Dala, the former becomes defunct. One should carefully apply the Nabhasa Yogas and should clearly note down which of the yogas lose their identity and which will prevail. The Nabhasa Yogas appear to be useful in the judgment of occupation. They will have important bearings on certain aspects of one's life depending upon the stress that is laid on particular bhavas by the dispositions of planets in or around them.

When the 10th and 11th lords occupy dusthanas, they cause Dur (103) and Daridra (104) Yogas respectively making the person selfish, deceitful, mean and poverty sticken. Lords of the 6th, 8th and 12th occupying the 6th, 8th and 12th will produce Harsha, Sarala and Vimala (105 to 107) respectively.

Combinations 108 to 117 pertain to the Lagna Bhava. By a certain disposition of the Lagnadhipathi, these yogas are formed, some producing health and happiness and others denoting a weak constitution, miserable existence and so on. Combinations for wealth (118 to 128) take into consideration not only the favourable disposition of the 2nd lord but also the existence of harmonious relationship between the lords of the 2nd, 5th, 11th, and 9th. A planet occupying the 5th identical with his own sign is indeed a powerful Dhana Yoga. Amassing of money, earning by one's efforts, access to wealth during certain specified periods, and through certain definite sources such as through father, mother, brothers, enemies and so on, and earning money with and without effort, have also their own special yogas and these are covered by combinations 129 to 143. Daridra Yogas (144 to 153) are of a variety and they denote dire poverty, wretchedness and miseries. Since the 2nd house has also reference to one's speech, Yogas 154 to 162 deal with such things as eloquence, sense of humour, want of character, capacity to influence people by one's oratorial powers, high learning and scholarship.

Combinations pertaining to the 2nd bhava (163 to 176) cover a variety of events such as dumbness, loss of sight, attractive and ugly appearance, generous instincts, eating condemned food, stammering, danger from serpents and death by poisoning. In all these cases, the 2nd lord's affliction in some form or other is considered. One will be happy on account of brothers who will themselves become prosperous, provided the third house, the third lord, or Mars is auspiciously disposed (177). Affliction to these factors result in the death of brothers (178). Then are given combinations for only one sister (179), 12 and 7 brothers and sisters respectively (180 and 181), one's courage (182), strategy in warfare (183), conduct before and after the commencement of war (184 and 185), and interest in religious discourses (186). Yogas pertaining to fourth bhava refer to very interesting topics. Combinations under which possession of good houses, innumerable mansions (187 and 188), acquisition of property without effort (189 and 190), destruction of houses (191 and 192), respect by relatives and friends (193 and 194) are given with suitable examples. One will be deserted by his relatives (195) if the 4th lord is afflicted occupying evil shashti-amsas. The mother lives upto a good age (196 and 197) or dies early in life (198 and 199) depending upon the strength or weakness of the Moon. If Matrugami (200) and Sahodaragami Yogas (201) are present, the person will be guilty of despicable behaviour towards his mother and sister respectively. Some people are hypocritic and some hate secrecy. This is revealed by combinations 202 to 206. One would be cruel or ill-disposed towards one's own mother. Yogas 207 and 208 help us to decide this. For the acquisition of material comforts and conveniences, Yogas 209 and 210 must be present. The 5th house has reference to children and intelligence. 25 Yogas (211 to 235) are devoted to this important bhava. Anapathya, Sarpasapa, Pitrusapa Sutakshaya, Matrusapa Sutakshaya, Bhratrusapa Sutakshaya, Pretasapa give causes for the loss of children. Bahuputra Yogas give combinations for judging the number of issues while the next two yogas give a clue to find out whether one, in the absence of the birth of an issue, would resort to adoption. Aputra Yogas, Ekaputra Yoga, Kalanirdesat Putra Yogas denote birth of no issues, birth of one issue and birth of issues at a particular period respectively. With the aid of Yogas 229 and 230, it is possible to say at what age a person would lose issues.

One's intelligence quotient is revealed by Yogas 231, 232, 233 and 234. Happiness from children is denoted by Putrasukha Yoga. Then we have yogas bearing on the 7th house. Jara Yoga (236) makes one go after women other than one's own wife.

When the man lacks the power of procreation, his wife getting an issue from another man goes under the name of Jarajaputra Yoga (237). Bahu Stree Yoga (238) gives the number of paramours one is likely to have. Happiness from wife and sexual perversions can be known from combinations 239 and 240. A man becomes fortunate by the presence of Bhagya Yoga (241). Father's death before birth of a person, generous instincts, bad reputation have reference to the next three yogas (242 to 244).

Raja Yogas are many and have several gradations. Combinations 245 to 263 deal with certain special Raja Yogas which make one a ruler or at least an equal to him. Three or more planets in exaltation or own houses (245) give rise to a ruler. Even a planet in debilitation can give rise to Raja Yoga (246) under certain conditions. 249 and 250 are Neechabhanga Raja Yogas denoting elevation from ordinary or low births. Then other important Raja Yogas (251 to 253) are dealt with. By a certain disposition of Saturn (254), Moon (255), lord of the 10th (256), Jupiter (257) and the lord of the Navamsa occupied by the Moon (258) another set of important yogas are formed. The next four yogas (260 to 263) deal with certain equally typical Raja Yogas.

Misfortunes are various and curious. Loss of wealth, prestige, children, position, incurable diseases, debts, imprisonment, humiliations, lunacy, poverty are all misfortunes going under the generic term of arishtas. Yoga 264 formed by the third being occupied by Mandi and Rahu or Mars in the shashtiamsa of Preta Puriha goes under the name of

Galakarna and this gives rise auditory troubles. When the 6th lord, being a malefic occupies Lagna, 8th or 10th, Vrana Yoga (265) is produced and this makes the person suffer from the dreadful disease of cancer. Sexual troubles are plenty and Sisna Vyadhi Yoga (266) which arises by Mercury's position in Lagna with the 6th and 8th lords comprehends all these troubles. Combinations 267 to 270, *viz.*, Kalatrashanda Yoga, Kushtaroga Yoga and Kshayaroga Yoga give clues for the detection of wife's impotency and previous predilections for leprosy and consumption. When the lords of Lagna and the 6th are in a trine or quadrant with Saturn, Rahu or Kethu, Bandhana Yoga (271) is formed. This makes the person undergo imprisonment. Karachcheda Yoga and Sirascheda Yoga (272 and 273) refer to punishment by way of one's limbs or head being severed. Accidental deaths happen under Durmarana Yoga (274) formed as a result of the Moon, being aspected by lord of Lagna, occupying dusthana with Saturn or Mandi. By a certain disposition and ownership of Mars, Yuddhe Marana Yoga (275) is formed, denoting death in battle-fields. Collective deaths are comprehended in Sanghataka Marana Yogas (276 and 277). The other important Arishta Yogas (278–294) are Peenasaroga Yoga (nasa trouble), Putrakalatraheena Yoga (loss of wife and children), Bharyasaha Vyabhichara Yoga (adultery), Vamsachcheda Yoga (family extinction), Guhyaroga Yoga (piles, hernia, etc.), Angaheena Yoga (bodily deformity), Swetakushta Yoga (white leprosy), Pisacha Grastha Yoga (trouble from spirits),

Andha Yogas (blindness), Vatharoga Yoga (windy complaints), Matibhramana Yogas (mental derangement). Judgment in regard to these yogas should not be pronounced in a haphazard manner, as unless the yoga is present *in toto* the results ascribed may not fully materialise.

Khalawata Yoga (295) caused by the ascendant being a malefic sign makes one bald-headed. The Moon-Saturn combination rendering one harsh in speech goes under the name of Nishturabhashi Yoga (296). Fall from high position is brought about by Rajabhrashta Yoga (297) which is formed when the lords of the Arudha Lagna and Arudha Dwadasamsa are in conjunction. Raja Yoga present in a horoscope gets cancelled or neutralised by the simultaneous presence of Raja Yoga Bhangas which arise when Lagna being Leo, Saturn is exalted but in a Neecha Navamsa (298) and when the Sun is in deep debilitation (299). The last combination dealt with goes under the name of Gohanta Yoga (300). This is formed by the presence of a malefic (devoid of benefic aspect) in a kendra and Jupiter occupying the 8th house.

The example horoscope given above contains the following yogas caused by the planets marked against them :—

Yoga	*Planets*
Gajakesari	Jupiter, Moon
Adhi Yoga	Jupiter
Rajalakshana Yoga	Jupiter, Venus, Moon Mercury
Amala Yoga	Jupiter

Yoga	*Planets*
Vesi Yoga	Mars, Venus, Mercury
Sankha Yoga	Moon, Mercury
Bheri Yoga	Venus, Saturn, Jupiter
Parijata Yoga	Venus
Bramha Yoga	Mercury, Venus
Kendra Yoga	All planets
	Saturn, Jupiter, Venus.

It will be seen from the above classification that some of the planets have caused more than one yoga. Jupiter, for instance, has been responsible for causing five important yogas, *viz.*, Gajakesari, Adhi Yoga, Rajalakshana Yoga, Amala and Bheri. Would he give the results of all these yogas in his Dasa or Bhukthi subject to the modification by the influences of the other planets involved? This is a difficult question to answer. But it would be reasonable to assume that because Jupiter has caused quite a number of yogas, there would be a blending of the effects of all the yogas. Adhi Yoga and Amala Yoga have merged with Gajakesari. So far as Bheri and other yogas are concerned, the more powerful of the planet or planets would give the effects. The following schedule gives an idea of the capacity or otherwise of the different planets to confer the effects due to the yogas caused by them :—

The Sun—

He is a benefic lord	....	1 unit
He is in a friendly sign	...	1 "
He is unassociated	....	0 "
Aspect strength	....	$-\frac{1}{4}$ "
Total	....	$1\frac{3}{4}$ units

Mars—

He is a benefic lord	....	1 unit
He is associated with Venus, another benefic lord	....	1 ,,
He is in a friendly sign	....	1 ,,
Aspect strength	....	—¼ ,,
Total	....	2¾ units

Mercury—

He is a neutral	....	0 unit
He is in a friendly sign	....	1 ,,
He is with 2 benefic lords	....	2 ,,
Aspect strength	....	—¼ ,,
Total	....	2¾ nnits

Jupiter 2¼ units

Venus—

He is a benefic lord	....	1 unit
He is in an inimical sign	....	—1 ,,
He is associated with a benefic lord Mars	....	1 ,,
Aspect strength	....	—¼ ,,
Total	....	¾ unit

Saturn—

He is a benefic lord	....	1 unit
He is in a friendly sign	....	1 ,,
He has joined a malefic lord	....	—1 ,,
Aspect strength	....	—½ ,,
Total	....	½ unit

Vesi Yoga has been caused by Mars, Venus and Mercury being in the 2nd from the Sun. Of these three planets, Mars and Mercury are the best benefics as judged above, and Venus is a benefic. The shadbala strength of Mars (6.4) and Mercury (6.3) are almost equal, while Venus is less strong (5.0). Therefore, Vesi Yoga could manifest to a larger extent in the (periods and) sub-periods, of Mars and Mercury and to a small extent during the sub-period of Venus. The bhavas involved are the 7th from Lagna and the 4th from the Moon. Therefore the native's fortune should show improvement and events pertaining to the 4th and 7th should receive a stimulus, Mercury's residential strength is 80% and the yoga can manifest to a great extent in his Dasa.

Taking Sankha Yoga, we find that it is caused by Mercury and the Moon. Mercury is definitely the best benefic, while the Moon is only a benefic. The inherent strength of the Moon is 8.9, much greater than that of Mercury. Consequently, during Moon's sub-period, the yoga can express itself but in a restricted manner as the Moon is only feebly benefic and moreover his residential strength is only 40%. On the other hand, Mercury can confer all the blessings of the yoga both as sub-lord and major lord as he is not only benefic *par excellence,* but has considerable residential strength. Taking again Bheri Yoga, the planets involved are Venus, Saturn and Jupiter. Of these, Jupiter is the best benefic, and Venus and Saturn are benefics. Jupiter and Saturn have more or less the same inherent and residential strengths.

Jupiter is the planet *par excellence* for conferring the blessings of this yoga, both as main and sub-lord.

It must be noted that the method of interpreting the yoga given above has no warrant in any classical works on astrology. It occurred to me in the course of examination of a number of horoscopes that a method, such as the one commended above, might possibly act as a fillip for the development of more accurate and reliable methods. Yogas like Parijatha, Bheri, etc., add general strength or vitality to the horoscope. It is the sum-total of the influences, good and bad, that should be the basis of making future predictions. The technique of prediction is an art and the successful astrologer is he, who has acquired the faculty of prediction by comprehensive study, vast experience and keen intellectual and mental discipline leading finally to intuitive capacity.

APPENDIX I

A NOTE ON KALA SARPA YOGA

Kalasarpa Yoga (KSY) is said to be formed if all the planets are situated between Rahu and Kethu. The results are that countries and rulers are destroyed and people become afflicted.

Strictly speaking KSY does not find a place in the classical astrological literature. How this yoga gained currency and gathered a sinister meaning is not clear.

I propose to make a few observations in the light of my own humble experience and it is left to the discretion of the readers to accept them for what they are worth.

The definition of KSY given above generally holds good. But what if all the planets are hemmed in between Kethu and Rahu? According to some, this does not constitute KSY. But in our view irrespective of whether the planets are between Rahu and Kethu or Kethu and Rahu the yoga technically exists. But in conferring results several variations are possible. The general belief is that KSY is evil restraining all the other good yogas present in the horoscope and that those having the yoga will have set-backs and reverses in life. It is also feared that *Kalasarpa Yoga* is capable of nullifying the most powerful *Dhanayogas* rendering a rich man poor.

In interpreting Kalasarpa Yoga, consideration should be given to the houses which are mainly involved, e.g., 1st and 7th, 2nd and 8th, 3rd and 9th, 4th and 10th, 5th and 11th, 6th and 12th, etc. In each case the results could be different, depending upon a number of other horoscopic factors. Generally it is found, other combinations warranting, the 6th-12th axis (i.e., Kalasarpa Yoga) could indicate incarceration, or spiritual elevation, depending upon the presence or absence of powerful *Bandhana Yogas*. If the axis involves the 1st and 7th houses, it is not good for marital happiness. The marital life may become oppressive and marred by frequent clashes and want of understanding. If the 7th lord or Venus is strongly placed and well disposed then the evil results should not be predicted. The marital troubles can be avoided. Knowing in advance, the implications of this yoga, one can regulate one's thinking and behaviour and develop an understanding.

Likewise if the houses involved are the 4th and 10th, setbacks may mark one's career unless the 10th house or the 10th lord is strong and well placed.

KSY has its bright shades. It makes one industrious, hard-working, aware of one's own ability-despite mental restlessness. It raises the natives to top positions in their respective fields *provided of course other* Raja Yogas are present. Rahu-Kethu axis favours rise in mundane life while Kethu-Rahu axis indicates elevation in spiritual matters. It is also found that KSY natives get betrayed by trusted friends and even relatives. Suffering due to developments in life strengthens the mind and mellows one's outlook. This is a bleassing of KSY.

Other important factors to be noted are :—(1) In a KSY horoscope, the evil gets intensified if the Lagna is between Kethu and Rahu ; (2) the evil gets almost neutralised if the Lagna is between Rahu and Kethu ; and (3) the yoga can be considered as defunct even if a single planet is with Rahu or Kethu or outside the axis.

The original sloka refers to *agre rahu*, i. e., Rahu must be the main or prominent planet which means the Yoga can become effective if planets are in between Rahu and Kethu. Another factor to be considered is if the planet associated with Rahu or Kethu is strongly disposed in his exaltation or own house, the intensity of the KSY gets reduced. The common fear that if Kalasarpa Yoga is fully present the effects of other good planetary combinations get nullified is not without justification. There are horoscopes with excellent yogas showing great advancement and prosperity but the natives continue to be mediocres. A brilliant career may suddenly end. Such cases may have KSY but it may not be the main cause for making one what he is. It may be one of the causes.

In the following horoscope KSY is present because of the situation of all the planets in between Kethu and Rahu. The Yoga is not really strong as the Kethu-Rahu axis is involved and Lagna is not behind Rahu. But the other afflictions—such as the political planet and lord of the 9th Sun being aspec-

Chart No. *Born 29th July 1883 at 2 p. m. L.M.T. Lat. 41° N. Long. 16° E.*

	Kethu	Moon Saturn Mars	Jupit.
	RASI		Sun Merc. Venus
	Lagna	Rahu	

			Moon Saturn Jupiter
Rahu	NAVAMSA		Mars Lagna Venus
			Kethu
	Mercury Sun		

Balance of the Moon's Dasa at birth : years 3-8-26.

ted by Saturn, and Saturn being in conjunction in the 7th with the lord of Lagna—gave a deep fall despite the fact the native rose to the highest position by virtue of other Raja Yogas, reckoned from both Lagna and Chandra Lagna. The end of Saturn Dasa gave a violent death. Mark the fact the Kethu-Rahu axis involves the 12th and 6th. The native was betrayed by his own trusted colleagues.

It occurs to me that undue importance need not be given to KSY. The view held by some astrologers that KSY affects longevity and adversely affects the operation of other yogas favouring rise in life, achievement and accomplishment is not tenable. The overall assessment of the horoscope is important. No single yoga, including KSY, is capable of marring or making a horoscope. In our view Kalasarpa Yoga plays an importan role in mundane astrology and is not of much importancet in individual charts.

APPENDIX II

INDEX OF YOGAS

90. Garuda Yoga	—	66	97
91. Gauri Yoga	—	28	60
92 & 93. Grihanasa Yogas	—	191 & 192	184
94. Griha Prapta Yogas, Ayatna	—	189 & 190	183
95. Griha Yoga, Uttama	—	187	180
96. Gohanta Yoga	—	300	304
97. Gola Yoga	—	68	100
98. Go Yoga	—	67	99
99. Guhya Roga Yoga	—	284	286
100. Hamsa Yoga	—	19	43
101. Harihara Brahma Yoga	—	51	76
102. Harsha Yoga	—	105	129
103. Indra Yoga	—	64	95
104. Jada Yoga	—	158	157
105. Jaya Yoga	—	58	85
106. Jara Yoga	—	236	226
107. Kahala Yoga	—	15	39
108. Kalanidhi Yoga	—	49	73
109. Kalatrashanda Yoga	—	267	265
110 to 112. Kapata Yogas	—	202 to 204	192
113. Karascheda Yoga	—	272	274
114. Kemadruma Yoga	—	5	22
115. Khalawata Yoga	—	295	300
116 & 117. Krisanga Yogas	—	112 & 113	132
118. Kshaya Roga Yoga	—	270	267
119. Kulavardhana Yoga	—	70	101
120. Kurma Yoga	—	54	80
121 & 122. Kushtaroga Yogas	—	268 & 269	265
123. Kusuma Yoga	—	52	77
124. Labha Yoga, Ayatnadhana	—	143	152
125. Lakshmi Yoga	—	27	58
126. Mahabhagya Yoga	—	25	55
127. Makuta Yoga	—	56	83
128. Malavya Yoga	—	20	48
129 to 140. Malika Yogas	—	32 to 43	65
141. Marana Yoga, Dur	—	274	277
142. Marana Yoga, Yuddhae	—	275	278

No.	Yoga			
283.	Vanchanachorabheethi Yoga	—	11	32
284.	Vasi Yoga	—	17	42
285.	Vasumathi Yoga	—	9	29
286.	Vatharoga Yoga	—	290	291
287.	Vesi Yoga	—	16	40
288.	Vakchalana Yoga	—	175	169
289.	Vichitra Saudha Prakara Yoga	—	188	181
290.	Vidyut Yoga	—	59	87
291.	Vikalangapatni Yoga	—	280	282
292.	Vimala Yoga	—	107	129
293.	Vishaprayoga Yoga	—	176	169
294.	Vishnu Yoga	—	62	90
295.	Vrana Yoga	—	265	260
296.	Yuddha Praveena Yoga	—	183	176
297.	Yuddhatpoorvadridhachitta Yoga		184	178
298.	Yuddhatpaschaddrubha Yoga	—	185	178
299 & 300.	Yukthi Samanwithavagmi Yogas	—	154 & 155	154

AN INDEX OF TECHNICAL TERMS

Adrishta	— Unseen, fortune, luck
Alpayu	— Short life
Annadana	— Free feeding
Anthara	— An astrological time-measure
Apoklimas	— 3, 6, 9 and 12 houses
Arishtayoga	— Combination of planets for misfortune
Aroodha Rasi	— The sign which is as distant from the lord as the lord is from the house concerned
Astha	— Combust
Ayurdaya	— Longevity
Bhagya	— Fortune, luck
Balarishta	— Infant mortality
Balishta	— Strong
Bhava	— House
Bhava Chakra	— House diagram
Bhavana	— House
Bhavasandhi	— Junction point of two adjacent houses or bhavas
Brahmin	— The first caste among Hindus
Bhrathrukaraka	— Mars—Indicator of brothers
Brihat Jataka	— A classical treatise on astrology
Brihat Samhita	— A classical treatise on natural phenomena
Budha	— Mercury
Budhaditya Yoga	— Sun-Mercury combination
Bhukthi	— An astrological time-measure
Chandra	— The Moon
Chandra Lagna	— The Moon-sign
Chandra Mangala Yoga	— Moon-Mars combination
Chara Rasi	— Moveable sign

Chathurthamsa — $\frac{1}{4}$th division of a sign
Chathushtaya — 4th house
Dhanayoga — Combination for wealth
Dasa — Planetary period, an astrological time-measure
Devendra — King of the celestials
Dhanakaraka — Indicator of wealth (Jupiter)
Dhanus — Sagittarius
Dharma — Righteousness
Digbala — Directional strength
Drekkana — 1/3 division of a sign
Dusthana — A malefic house (6th, 8th and 12th)
Dwadasamsa — 1/12th division of a sign
Dwadasaroodha — **Aroodha** Rasi of the 12th sign
Dwirdwadasa — Mutual 2nd and 12th positions of planets
Dwiswabhava Rasi — Dual sign
Gnanayoga — Planetary combination for higher wisdom and knowledge
Gopuramsa — A distinction attained by a planet when it occupies 8 own vargas or divisions
Gulika — A secondary planet
Guru — Jupiter
Hora — $\frac{1}{2}$ division of a sign
Hala — Plough
Jatakachandrika — An ancient astrological treatise
Jatakadesamarga — -do-
Jataka Tatwa — - do-
Jaya — Victory
Kalabala — Temporal strength of planets
Kalatra — Wife
Kanya — Virgo
Karma — Doctrine of rebirth, action, etc.
Karaka — Indicator

Kendra	— A quadrant
Kendradhipathya dosha	— Affliction due to ownership of a quadrant
Kuta	— Mars
Kumbha	— Aquarius
Lagna	— Ascendant
Lagnadhipathi	— Ascendant-lord
Labha	— Gain, the 11th house
Makara	— Capricorn
Makuta	— Crown
Mandi	— A secondary planet for Saturn
Maraka	— Death-dealing planet
Matsya	— Fish
Meena	— Pisces
Mesha	— Aries
Mithuna	— Gemini
Moksha	— Salvation
Moolathrikonadhibala	— Strength obtained by a planet due to residence in the various vargas or divisions
Mridwamsa	— A certain sensitive point in a sign
Naisargikabala	— Natural strength
Navamsa	— 1/9th division of a sign
Neecha	— Debilitation, debilitated
Neechabhanga	— Cancellation of debilitation
Nirayana	— Sidereal or fixed zodiac
Panapara	— 2, 5, 8 and 11 signs
Panchamahapurusha Yoga	— A special combination
Parakrama	— Valour
Parivarthana	— Exchange of places
Parvathamsa	— A planet occupying its own vargas three times
Pithrukaraka	— Sun—indicator of father and paternal affairs

Pretasapa — Curse by manes
Putra — Son
Rajayoga — A special planetary combination for eminence
Randhra — 8th house
Rasi — Sign (zodiacal)
Rasi Chakra — The sign diagram
Ravi — The Sun
Sambhuhoraprakasika — An ancient astrological treatise
Samudra — Ocean, Sea
Sani — Saturn
Sapthamsa — 1/7th division of a sign
Sapthavargajabala — Strength due to residence of a planet in different vargas
Saravali — A classical astrological treatise
Sarpasapa — Curse by serpent
Satayogamanjari — An ancient astrological treatise
Satru — Enemy
Sayana — Tropical or moveable zodiac
Shadbala Pinda — The sum-total of six sources of strength of planets
Shashtiamsa — 1/60th division of a sign
Shodasavarga — 16 divisions of a sign
Simha — Leo
Simhasanamsa — A planet occupying its own varga 4 times
Sukha — Comforts, happiness
Sukra — Venus
Sukranadi — A classical treatise in applied astrology
Sutakshaya — Extinction of progeny
Swakshetra — Own sign
Swa-Varga — Own division
Tatkalika — Temporary
Thridoshas — The 3 primary humours in the human system

Thrikalagnana	— Knowledge of past, present and future
Thrikona	— Trine
Thula	— Libra
Vahana	— Vehicle, conveyance
Vahanastana	— House indicating conveyance (4th)
Vakra	— Retrograde
Vedha	— Obstruction
Vihaga	— Bird
Vikrama	— 3rd house
Vishnu	— The sustaining aspect of the Hindu Trinity
Vraya	— Loss or expenditure
Vrischika	— Scorpio
Vrishabha	— Taurus
Upachaya	— 3, 6, 10 and 11 signs
Uchcha	— Exaltation
Yoga	— Planetary combination
Yogakaraka	— Conferor of fame
Yogee	— Saint, one who has attained mental equanimity